PRACTISING SHAME

Manchester University Press

Series editors: Anke Bernau, David Matthews and James Paz

Series founded by: J. J. Anderson and Gail Ashton

Advisory board: Ruth Evans, Patricia C. Ingham, Andrew James Johnston, Chris Jones, Catherine Karkov, Nicola McDonald, Sarah Salih, Larry Scanlon and Stephanie Trigg

Manchester Medieval Literature and Culture publishes monographs and essay collections comprising new research informed by current critical methodologies on the literary cultures of the Middle Ages. We are interested in all periods, from the early Middle Ages through to the late, and we include post-medieval engagements with and representations of the medieval period (or 'medievalism'). 'Literature' is taken in a broad sense, to include the many different medieval genres: imaginative, historical, political, scientific, religious. While we welcome contributions on the diverse cultures of medieval Britain and are happy to receive submissions on Anglo-Norman, Anglo-Latin and Celtic writings, we are also open to work on the Middle Ages in Europe more widely, and beyond.

Titles available in the series

14. *Love, history and emotion in Chaucer and Shakespeare:* Troilus and Criseyde *and* Troilus and Cressida
    Andrew James Johnston, Russell West-Pavlov and Elisabeth Kempf (eds)
15. *The Scottish Legendary: Towards a poetics of hagiographic narration*
    Eva von Contzen
16. *Nonhuman voices in Anglo-Saxon literature and material culture*
    James Paz
17. *The church as sacred space in Middle English literature and culture*
    Laura Varnam
18. *Aspects of knowledge: Preserving and reinventing traditions of learning in the Middle Ages*
    Marilina Cesario and Hugh Magennis (eds)
19. *Visions and ruins: Cultural memory and the untimely Middle Ages*
    Joshua Davies
20. *Participatory reading in late-medieval England*
    Heather Blatt
21. *Affective medievalism: Love, abjection and discontent*
    Thomas A. Prendergast and Stephanie Trigg
22. *Performing women: Gender, self, and representation in late-medieval Metz*
    Susannah Crowder
23. *The politics of Middle English parables: Fiction, theology, and social practice*
    Mary Raschko
24. *Contemporary Chaucer across the centuries*
    Helen M. Hickey, Anne McKendry and Melissa Raine (eds)
25. *Borrowed objects and the art of poetry: Spolia in Old English verse*
    Denis Ferhatović
26. *Rebel angels: Space and sovereignty in Anglo-Saxon England*
    Jill Fitzgerald
27. *A landscape of words: Ireland, Britain and the poetics of space, 700–1250*
    Amy Mulligan
28. *Household knowledges in late-medieval England and France*
    Glenn D. Burger and Rory G. Critten (eds)
29. *Practising shame: Female honour in later medieval England*
    Mary C. Flannery

Practising shame
Female honour in later medieval England

MARY C. FLANNERY

Manchester University Press

Copyright © Mary C. Flannery 2020

The right of Mary C. Flannery to be identified as the author of this work has been asserted by her in accordance with the Copyright, Designs and Patents Act 1988.

Published by Manchester University Press
Oxford Road, Manchester M13 9PL
www.manchesteruniversitypress.co.uk

British Library Cataloguing-in-Publication Data
A catalogue record for this book is available from the British Library

ISBN 978 1 5261 1006 0 hardback
ISBN 978 1 5261 1007 7 paperback

First published 2020

The publisher has no responsibility for the persistence or accuracy of URLs for any external or third-party internet websites referred to in this book, and does not guarantee that any content on such websites is, or will remain, accurate or appropriate.

Typeset
by Toppan Best-set Premedia Limited

*For George, Joseph, Jacob, and Mathieu –
may you grow into men who know the meaning and value of honour.*

Contents

Preface	*page* viii
Acknowledgements	xi
Abbreviations	xiv
Introduction	1
1 Show and tell: shame and the subject of women's bodies	34
2 Lessons in shame	60
3 Shame under suspicion, shame under siege	90
4 Death or dishonour: the problem of exemplary shame	122
5 Shamefast Hoccleve and shameless craving	160
Afterword	186
Bibliography	192
Index	210

Preface

I have been wondering about the meaning of honour for more than twenty years. Although this book emerges out of my longstanding interest in rumour and reputation, the story of its writing might be said to have begun at a gas station in California, when I was in high school. A family friend spotted me when I pulled up to the pump with my boyfriend and decided to introduce himself. After greeting me, he squinted sternly into the car and asked my companion, 'Do you know what honour is?' Receiving no immediate reply (which was, under the circumstances, not entirely surprising), he answered his own question: '... Deserved good reputation.'

I don't remember precisely how that encounter ended, but I have been reflecting on those three words ever since. I remember the certainty in the voice of an older man explaining honour to a younger one, and I remember that my immediate internal response was doubt (as well as some irritation). 'Deserved good reputation' might cover one aspect of honour, but it didn't explain what it meant to have a *sense* of honour, nor did it explain what that good reputation was founded on. It didn't explain who determined which people were deserving of a good reputation, or why. It didn't explain what made a reputation 'good' in the first place.

I have been circling the subject of honour in my research ever since.

The question of whether or not someone is 'honourable' concerns not only the state of that person's reputation, but also whether or not that person values a good reputation, and how that value guides his or her behaviour. This book argues that, in the case of medieval women (whose honour was believed to reside primarily in their chastity), being honourable and valuing honour meant practising shame-avoidance in a way that reinforced their own chaste habits of mind and communicated their honourable chastity to those around them. Thus, for the purposes of this book, 'practising shame' is not about feeling ashamed or disgraced, but rather about enacting and honing one's *sense of shame*, one's anticipative sensitivity to the prospect of disgrace. In this respect, this study is not about an emotion at all, but rather about what goes on around that emotion, and how this peripheral activity was, in the literature of medieval England, constitutive of female honour.

Although the study of shame and honour continues to flourish, it has been suggested that shame and honour are themselves somewhat outmoded in Western culture. One prominent historian of emotion has suggested that honour is so much a thing of the past that we might consider it to be 'a lost emotion'.[1] By contrast, researcher Brené Brown (whose TED talks on the subject of shame have been viewed by millions) characterizes shame as something that should be *made* a thing of the past, a 'silent epidemic' that must be eradicated.[2] Yet there is a lingering awareness that a sense of shame remains important in the present day. In February 2018, David A. Graham wrote an article for the *Atlantic* in which he suggested that recent political events in the United States had exposed the extent to which we rely on politicians' presumed sense of shame as an 'enforcement mechanism' that will ensure they follow the unwritten rules of politics. While noting the potential limitations of such a mechanism for enforcing morality in politics, Graham observed, 'A system where politicians are immune to shame is almost certainly not a good one.'[3]

As this remark suggests, while some might view honour as outdated or shame as unhealthy, we continue to rely on susceptibility to shame as a mechanism that will encourage 'good' behaviour and discourage 'bad' behaviour. Yet what it has meant to be susceptible to shame in different historical contexts, and how one might develop or demonstrate this sense of shame in such contexts, remains little understood.[4] The present study aims to illuminate how this mechanism operated in the literature of medieval England, and how it participated in and contributed to constructions of honourable femininity in the later Middle Ages. Although it is unclear to what extent susceptibility to shame continues to shape ideas concerning female goodness and honour today, there is much in what this study uncovers that I believe will resonate with contemporary debates on subjects ranging from rape prevention to the perception of women in the workplace. As I will show, the fears and expectations that attend honourable female chastity place the burden of its defence squarely on women, leaving the world full of threats to this ideal and making it women's job to avoid, combat, or placate those threats. What is overlooked in the present as often as it was in the past is that these 'necessities' of female behaviour will remain in place as long as women alone remain both the problem and the solution. My greatest hope for this book is that its arguments will contribute not only to our understanding of the ethical construction of femininity in the past, but also to the way we think about honourable womanhood now and in the years to come.

Notes

1 Ute Frevert, *Emotions in History – Lost and Found* (Budapest: Central European University Press, 2011), p. 10.
2 See, for example, Brené Brown, *I Thought It Was Just Me (But It Isn't): Making the Journey from 'What Will People Think?' to 'I am Enough'* (New York, NY: Avery, 2008), previously published as *I Thought It Was Just Me*. Brown's most-viewed TED talk, 'The power of vulnerability', delivered at TEDxHouston (June 2010), may be found online: www.ted.com/talks/brene_brown_on_vulnerability?referrer=playlist-the_most_popular_talks_of_all [accessed 18 April 2018].
3 David A. Graham, 'What If Voters Don't Care About Infidelity At All?', the *Atlantic* (17 February 2018) www.theatlantic.com/politics/archive/2018/02/presidential-infidelity-shame/553559/ [accessed online 18 April 2018].
4 In his recent history of shame, Peter N. Stearns argues that 'we need to register on the *anticipation* aspect that extends shaming's social utility, which has gained less attention, historically, than shame itself' (*Shame: A Brief History* (Urbana, IL: University of Illinois Press, 2017), p. 8).

Acknowledgements

This book has been in progress for more than a decade. The risk one runs at the end of any project that lasts this long is that of forgetting one or more parties to whom thanks are due. That risk is particularly great in my case, since I have had the good fortune to enjoy the support not only of those institutions with which I have been affiliated during this project, but of a remarkable group of colleagues, friends, and family members.

My work on shame began to take shape in the wake of conversations with Helen Cooper, who was the first to suggest that, having already explored the topic of 'fame', I might be interested in investigating one of its antonyms. I remain extremely grateful to her for that initial suggestion.

Not long afterward, I learned that there was an entire field of study devoted to precisely the phenomena to which I was turning my attention: the history of emotions. I have benefited considerably from collaborations, conversation, and correspondence with scholars working in this field, particularly those based at the Australian Research Council's Centre for the History of Emotions (the ARC CHE, where I held a Visiting Research Fellowship at the University of Melbourne in 2013) and at the Centre for the History of Emotions at Queen Mary University of London (QMUL), which was launched the same year that I took up a post in the QMUL School of English and Drama. Without the encouragement of the late Philippa Maddern, I never would have dared to apply for a visiting fellowship to the ARC CHE in the first place – I cannot express how grateful I am to her for her support. I would also particularly like to convey my thanks to Stephanie Trigg, who was an extraordinary mentor during my time at the ARC CHE, and who remains one of the chief sources of inspiration for my work on emotion. I continue to benefit from the expertise and generosity of my ARC CHE colleague Stephanie Downes, to whom I am forever grateful for her advice and encouragement. I would also like to extend my thanks to Louise

D'Arcens, Thomas Dixon, Andrew Lynch, Anne McKendry, Rebecca McNamara, Una McIlvenna, Sarah Randles, Juanita Ruys, Katrina Tap, and Helen Young.

Research for this book would not have been possible without the backing of my home institutions. I was honoured to be a member of the School of English and Drama at Queen Mary University of London for four years, and of the University of Lausanne's (UNIL) English Department for five years – I remain extremely grateful to my colleagues and students at both institutions. The final stages of research and writing were funded by two generous grants I received from UNIL in 2014: a 'Subvention égalité' and a 'Subvention Tremplin', for which I extend my fervent thanks. I would also like to express my gratitude to Elizabeth Morrison and my other former colleagues at the J. Paul Getty Museum in Los Angeles for their kind permission to use the image of bathing Bathsheba (Getty MS 79, recto) as the cover image for this book.

I am extremely grateful to the many colleagues who have shared their time and expertise with me during the writing of this book. In particular, I would like to thank Ruth Ahnert, Sarah Baccianti, Alcuin Blamires, Julia Boffey, Guillemette Bolens, Sarah Brazil, Amy Brown, Daniel DiCenso, Stephanie Downes, Irina Dumitrescu, Lukas Erne, Monica Green, Carrie Griffin, Sarah Kelen, Einat Klafter, Carolyne Larrington, Camille Marshall, Denis Renevey, Hannah Ryley, James Simpson, Stephanie Trigg, Juliette Vuille, Daniel Wakelin, and Katie Walter. Sarah Brazil, Stephanie Downes, and Katie Walter were kind enough to read early drafts of the complete manuscript before I submitted it to Manchester University Press – I cannot thank them enough for their generosity and invaluable feedback. Annette Kern-Stähler oversaw the preparation of this book for submission to the University of Bern as my *Habilitationsschrift*, and shepherded me through the unfamiliar 'habilitation' process, for which I owe her tremendous thanks indeed. Anne Yardley ensured that this book and its revisions got done, and I can never thank her enough.

I am absolutely delighted that this book is appearing in the Manchester Medieval Literature and Culture series, and am extremely grateful to Anke Bernau, David Matthews, and the series editorial board for their support of the project. The anonymous readers provided tremendously helpful feedback on the proposal materials and on the draft manuscript – I owe them a great debt of thanks. Any infelicities or errors that may remain in the final product are entirely my own. I would also like to thank the editorial team at Manchester University Press (particularly Meredith Carroll and Alun Richards) for their assistance in shepherding this manuscript through production.

As I have indicated in the notes to the appropriate chapters, portions of this book are adapted from previous publications: 'Emotion and the Ideal Reader in Middle English Gynecological Texts', in Rachel Falconer and Denis Renevey (eds), *Literature, Science and Medicine in the Medieval and Early Modern Periods* (Turnhout: Swiss Papers in English Language and Literature (SPELL), 2013), pp. 103–15; 'The Shame of the *Rose*: A Paradox', in Jennifer Chamarette and Jennifer Higgins (eds), *Guilt and Shame: Essays in French Literature and Culture* (Oxford: Peter Lang, 2010), pp. 51–69; and 'A Bloody Shame: Chaucer's Honourable Women', *The Review of English Studies* 62 (2011), 337–57. My thanks to the publishers and editors of these publications for their permission to incorporate this material.

One always expects that a first book will be a bit of a challenge, but I must confess that I never expected that my *second* book would be such a hurdle (Alex Gillespie knows my pain). That I have managed to get here in the end is entirely down to the support and encouragement of more family members, friends, colleagues, and co-conspirators than I can count (you know who you are). At the head of this merry band is my husband, Thibaud Kössler. Not only has he been a vital sounding board at many stages in the writing process, he has given me love and patience when I needed it most, and faith when I had lost my own. *Merci de tout mon coeur, mon ange.*

Since I began writing this book, my extended family has welcomed four new members: my three nephews and my son. All three have been in my mind during the final stages of this project. One of the central arguments of this book is that what we teach women about honour and shame is intimately connected to what we teach men about these matters, sometimes in deeply problematic ways. As I continue to flounder my way through aunt-hood and parenthood in the coming years, I hope I will be able to share my curiosity about and interest in these subjects with my family. It is for these reasons and more that this book is dedicated, with all my love, to Joseph, Jacob, Mathieu, and most especially George.

Abbreviations

EETS	Early English Text Society
EETS ES	Early English Text Society, Extra Series
EETS OS	Early English Text Society, Original Series
ELH	*English Literary History*
ELN	*English Language Notes*
MED	*Middle English Dictionary*
n. s.	new series
OED	*Oxford English Dictionary*
PLoS	*Public Library of Science*
PMLA	*Proceedings of the Modern Language Association*
STC	Short Title Catalogue
TEAMS	Teaching Association for Medieval Studies
TSE	*Tulane Studies in English*

Introduction

> [W]omenis honore is tendyr and slyddyr,
> And raithar brekis be mekil thinge,
> As farest ross takis sonest faidinge.
> A woman suld ay have radour
> Of thinge that gref mycht hir honoure[.]
> *(The Thewis of Good Women,* C 8–12)[1]

> In habit maad with chastitee and shame
> Ye wommen shul apparaille yow[.]
> *(The Wife of Bath's Prologue,* 342–3)[2]

How can one know whether a woman is honourable? Such a question raises a number of problems, not the least of which is the definition of honour itself. The Middle English word *honour* encompassed good repute, respectability, and nobility of character, as well as position or rank, but in medieval culture female honour rested most heavily on a single determinant: confirmed sexual continence.[3] Therein lay the *real* problem, for how could one be absolutely sure of a woman's chaste nature? Whether wife, widow, or virgin, a woman's chastity was a function not only of her bodily integrity, but also of her inner thoughts and her outward comportment, only the latter of which could be observed and used as data from which conclusions might be drawn.[4] The fact that women were believed to be inherently bodily creatures (as opposed to men, who were believed to be more intellectual and less bound by their bodily impulses) contributed to the belief that they were less inclined to remain chaste – their bodies were considered porous, pregnable, and governed by the senses and sensuality.[5] Moreover, as medieval authors were quick to point out, appearances could be misleading. Virtuous behaviour could conceal a vicious heart. The precariousness of female honour is captured by the Middle Scots epigraph above, which notes that female honour is 'tendyr and slyddyr [slippery, treacherous]' – it is vulnerable, fragile, and at its worst deceitful, a quality that cannot be taken at face value.[6] As a consequence, women are compelled to 'ay have radour', to always be afraid of anything that has the potential to 'gref' their honour.[7] If they want to secure their honour, women must *beware*.

The idea that a woman must be continually on her guard against potential threats to her reputation or to her person continues to be invoked today in the context of debates concerning topics such as sexual harassment or rape prevention. Although the subject of female honour may not be raised explicitly in these cases, such debates consistently place female behaviour under scrutiny. This scrutiny stems from the assumption that a woman's extreme vigilance – concerning her conduct, what she consumes, her surroundings, or her appearance – is the surest way for her to prevent her own harassment or assault. As I will demonstrate over the course of this book, this emphasis on female circumspection is shared by medieval texts, which depict honour as something that women must safeguard by cultivating and exhibiting their hypervigilance against the possibility of shame.

This book investigates the practices that underpin medieval understandings of female honour, and literature's role in shaping and articulating those practices in later medieval England. While thirteenth-century texts such as *Hali Meiðhad* (a treatise on virginity) and *Ancrene Wisse* (a guide for anchoresses) had held up virginity and the vowed life as the surest means by which women might hope to perfect their virtue, conduct literature and other texts composed in the fourteenth and fifteenth centuries suggest that women who were neither virgins nor female religious might achieve a comparable level of spiritual *and* social virtue.[8] I aim to show that conduct texts, courtly poems, classical exempla, and other forms of medieval English literature produced in this later period encouraged women to secure honour by practising behaviour designed to perfect and maintain a specific emotional disposition: a hypervigilance against the possibility of disgrace that was commonly referred to in Middle English as *shamefastness*, and which was believed to safeguard women against the loss of their chastity and their honour.[9] The word *shamefastness* was in use from the beginning of the thirteenth century but has long since become obsolete, transformed via an etymological misinterpretation into the modern English *shamefacedness* sometime in the sixteenth century.[10] It is typically used to describe hypersensitivity to disgrace; to be 'shamefast' is to be modest, hesitant, bashful, and afraid of being shamed. In this respect, it refers not to the experience of shame, but rather to what Peter N. Stearns has described as 'the *anticipation* aspect' that is attached to shame and enhances its social utility, a subject that has received significantly less scholarly attention from historians than shame itself.[11] The suffix *-fast* is suggestive of both stability and security, a reflection, perhaps, of the idea that a steadfast fear of shame might help to foreclose the possibility of disgrace.[12] But at the same time that later medieval English texts depict the practice of shamefastness as essential for the preservation of female honour, they also depict it as highly problematic. Writing in the middle of what has been described as a crisis of thought regarding the cultivation of virtue, fourteenth- and fifteenth-century English writers persistently return to the idea that, because shamefastness is linked to certain conventions of behaviour and appearance, it is something that can be counterfeited or 'feigned', potentially in order to conceal a woman's lust or other vices.[13] And when a woman's shamefastness *is* genuine, it confirms not only her status as an honourable woman but also her status as a violable subject, someone whose chastity must be conquered by the persuasion, wiles, or violence of men. Assailed on one side by suspicion and on another side by the possibility of violence, female shamefastness remains an unfinishable work-in-progress in medieval literature.

Practice and the history of emotions

Shamefastness is not an emotion, but is rather a disposition towards and susceptibility to shame: a state of vigilance that simultaneously guards one against shame and makes one more sensitive to it. Medieval literature reveals shamefastness to be a mandatory matter of practice for honourable women, something to be interiorized through reflection and mindfulness, and exteriorized through specific conventional gestures and behaviours. As I will show, while it is unclear whether interiorization or exteriorization must come first, neither can be omitted if the practice of shamefastness is to be perfected.

In writing of shamefastness as a practice, I am contributing to a body of scholarship that is attempting to effect a theoretical shift away from the notion that emotions are something that we 'have' (or do not have) and towards the idea that emotions are something that we *do*. Advocates for this shift include philosopher Robert C. Solomon (who has argued that emotions 'are not entities *in* consciousness', but rather '*acts* of consciousness') and historian

William M. Reddy, whose groundbreaking work has shed light on some of the ways that language enables us to 'do' emotion.[14] Reddy contends that we ought to incorporate 'first-person, present tense emotion claims' into a unique category of speech act: *emotives*, which he defines as 'instruments for directly changing, building, hiding, intensifying emotions, instruments that may be more or less successful'.[15] These and related developments in emotion studies have been especially valuable to those scholars of literature who have sought to carve out a place for literary texts and literary analysis within the history of emotions. As has often been noted, literature poses problems for the historian of emotion, since literary texts cannot be read as records of historical experience or as 'straightforwardly mimetically accurate' in their portrayal of emotions.[16] Medievalist Sarah McNamer is one of several scholars who have attempted to resolve the problems posed by literature for the history of emotions.[17] As she puts it, from the perspective of historians of emotion

> the literary is, by its very nature, thought to be untrustworthy: disorienting in its instability, disarming in its beauty, never meaning what it says – in short, a tease. If the goal is to discover the historical truth through the veils of compromised sources, the less opaque those veils, the better.[18]

The problem McNamer highlights here is that historians of emotion have tended to approach texts for factual evidence of past emotions; under these conditions, literature is often viewed as obscuring the truth – or at least dressing it up in a misleading way. This problem of 'literariness' is one to which McNamer has also drawn attention in her work on the affective impact of the anonymously authored fourteenth-century poem *Pearl*, noting that 'the very features that make this poem so magnificent as art – the lushness of its language, the richness of its wordplay, its formal intricacies, its wildly imaginative departures from the real ... – are precisely what make it such a challenge to bring into conversation with the history of emotion as the field is currently configured'.[19] In her study of 'affective meditations on the Passion', she makes a powerful case for viewing these texts as 'iterations of what William Reddy has called "emotives"', arguing that they function as 'mechanisms for the production of emotion' (what McNamer terms 'intimate scripts').[20] Her aim, as she describes it, is to continue 'building a case for a performative model of affect as the default mode' between the

Introduction

eleventh and sixteenth centuries. The affective meditations composed during this period, she argues, are founded on the assumption that emotions can be 'willed, faked, performed through the repetition of scripted words. It is through such manifest fakery, this genre insists, that compassion can be brought into being, can come to be "true"'.[21]

Both in her study of affective meditations and in her other scholarship, McNamer proposes that it is exactly the ornamental features of literature – its 'literariness' – that enable some literary texts to function as scripts for the performance of emotion. While acknowledging that the word 'script' is often used metaphorically to refer to the role of discourse in shaping the emotional norms of specific groups, McNamer proposes that we approach some Middle English texts as 'literal scripts that vigorously enlist *literariness*' to generate feelings, and suggests that we 'combine the usual forms of textual research with considerations of what is likely to have been seen, heard, touched, even *tasted* at the moment of a text's performance'.[22]

As McNamer is the first to acknowledge, such an approach is necessarily somewhat speculative; but it nevertheless points tantalizingly towards one way we might begin to theorize a link between what is on the page and what comprises lived emotional experience. Further support for such an approach may be found in the work of ethnohistorian Monique Scheer, who has argued for viewing emotion as 'a kind of practice' that is dependent on and intertwined with 'doings and sayings' such as 'speaking, gesturing, remembering, manipulating objects, and perceiving sounds, smells, and spaces'. Scheer terms these 'doings and sayings' 'emotional practices', which 'build on the embodied knowledge of the habituated links that form complexes of mind/body actions':

> Emotional practices are habits, rituals, and everyday pastimes that aid us in achieving a certain emotional state. This includes the striving for a desired feeling as well as the modifying of one that is not desirable. Emotional practices in this sense are manipulations of body and mind to evoke feelings where there are none, to focus diffuse arousals and give them an intelligible shape, or to change or remove emotions already there.[23]

Scheer makes a strong case for viewing emotions as 'practices involving the self (as body and mind), language, material artifacts, the environment, and other people'.[24] Her theory of emotion-as-practice enables us to explore how emotions might both shape and be shaped by literary and non-literary texts, as well as other cultural artefacts:

> The objects used in emotional practices of the past – images, literature, musical notation, film, or household items – may still be available for direct observation and analysis. Fictional representations in literature, theater, and film can be analyzed as artifacts used by actors in their emotional practices, as providers of templates of language and gesture as well as mediators of social norms. Texts will remain the main sources, not only for discourses and implicit orders of knowledge, but also for emotives and other emotional practices.[25]

By bringing Scheer's concept of emotion-as-practice into conversation with McNamer's account of the performative nature of medieval emotion, I aim to reveal the many different ways that literary and non-literary medieval English texts shape the idea and practice of female honour. As I will show, shamefastness is an emotional disposition and state of emotion-proneness that relies on and is intertwined with emotional practices as Scheer outlines them here, as well as the kind of 'manifest fakery' that McNamer identifies as a key component of performing 'true' emotion. And it is the skillful practise of shamefastness that, in turn, underpins medieval concepts of honourable femininity. In some instances, Middle English texts are written in such a way as to *produce* a sense of shame in female audiences, whether hypothetical or real; conduct texts for women, for example, instruct them to reflect on all they have to lose if they do not safeguard their honour, and advise them how to dress and behave in order to reinforce and broadcast their shamefastness (leading one medievalist to describe conduct manuals as 'shame scripts').[26] In these instances, a sense of shame is something that can be developed and enhanced through reflection and careful behaviour until it becomes a matter of honourable habit. Other texts shape how the practice of female shamefastness is viewed, presenting it as a complication for medical practitioners, an obstacle to would-be lovers, an empty performance that anyone might mimic, or even a potential danger to women themselves. In these instances, texts do not function solely as scripts for emotion (producing feelings *about* shamefastness, or a sense of shame itself), but reflect and shape social norms concerning the practice of shamefastness. Through sustained close reading of a wide range of later medieval genres, I bring these textual mechanisms and strategies into view.

Because of my study's emphasis on the ways that a sense of shame can be consciously honed and reinforced through reflection and behaviour, I set aside terms such as *affect* (which tend to emphasize an automatic, pre-cognitive state of feeling) in favour of *emotion* when referring to mental and somatic states such as shame, fear, etc.[27] In so doing, I am not only employing a word whose precise meaning and scope has long been debated, but also using a term that would have been entirely unfamiliar to medieval men and women, although medieval writings on the subject of emotion abound.[28] In place of *emotion* (a postmedieval term), medieval theological and philosophical texts make reference to categories of feeling such as *affectus, passiones, affectiones*, and *perturbationes*, among others.[29] Prudentius's *Psychomachia* (early fifth century), discussed in Chapter 3, labels personified feelings *Sensus* (sentiments, senses) and *Furores* (passions) in its description of battle between the virtues and vices. Augustine (354–430), who argued that the emotions are dependant on acts of will, used *affectiones, perturbationes*, and *passiones* in his discussion of emotions in *The City of God Against the Pagans*.[30] Thomas Aquinas (1225-74) used *passiones, affectus*, and *animi concitatio* to refer to emotions in his *Summa Theologiae*, and described emotions as the movements of the sensitive appetite.[31] As these various emotion theories indicate, medieval writers differed in their opinions concerning the precise relationship between emotion and conscious or unconscious action.[32] A similar lack of consensus obtains among contemporary scholars, who have been unable to agree on a preferred critical term for emotions.[33] Whereas *feeling* and *affect* have been embraced by different camps of historians and emotion scholars, and although *passion, movement, sensation,* or *affection* might more closely resemble the Latin terms in use during the Middle Ages, my objective is not to situate honour, shame, or shamefastness in relation to the more learned, Latinate, and/or theological theories of emotion. My interest is rather in the muddier waters of vernacular territory, in specifically lay interpretations of how one might develop and perform one's predisposition to virtuous feelings, impulses, and behaviour that would secure female honour. As a consequence, *emotion* will be my preferred critical term throughout this study. As I will show, however, the importation of Latinate monastic concepts of virtue into the language and literature of later medieval England rendered the practice and performance of virtue potentially suspect. By focusing on the nature of female shamefastness as a practice, I hope to uncover both the ways in which such practices could be perceived both as 'a means for positive intervention in the ethical production of embodied identities' *and* as potentially misleading performances of feigned virtue.[34]

The problem with practice

While the practice of shamefastness was believed to be the most effective tool for the preservation of female chastity, it was also a potential source of anxiety and even suspicion. The problem with the practice of shamefastness was precisely the fact that it could be *practised* – it could be studied, rehearsed, and imitated. In her discussion of medieval English conduct literature, Claire Sponsler identifies two key problems with the genre that are particularly applicable to the idea of a practice of shamefastness. The first problem relates to the 'supposed congruence between inner and outer forms of behavior'; for if one can change one's behaviour to match whatever is currently deemed acceptable or fashionable, that congruence can no longer be presumed to exist. The second problem relates to the idea that good behaviour can be learned; if this is the case, then it can be learned not only as a means of being virtuous, but also as a means of counterfeiting virtuous behaviour 'as a form of disguise in order deliberately to mask true, inner nature'.[35]

This uncertainty regarding the authenticity of ostensibly virtuous behaviour becomes clearer when considered in the light of contemporaneous shifts in thinking about virtue and *habit*, an emerging, unstable term in later medieval England. Throughout the early Middle Ages, the Latin word *habitus* had designated an internalized virtue that was specifically Christian, and to which only those who *wore* the habit – male and female religious – could ever hope to aspire.[36] These associations linger on in the earliest recorded uses of Middle English *habit* in the thirteenth century (recorded, coincidentally, in the *Ancrene Wisse*), and from that time until the end of the fourteenth century the word was most frequently used to refer to the clothing characteristically worn by male and female religious. During this period, Katharine Breen has argued, '*habit* describes only the relatively small part of [*habitus*] that was visible to lay people, while leaving the senses of *habitus* as internalized Christian ethics, and even settled disposition, untranslated and inaccessible'.[37] But as the fourteenth century became the fifteenth century, authors increasingly used *habit* to refer to 'mental condition, mental or moral disposition' as well as 'customary practice', as Breen explains:[38]

> the normative behavior of lay people, whether marked by appropriate clothing or a suitable mental disposition, becomes linguistically continuous with the normative behavior of the clergy. Instead of belonging to distinct languages or verbal registers, the two realms began to shade into each other by way of a hard-to-define middle ground occupied by devout anchoresses, corrupt friars, and traveling monks. In the process, *habit* itself spread from narrow, philosophical uses into a broader English moral lexicon.[39]

Breen traces this gradual shift in meaning, the importation of *habitus* into the Middle English *habit*, and then the vernacular term's accumulation of the various behavioural connotations of its Latin forebear.[40] Notably, she observes that the medieval concept of *habitus* is of a *consciously learned or cultivated* 'mental or moral disposition', 'customary practice', and 'innate property'.[41] As well as contrasting with the more contemporary understanding of habit as something unconsciously 'picked up', this medieval concept of *habitus* overlaps with and differs from Pierre Bourdieu's notion of 'habitus' as 'systems of durable, transposable *dispositions* … which can be objectively "regulated" and "regular" without in any way being the product of obedience to rules, objectively adapted to their goals without presupposing a conscious aiming at ends or an express mastery of the operations necessary to attain them'.[42] Key to Bourdieu's theory of habitus is the notion that, because the actions of an individual 'are the product of a *modus operandi* of which he is not the producer and has no conscious mastery',

> they contain an 'objective intention', as the Scholastics put it, which always outruns his conscious intentions. The schemes of thought and expression he has acquired are the basis for the *intentionless invention* of regulated improvisation.[43]

Thus, not only are an individual's actions a series of 'regulated improvisations', but they are also the product of structures of which he is unaware and in the perpetuation of which he unconsciously participates. By contrast, whereas for Bourdieu habitus works in a largely unconscious way, medieval philosophers and theologians viewed *habitus* as 'a conscious tool for reforming or perfecting behaviour'.[44]

Despite its associations with virtue, Latin *habitus* could still be perceived as a slippery concept in medieval England. As *habitus* evolved into Middle English *habit*, this shift was accompanied by a kind of outward conceptual spreading (or, to use Breen's word, 'expansion') of both language and ideas from the Latin, clerical *habitus* into a correspondingly flexible vernacular equivalent.[45] Thus, by the mid fifteenth century Reginald Pecock (c. 1395–c. 1461) wrote in *The Folewer to the Donet* that when a 'disposicioun is comen into þis now seid degre of stabilnes and of vnremouabilnes, þanne it is clepid an "habite"'.[46] However, at the same time that the various meanings of *habitus* were being translated into English, religious controversy within England transformed the concept into 'an important site of moral and religious contest'.[47] Hence a common Middle English proverb warned, 'Abit ne makith neither monk ne frere' (or, in medieval Latin, 'habitus non facit monachum').[48]

The emergence of new vernacular concepts of *habit* in later medieval England helps to explain the admixture of admiration and suspicion that attended the practice of female honour in Middle English texts written during this period. The fact that female honour depended to such an extent on the practice of shamefastness made it a precarious concept, encompassing both a sense of stable interior virtue and a potentially misleading outward appearance of virtue (and scepticism was further exacerbated by centuries of misogynist writing depicting women as temptresses, seductresses, and deceivers).[49] The persistence with which conduct texts for women deploy the language of *habit* in their references to virtuous *customs*, *thewis*, and, as in Pecock, *disposicions*, suggests the extent to which women were encouraged to be perfectly shamefast inside and out. This language requires and repays close attention, which uncovers the uneasy relationship between *habit* and the description and depiction of female shamefastness in later medieval texts. At the same time, as my second epigraph illustrates, the idea of a shamefast *habit* inevitably raises questions concerning 'the supposed congruence between inner and outer behaviour'; in *The Canterbury Tales*, Alison the Wife of Bath describes how she would anticipate and forestall any objections her husbands might raise concerning her interest in wearing beautiful clothing:

> Thou seyst also, that if we make us gay
> With clothyng, and with precious array,
> That it is peril of oure chastitee;
> And yet – with sorwe! – thou most enforce thee,
> And seye thise wordes in the Apostles name:

Introduction

> 'In habit maad with chastitee and shame
> Ye wommen shul apparaille yow,' quod he,
> 'And noght in tressed heer and gay perree,
> As perles, ne with gold, ne clothes riche.'
> After thy text, ne after thy rubriche,
> I wol nat wirche as muchel as a gnat.
> *(The Wife of Bath's Prologue* 337–47)

Chastity is the key issue here, and too much 'precious array' is deemed to put it at risk. Alison maintains that her husband identifies a 'habit maad with chastitee and shame' as the only finery to which a woman should aspire, the only ornament that is both honourable and protects the foundation of a woman's honour. The passage's reference to 'the Apostles name' points us to Alison's husband's purported source text, the first epistle of St Paul to Timothy, in which Paul declares that women should clothe themselves in virtue rather than in finery:

> [volo] mulieres in habitu ornato cum verecundia et sobrietate ornantes se non in tortis crinibus aut auro aut margaritis vel veste pretiosa sed quod decet mulieres promittentes pietatem per opera bona.
>
> I wolle þat wymmen ben in covenable abite, wiþ schamefastnesse and sobirnesse ournynge hem or makynge fair, not in wriþen here, ne in gold, ne in margery stones, or perlis, ne in precious cloþ, but þat þat bicomeþ wymmen bihetynge pite, bi goode werkis.[50]

In Chaucer's source text, a virtuous habit is a metaphorical garment, a gleaming marker of virtue more precious than cloth interwoven with gold or gems. Such manifest virtue is the highest form of *ournynge* (adornment) a woman can display, and therefore, Alison's husband would claim, is the most 'precious array' a woman should exhibit; it is also the most secure, since it will not imperil chastity.[51] At the same time, however, the passage's emphasis on the importance of 'schamefastnesse', 'sobirnesse', and 'goode werkis' suggests that this garment is the product of a woman's comportment and disposition, a reflection of the alternate definitions of the Middle English word *habit* as one's mental or moral disposition, or customary practice.[52] Alison's use of the word 'shul' ('should', a modal auxiliary conveying duty or a command) plays upon these behavioural connotations, implying that women have an obligation to cultivate a sense of shame until it becomes habit.[53] Being in the habit (*in habitu*) of shamefastness requires more than merely keeping up appearances: it requires the regular practice of particular behaviours in order to reinforce and demonstrate a virtuous disposition. Yet the passage's opening references to splendid garments gestures towards some of the ways in which the virtue of shamefastness might also be mistaken for something to be put on (and, later, taken off) like an article of clothing or an accessory, serving no other purpose than to temporarily dazzle the onlooker. This poses a significant problem, for how then can we tell one kind of 'habit' from the other?

These questions were especially urgent at the moment when Chaucer was writing. Between the fourteenth and fifteenth centuries, ideas about female virtue and the practice thereof were undergoing fundamental shifts. Prior to the fourteenth century, a clear hierarchy of female virtue is consistently in evidence in medieval texts: in descending order, the three honourable categories that women could occupy in medieval Europe were those of virgin, widow, or wife.[54] Virginity was the unchallenged gold standard of spiritual virtue for women within this hierarchy, and something to which not many women outside of a nunnery, anchorhold, or beguinage could aspire.[55] Thus, the thirteenth-century Middle English prose text now known as *Hali Meiðhad* informs its readers that 'alswa as a charbucle is betere þen a iacinct i þe euene of hare cunde ... alswa passeþ meiden, onont te mihte of meiþhad, widewen ant iweddede' (although it also warns that 'tah is betere a milde wif oþer a meoke widewe þen a prud meiden').[56] Over the last two decades, however, scholarship on late medieval conduct literature produced in England and France has shed light on how this genre transformed the household into a new site for the cultivation of spiritual and social female virtue in the context of the married life.[57] Most recently, Glenn Burger has argued that conduct literature for women redefines 'woman and the feminine such that the benefits of chastity can be made available to a much wider group of women than virgins, martyrs, or nuns':

> It is especially in the literate practices surrounding private devotion that the laywoman, living not in a nunnery or anchorage or beguinage but fully in the world of the married household, can find a space and time where her conduct can most effectively show the full potential of her nature, where the good wife can equal, or even excel, the virgin nun in her excellence as a fully formed ethical subject. Such texts and the practices that they engender open up a space and time for her labor in ways that rework the formerly hierarchized relation of virgin, widow, wife and reconceptualise the good wife's place in that symbolic imaginary.[58]

Introduction

Thus, just as *habit* was migrating from Latinate, monastic contexts to vernacular, lay contexts, the question of what chaste female excellence might consist of, and of who might practise it (and how), was generating new answers. The discourse surrounding the practice of female shamefastness in later medieval English texts suggests that, in light of these changes, the same issue of authenticity which had dogged *habitus* also attended the habit of shamefastness, not least because it had to be practised, not within a religious enclosure, but in the open and comparatively unregulated spaces of the community.

The Wife of Bath's reference to habit bears witness to the shifts and complications that attended concepts of female virtue in this period. The word *habit* in *The Wife of Bath's Prologue* evokes not only the image of shamefastness as a protective garment, but also the Latin concept of *habitus*, a morally virtuous inner disposition moulded by – and reflected in – consistent, disciplined practice. But Alison rejects 'the Apostles'' idea of habit as outwardly visible inner virtue in favour of material clothing that, in the eyes of many misogynist writers, would be an accurate reflection of women's material priorities. This is unsurprising, given that the Wife of Bath is largely a composite of anti-feminist convention and satire drawn from other texts; but her reference to this passage from the letter of St Paul threatens to reduce the terms habit and *habitus* to nothing more than sartorial signifiers. By extension, this would reduce a practice or 'habit' of chastity and shamefastness to nothing more than an act, the mere appearance of virtue. Such a reduction would, ironically enough, recall shame's etymological associations with clothing and covering: the form of the Old English words (*scamu*, *sceamu*, *scomu*, etc.) from which Middle English *shame* originates derives ultimately from a Proto-Indo-European verb meaning 'to cover', a gesture that has long been associated with the sense of exposure that characterizes shame, and the instinctive response to that sense of exposure.[59] As Sara Ahmed has put it, shame 'involves an impulse to "take cover" and "to cover oneself". But the desire to take cover and to be covered presupposes the failure of cover; in shame, one desires cover precisely because one has already been exposed to others'.[60] In medieval Christian culture, the archetypal image of bodily concealment was also the moment at which shame was believed to have become a part of the human condition: the moment when Adam and Eve realized their nakedness and covered themselves with fig leaves. As I suggest in Chapter 1, the practice of shamefastness involves women in a complex of antithetical gestures characterized by covering and withdrawal on the one hand and, on the other, the exhibition of this covering and withdrawal as evidence of their chastity. And while this practice is presented as something that can be achieved through discipline and effort, it is perceived as most genuine, most trustworthy, when it appears most artless and effortless to others.

As I hope this study will show, textual treatments of female shamefastness demand in-depth reading not only because they bear witness to the emerging Middle English discourse of habit (particularly as it pertains to female virtue), but also because of the role that these texts played in shaping habit. This role was very familiar to medieval English authors such as Thomas Hoccleve, as David Watt has shown in his study of Hoccleve's *Series* (1420–21). Watt employs the term 'information technology' to describe the function of the *Series*, which he suggests was 'designed to contribute to the re-formation of the English character'.[61] Watt derives his term from the way that writers such as Hoccleve, Gower, and Chaucer use the word *information* in their writings to refer to ways of shaping one's character via the communication of knowledge. As he notes,

> Character development in the early fifteenth century was often understood as a process through which the substance of memory could be informed (i.e., formed inwardly) through the communication of instructive knowledge. The book, which is a technological form, is an important medium in the communication of knowledge.[62]

Watt's interpretation of the medieval concept of 'in-formation' reads it as an active, conscious process of character development, one for which books function as crucial tools. These later medieval beliefs concerning character development owe much to monastic traditions concerning the importance of memory and memory work to the cultivation of moral character, a subject most thoroughly explored in the work of Mary Carruthers.[63] Carruthers has shown that medieval texts characterize memory and cognition as arts or crafts that employ a range of tools including images, meditation, and emotions. According to Carruthers, '[i]n the idiom of monasticism, people do not "have" ideas, they "make" them'.[64] In her reading of Aristotle, Carruthers identifies 'emotional colouring' as key to the formation of a virtuous *habitus*: one's '*hexis* or *habitus* is a matter of custom, particular emotional responses and acts performed in the past and remembered, which then predispose it to the same response in the future. Both vices and virtues are habitual dispositions, formed in this way.'[65] The content and popularity of medieval conduct texts and exemplary narratives suggest that similar practices could be adapted to the cultivation of virtues such as shamefastness in lay audiences. The strategies employed by these texts seem calculated to inculcate shamefastness by presenting it as admirable and even desirable, or by inviting women to contemplate how shameful it would be to be judged unchaste. In the latter case, medieval texts serve as something like a controlled environment for emotional experimentation, a virtual space within which women might vicariously experience shame through specific characters or scenarios without experiencing shame directly.

By practising shamefastness, women constructed a habit with which they might hope to secure their honour. Literature was a tool for this habituation insofar as it extolled the value of female shamefastness, reinforced the idea that shamefastness lay at the heart of female honour, offered models of shamefast behaviour (and counterexamples of shameless women), and described how a shamefast practice could be developed and reinforced. But what was the honour to which medieval women were being encouraged to aspire, and how could shamefastness help them to secure it?

Understanding shame

Historian Ute Frevert has described honour as 'a lost emotion, or, to be more precise, as a disposition whose emotional power has more or less vanished' even though the word remains in our vocabulary.[66] The inverse might be said of shamefastness: the word is now obsolete, but the degree to which shamefastness still exists today – and the degree to which it has emotional power, or to which it is gendered – might be said to be a function of the social, geographical, or religious context in question. Its association with chastity – one of the more important determinants of female honour in the Middle Ages – is certainly nowhere near as universal today as it would have been in medieval England (not overtly, at any rate, although it still underpins contemporary understandings of female virtue in highly problematic ways). The belief that female chastity was almost constantly at risk reinforced the belief that constant vigilance was needed against the prospect of its violation. A sense of shame was therefore something that women needed to maintain and demonstrate consistently, rather than something acquired or demonstrated on a one-time-only basis.

At the same time, a sense of shame was not *exclusive* to women. Biblical history traced the origins of shame back to original sin and the fall of man, before which Adam and Eve 'shameden noȝt', in spite of their nakedness.⁶⁷ But although shame is a consequence of the fall of man, in it also lies the possibility for human redemption; as Valerie Allen notes, 'Christian morality valorizes shame ... because it seeks to compensate for and protect against the spiritual frailty that is our universal condition'.⁶⁸ According to the authors of fourteenth-century devotional texts, shame was one of the most effective emotional weapons against sin, particularly the sin of pride. The opening invocation of *Handlyng Synne*, a treatise translated from an Anglo-Norman source by Robert Mannyng (died c. 1338), suggests that shame is fundamental both to moving the penitent to confession and to eventually triumphing over 'þe fende':

> Fadyr, and Sone, & holy goste,
> Þat art o god of myȝtes moste,
> At þy wurschyp shul we bygynne,
> To shame þe fende & shew oure synne;
> Synne to shewe, vs to frame,
> God to wurschyp, þe fende to shame.⁶⁹

And as Walter Hilton's (c. 1343–96) *The Scale of Perfection* shows, shame can also forestall the possibility of pride:

> Thanne yif thou feele a stirynge of pride, or ony othir spice of it, be soone waar yif thou mai, and suffre hit not lightli passe awai, but take in thi mynde and rende it, breke it and dispice it, and doo al the shame that thou mai therto.⁷⁰

Here, Hilton's words deploy shame against pride in a psychomachic struggle over the Christian soul. In this context, shame is a weapon to be used by the reader 'in thi mynde' to combat sin.⁷¹ This redemptive function notwithstanding, in the medieval imagination shame remained linked with the exposure of the human body's most private parts to the eyes of others.

Within the past decade, shame has attracted increasing attention from medievalists,⁷² as well as from cultural and literary theorists whose studies have profoundly influenced the history of emotions.⁷³ These studies have raised shame's profile in medieval scholarship, to the point where Allen has stated that 'we might even call shame the primal medieval emotion, so ubiquitous and various are its applications'.⁷⁴ In his recently published history of shame, Stearns begins his chapter on premodern shame by making reference to the Middle Ages, a sign, perhaps, of the extent to which the emotion and the epoch have become yoked together in the minds of scholars.[75] Yet the concept of shamefastness is often absorbed into discussions of medieval shame without any acknowledgement of its distinctiveness as an emotional disposition, nor of its role in the establishment and safekeeping of female honour.[76]

In the case of medieval English literary studies, one possible reason for this oversight may be the imbalance between the relatively limited availability of Middle English vocabulary for shame and related concepts in comparison with the abundance of such terms in Latin and in continental vernaculars. Thus, for example, Thomas Aquinas used *verecundia* and *pudicitia* to refer to different kinds of shame; whereas *verecundia* refers to 'a recoil[ing] from the disgrace that is contrary to temperance', Aquinas uses *pudicitia* in his discussion of chastity:[77]

> [P]udicitia attenditur proprie circa venerea, et præcipue circa signa venereorum, sicut sunt aspectus impudici, oscula et tactus. Et quia hæc magis solent deprehendi, ideo pudicitia magis respicit hujusmodi exteriora signa; castitas autem magis ipsam veneream commixtionem. Et ideo pudicitia ad castitatem ordinatur, non quasi virtus ab ipsa distincta, sed sicut exprimens castitatis circumstantiam quamdam. Interdum tamen unum pro alio ponitur.
>
> [P]urity [*pudicitia*] or modesty properly speaking regards sex activity, and chiefly its secondary manifestations, such as looks, kisses, and touches. Usage applies it to these, and chastity rather to the act of intercourse. Purity is ordained to chastity, not as a distinct virtue, but as dealing with what surrounds it. Sometimes, however, the terms are used interchangeably.[78]

Whereas Latin texts such as Aquinas's *Summa Theologiae* might navigate between such distinct terms as *verecundia*, *pudor*, *pudicitia*, and *modestia* (and French texts, for example, between such terms as *vergoigne*, *honte*, and *pudeur*), writers using Middle English were limited almost entirely to *shame* and *shamefastness*, each of which could encompass a number of concepts.[79] The definitions of *shamefast* provided by medieval English–Latin and Latin–English dictionaries and word lists suggest that *verecundia* may have been perceived as the nearest Latin equivalent: in an early Middle English copy of Aelfric's *Grammar* and *Glossary* contained in a thirteenth-century manuscript in Worcester Cathedral, '*Uerecundus*' is glossed as 'sceomefest' (and '*Inpudens*' as 'unsceomefest'), while a copy of the fifteenth-century English–Latin *Promptorium parvulorum* in London, British Library MS Harley 221 defines '*Schamefast*' as 'Verecundus, verecundiosus, pudorosus'.[80] Alternatively, another fifteenth-century Latin–English vocabulary list contained in Trinity College Cambridge MS O.5.4 presents 'shamfast' as the equivalent of *'Rubescens'*, linking the concept of shamefastness to the red of a blushing face.

The Middle English noun *shame* has a particularly wide range of potential meanings, including fear of disgrace; 'the feeling of having done something disgraceful'; modesty or timidity; humiliation; immoral behaviour; nakedness, or the genitals; a verbal insult; loss of virginity; or the sexual violation of a woman.[81] While *shamefastness* has many fewer possible definitions, these meanings still include modesty, bashfulness, and shyness, as well as regret and remorse.[82] Thus, even if at first blush we might be tempted to equate shamefastness very broadly with modesty or humility, the terms are not so easily interchangeable. The translation of concepts between languages, and the evolution of *shamefastness* within the English language, might seem to situate shamefastness among emotions such as *acedia* or *melancholia* or dispositions like honour that Frevert views as having been lost to the past:

> [e]ven if there are signs of *acedia*, *melancholia* and depression that resemble each other, the labeling, framing and contextualizing of those signs are vastly different. Relating the symptoms to diverse systems of reference (magic, religion, arts and sciences, neurobiology) affects the value attributed to them. This in turn affects the appraisal and experience of those states. Seen from this perspective, *acedia* and *melancholia* are indeed 'lost emotions,' lost in translation to a new emotional state called *depression*.[83]

Frevert is right to draw attention to the ways that emotion-words and -concepts fall in and out of use over time, but to refer to them as 'lost' risks obscuring the ways in which they inform and shape successive emotion-concepts, dispositions, attitudes, and identities. Such is the case with regard to shamefastness: whether as *verecundia* or *pudicitia*, a sense of shame was esteemed more highly by medieval Christianity than it had been in classical philosophy. In his *Nicomachean Ethics*, Aristotle argued that shame should not be 'described as a virtue' because 'it is more like a feeling than a state of character'. He defines shame as 'a kind of fear of dishonour' and contends that it is more becoming to youth than to age:

> For we think young people should be prone to the feeling of shame because they live by feeling and therefore commit many errors, but are restrained by shame; and we praise young people who are prone

to this feeling, but an older person no one would praise for being prone to the sense of disgrace, since we think he should not do anything that need cause this sense. For the sense of disgrace is not even characteristic of a good man, since it is consequent on bad actions (for such actions should not be done; and if some actions are disgraceful in very truth and others only according to common opinion, this makes no difference; for neither class of actions should be done, so that no disgrace should be felt); and it is a mark of a bad man even to be such as to do any disgraceful action.[84]

In medieval interpretations of Aristotle's arguments, a sense of shame is increasingly dissociated with masculinity and *associated* with honourable femininity. In book 4 of his *Il Convivio*, for example, Dante glosses Aristotle's *Ethics* when he declares that shame ('vergogna') is 'good and praiseworthy' ('buona e laudabile') 'in women and in young people' ('nelle donne e nelli giovani').[85] Commenting on the distinction between Aristotle's depiction of shame and Aquinas's treatment of *verecundia*, Allen has argued that the latter carries a 'heightened sense of modesty'; it 'protects' rather than 'constrains':

> By virtue of its doctrine of original sin, Christian morality valorizes shame, which for Aristotle is a mark of privation and weakness, because it seeks to compensate for and protect against the spiritual frailty that is our universal condition. Doubly frail because she is weaker in reason and body than is a man, woman needs shame to cover and support her.[86]

Nevertheless, even Aquinas debated the question of whether shame was a passion or a virtue, ultimately deciding that it possessed aspects of both.[87]

Over the course of my discussion, it will become clear that the shame and shamefastness I am describing cannot always be thoroughly disentangled from neighbouring emotions such as guilt or embarrassment. As some of the texts considered here suggest, these emotional fields can occasionally blur together, or perform similar work. My aim is not to throw up rigid barriers between these concepts, nor to lay out precisely how we ought to relate them to one another.[88] The practice of shamefastness as I outline it here does not rely on hard-and-fast definitions of isolated emotions, but is rather made up of a network of ideas that were constantly being rearticulated, redefined, and redeployed by those who wrote about them.

Chapter synopses

My emphasis throughout this book is on how Middle English texts shape, enable, and reflect the female practice of shamefastness. Not all of the texts discussed here would be universally recognized as 'literary' (although they have all attracted the attention of literary scholars), but by closely reading literary texts in the broader context of writing for and about women, I hope to demonstrate what discourses and imagery literary texts share with non-literary material, as well as some of the distinctive ways that literary texts in particular shape emotion practices and norms. In generic terms, the texts I examine move from the more practical subjects covered by medical treatises and conduct texts to the more strictly literary realm of courtly poetry, classical exempla, and petitionary verse as my argument unfolds. At the same time, the focus of my argument moves from female honour's grounding in the gestures of the female body, through the effects of shamefast practice on women, and, ultimately, to the staging of a shamefast persona by a male author. The texts I consider shape and facilitate shamefastness in various ways: by articulating the connection between shamefastness and gestures of concealment and exhibition; by functioning as guides for practising shamefastness; by depicting female shamefastness as an adversary of male desire; and by depicting models of honourable female shamefastness. They also reveal the ways in which the idea of shamefastness *as* a practice made it a potentially unreliable sign of female virtue, as well as a performance that might be reappropriated by male authors.

Chapter 1 examines the embodied nature of female honour. Because the chief determinant of a woman's honour was her degree of sexual continence, women's bodies and even their most private parts simultaneously required concealment and direct or indirect scrutiny. In order to show how this paradox both necessitated and complicated the practice of shamefastness, I begin by considering the ways in which the language of shame was applied to women's bodies (most specifically to their private parts or *shamefuls*). I then examine how beliefs concerning the postlapsarian origins of shame contributed to medieval understandings of both pain and shame as universal features of women's experience of childbirth. In the final part of this chapter, I consider how the prologues of two Middle English gynaecological treatises, *The Knowing of Woman's Kind in Childing* and *The Sickness of Women*, point to the social and emotional risks women faced in exposing their bodies even for the ostensibly innocent purposes of medical diagnosis and treatment. In their efforts to mitigate these risks on behalf of female patients, these prologues reveal the complications that arise in the 'show and tell' of gynaecological practice and even the writing of gynaecological texts. I argue that this dynamic mirrors that of the practice of female shamefastness, which simultaneously requires the concealment and withdrawal of women's bodies and the exhibition of their shamefast chastity.

In Chapter 2, I turn to conduct literature for women and investigate how Middle English examples of this genre lay out practical advice for the cultivation of female shamefastness. Medieval conduct literature for women was primarily concerned with issues of proper comportment and behaviour, the makings and markers of a 'good' honourable woman. Since incontrovertible sexual continence was the surest foundation of female honour, conduct texts for women inevitably concentrate on promoting the development of a strong sense of shame. As fear of disgrace, shamefastness operated as a restraint on female behaviour which, when properly and regularly practised, helped women to safeguard their good name. This chapter considers *The Book of the Knight of La Tour Landry* (a Middle English translation of the prose treatise *Le livre du Chevalier de la Tour Landry pour l'enseignement de ses filles*) alongside several Middle English and Scottish conduct poems addressed to or concerning women in order to show how these texts valorize shamefastness, which they present as a practice made up of and reliant on patterns of behaviour aimed at producing and communicating a specific emotional state. I propose that we can read texts like these as guides for the development of a strong sense of shame, guides that on occasion harness startlingly literary tropes, devices, and techniques in order to promote the disciplined practice of female shame.

In Chapter 3, I examine the ways that medieval texts also present female shamefastness as problematically 'practised' – that is, as behaviour that might be learned and faked by women hoping to present the appearance of virtue. Suspicion of female shamefastness was exacerbated by anti-feminist literary traditions surrounding courtly erotic desire that presented women as inherently lustful creatures longing to be sexually conquered by men, and which suggested that, if shamefastness did not exist, men would not need to lay siege to women in order to enjoy their sexual favour. Texts such as the *Roman de la rose* and its Middle English translation depict shamefastness as a personified figure hindering men in the pursuit of their desire, an obstacle who must be overcome at all costs, even if by force. I begin by considering the origins of the adversarial dynamic between desire and shamefastness in influential personification allegories such as Prudentius's *Psychomachia* and, later, the *Roman de la rose*. I then show how the *Roman* and its Middle English translation draw on anti-feminist suspicion of female shamefastness, suspicion that later informs John Lydgate's depiction of Medea's infatuation with Jason in his *Troy Book*. As I show, Lydgate depicts Medea as a figure of both cunning and lust, a woman who exploits the conventions of shamefast behaviour in order to conceal her desire, and a troubling example of the ways in which shamefast practice was an object of potential suspicion as well as a potential source of honour.

Chapter 4 continues to unpick the problematic nature of honourable female shamefastness by turning to two exemplary shamefast women: Virginia and Lucretia. Medieval readers and writers were alternately fascinated and horrified by the stories of Virginia and Lucretia, classical examples of women faced with the prospect of either death or dishonour. Underlying the mixed reader responses to these narratives is an urge to indulge in counterfactual fantasy – to imagine what *might* have happened under different circumstances. But I argue that, at the same time that these stories invite readers to create counterfactual versions, they foreclose the possibility of doing so. This foreclosure is the result of the problematic binary at the heart of these narratives: the assumption that honourable shamefast women who are faced with the possibility of disgrace must endure either death or shame. This chapter takes up the troubling relationship between the model of hardy masculinity set forth in such texts as the *Roman de la rose* and the practice of female shamefastness, and considers its disturbing implications for exemplary female chastity. I argue that, in his retellings of the stories of Virginia and Lucrece, Chaucer highlights and critiques the inevitability of their deaths by aligning it with the tension between the expectations of masculinity and female honour. Building on the arguments I have put forward elsewhere concerning the depiction of honourable women in Chaucer's work, this chapter considers how and why Chaucer's *Physician's Tale* and *Legend of Lucrece* deviate from classical narratives, and from the versions of these stories included in John Gower's *Confessio Amantis* (composed during the same period as Chaucer's stories).[89]

Chapter 5 considers the works of one male fifteenth-century author who was particularly adept at adopting a mantle of feminine shamefastness when it suited him: Thomas Hoccleve (c. 1368–1426).

'Embarrassment' has come to be thought of as a characteristic feature of Hoccleve's poetics, but I argue for closer attention to the role played by the language and imagery of shame and shamefastness in shaping this poetics.[90] I begin by considering the Middle English language of 'manhood' and 'manliness', which frequently contrasts masculine boldness with feminine bashfulness and hesitation. I then explore the ways in which Hoccleve's scepticism concerning the reliability of appearances (articulated in his *Letter of Cupid*) informs his engagement with the binary that links masculinity with boldness and aggression, and femininity with shamefastness. I argue that in his early poem, *La Male Regle*, Hoccleve exploits the nature of shamefastness as a potentially suspicious practice, turning what medieval women were encouraged to make an apparently artless performance of virtue into a performance of conspicuous artifice.

The chapters that follow demonstrate the extent to which the literature of medieval England presents female honour as a matter of *feeling* like an honourable woman.[91] As I hope I will make clear, the idea of 'feeling like an honourable woman' denotes an ethical and emotional construction of gender that is potentially imitable by others, and capable of being reappropriated for other purposes. At the same time, its very imitability, and the potential for its reappropriation, rendered shamefastness a difficult and even dangerous habit for medieval women to acquire.

Notes

1 Quotations from *The Thewis of Good Women* are taken from the editions of the two versions of the poem contained in *The Good Wife Taught Her Daughter, The Good Wyfe Wold a Pylgremage, The Thewis of Gud Women*, ed. Tauno E. Mustanoja (Helsinki: Suomaleisen Kirjallisuuden Seuran, 1948), presented in parallel at pp. 176–95. The poem survives in two manuscripts: Cambridge, Cambridge University Library MS Kk.1.5 (fols 49–53; hereafter referred to as C), and Cambridge, St John's College G.23 (fols 164–67v; hereafter referred to as J). Citations from the text will be taken from Mustanoja's edition, and cited above by version and line number.
2 All citations of Chaucer's works in this study are drawn from *The Riverside Chaucer*, ed. Larry D. Benson *et al.*, 3rd edn (Oxford: Oxford University Press, 2008), and will be cited above by line number.
3 *MED*, s. v. *honour*.
4 Throughout this book, I will use 'chastity' to refer to sexual continence, the parameters of which depend on a woman's marital status, as I discuss in Chapter 2.

5 Medieval anxieties concerning the 'openness' of the female body contribute to what Caroline Walker Bynum has identified as the medieval view that 'the good female body is closed and intact; the bad woman's body is open, windy and breachable' ('The Female Body and Medieval Religious Practice in the Later Middle Ages', in Michel Feher, with Ramona Naddaf and Nadia Tazi (eds), *Fragments for a History of the Human Body* (New York, NY: Zone Books, 1989), pp. 181–238 (p. 212, n. 98). Gail Kern Paster has also explored anxieties concerning the 'leakiness' of the female body in *The Body Embarrassed: Drama and the Disciplines of Shame in Early Modern England* (New York, NY: Cornell University Press, 1993). Misogynist stereotypes concerning the sensual nature of women are recorded in many of the sources edited in *Woman Defamed and Woman Defended: An Anthology of Medieval Texts*, ed. Alcuin Blamires, with Karen Pratt and C. W. Marx (Oxford: Clarendon Press, 1992).
6 *MED*, s. v. *slider*.
7 See *MED*, s. v. *radnesse* (fear, terror) and *rade* (afraid, frightened because of).
8 This shift is discussed by Glenn D. Burger in *Conduct Becoming: Good Wives and Husbands in the Later Middle Ages* (Philadelphia, PA: University of Pennsylvania Press, 2018), in which Burger argues that, while treatises like *Hali Meiðhad* had reinforced 'a traditional medieval hierarchy of women's roles founded on the absolute value of chastity within the enclosed life', the lay spiritual guidance offered by texts composed in and after the fourteenth century 'promise a rule for devout laypeople that can – at least potentially – come close to that achieved by those contemplatives living enclosed lives' (p. 39). Burger pays particular attention to the continental origins of this shift in texts like the fourteenth-century *Livre du Chevalier de la Tour Landry pour l'enseignement de ses filles* and its sources, in which (to quote Anne Marie De Gendt) '[l]a chasteté devient donc une vertu non seulement morale, mais aussi sociale' ('chastity thus becomes a virtue that is not only moral, but also social'; *L'Art d'éduquer les nobles damoiselles: Le Livre du Chevalier de la Tour Landry* (Paris: Champion, 2003), p. 158; quoted in Burger at p. 217 n. 48, whose translation on p. 95 I have adapted here). See also Lynn Staley, *Languages of Power in the Age of Richard II* (University Park, PA: The Pennsylvania State University Press, 2005), who maintains that conduct texts such as *Le livre du Chevalier* offer 'a view of the world in which a young woman may find in marriage the spiritual fulfilment she might have sought in a nunnery' (p. 271).
9 This is not to say that a sense of shame was considered universally useful; a number of texts suggest that too much shame could prevent one from confessing to sin, for example, as in the account of a woman who was damned because she did not confess to having had sex with a monk 'for drede of encursinge, dredinge shame and the bobaunce of

the worlde, more thanne spirituel uengeaunce of myn synne' (Geoffrey de la Tour Landry, *The Book of the Knight of La Tour Landry*, ed. Thomas Wright, EETS OS 33 (London: N. Trübner & Co., 1868), pp. 12–13). The Middle English word *shame* is occasionally used to refer to a sense of shame, rather than to the experience of disgrace, but in order to avoid confusion I will use *shamefastness* and 'a sense of shame' interchangeably, and I will clarify whenever a Middle English text is using *shame* to refer to this sense of shame (as in the epigraph taken from *The Wife of Bath's Prologue*, discussed later in this introduction).

10 *MED*, s. v. *shamefast, shamefastness*; *OED*, s. v. *shamefaced*. Although *shamefastness* most frequently describes a fixed fear or regular avoidance of disgrace, the word is occasionally used to refer to the experience of disgrace, which may explain the eventual evolution of 'shamefast' into 'shamefaced'.

11 Stearns, *Shame: A Brief History*, p. 8. The body of scholarship on shame is vast; Stearns provides a useful starting point in his list of suggested texts for further reading (pp. 155–8). Although the power of anticipative shame has been little explored in historical studies, it has been the subject of several psychological studies: see, for example, Vanessa M. Patrick, HaeEun Helen Chun, and Deborah J. Macinnis, 'Affective Forecasting and Social Control: Why Anticipating Pride Wins Over Anticipating Shame in a Self-regulation Context', *Journal of Consumer Psychology* 19 (2009), 537–45; Lee Shepherd, Russell Spears, and Antony S. R. Manstead, '"This Will Bring Shame on Our Nation": The Role of Anticipated Group-based Emotions on Collective Action', *Journal of Experimental Psychology* 49 (2013), 42–57; Lee Shepherd, Russell Spears, and Antony S. R. Manstead, 'When Does Anticipating Group-based Shame Lead to Lower Ingroup Favoritism? The Role of Status and Status Stability', *Journal of Experimental Psychology* 49 (2013), 334–43; and T. Bonavia and J. Brox-Ponce 'Shame in Decision Making Under Risk Conditions: Understanding the Effect of Transparency', *Public Library of Science (PLoS) ONE* 13 (2018), e0191990, https://doi.org/10.1371/journal.pone.0191990 [accessed 19 April 2018].

12 *MED*, s. v. *fast*.

13 On the crisis of *habit* and *habitus* (internalized Christian virtue) in later medieval England, see Katharine Breen, *Imagining an English Reading Public, 1150–1400* (Cambridge: Cambridge University Press, 2010), discussed more fully below.

14 Robert C. Solomon, *True to Our Feelings: What Our Emotions Are Really Telling Us* (Oxford: Oxford University Press, 2007), p. 157; William M. Reddy, *The Navigation of Feeling: A Framework for the History of Emotions* (Cambridge: Cambridge University Press, 2001).

15 Reddy, *The Navigation of Feeling*, pp. 104–5; see also his earlier articulation of these arguments in 'Against Constructionism: The

Historical Ethnography of Emotions', *Current Anthropology* 38 (1997), 327–51 (p. 331).

16 Patrick Colm Hogan, 'Fictions and Feelings: On the Place of Literature in the Study of Emotion', *Emotion Review* 2 (2010), 184–95 (p. 185).

17 See, for example, Hogan, 'Fictions and Feelings', which considers the ways that literature encodes and represents emotion; Carolyne Larrington, 'The Psychology of Emotion and Study of the Medieval Period', *Early Medieval Europe* 10 (2001), 251–6, which contends that imaginative literature permits 'access to the protagonists' interior processes, processes which are of course imagined, but not randomly so' (p. 254); and Mary C. Flannery, 'Personification and Embodied Emotional Practice in Middle English Literature', *Literature Compass* 13 (2016), 351–61, which argues for focusing on literary tropes and forms in order to incorporate literature into the history of emotions. (I also make a broader case for the centrality of textual evidence to the history of emotions in my introduction to Mary C. Flannery (ed.), *Emotion & Medieval Textual Media* (Turnhout: Brepols, 2019).) Despite historians' misgivings concerning the potentially misleading nature of literary evidence, several historical studies of emotion have made use of literary texts. Reddy has been foremost among those to do so: see for example *The Navigation of Feeling* and *The Making of Romantic Love: Longing and Sexuality in Europe, South Asia, and Japan, 900–1200 CE* (Oxford: Oxford University Press, 2012).

18 Sarah McNamer, 'Feeling', in Paul Strohm (ed.), *Oxford Twenty-First-Century Approaches to Literature: Middle English* (Oxford: Oxford University Press, 2007), pp. 241–57 (p. 243).

19 Sarah McNamer, 'The Literariness of Literature and the History of Emotion', *PMLA* 130 (2015), 1433–42 (p. 1435).

20 Sarah McNamer, *Affective Meditation and the Invention of Medieval Compassion* (Philadelphia, PA: University of Pennsylvania Press, 2010), pp. 1, 12–13.

21 *Ibid.*, p. 13.

22 McNamer, 'Feeling', pp. 245–7 (original emphasis), referring particularly to metaphorical references to emotion scripts in the work of Reddy on 'emotional regimes' (*The Navigation of Feeling*) and Barbara Rosenwein on 'emotional communities' (*Emotional Communities in the Early Middle Ages* (Ithaca, NY: Cornell University Press, 2006)).

23 Monique Scheer, 'Are Emotions a Kind of Practice (And Is That What Makes Them Have a History)? A Bourdieuian Approach to Understanding Emotion', *History and Theory* 51 (2012), 192–220 (p. 209). I remain extremely grateful to Stephanie Trigg for originally drawing my attention to Scheer's argument in 2013. Scheer is also cited (though not discussed) by McNamer in 'The Literariness of Literature', p. 9.

24 Scheer, 'Are Emotions a Kind of Practice', p. 193.

Introduction 27

25 *Ibid.*, pp. 217–18.
26 Wan-Chuan Kao, 'Conduct Shameful and Unshameful in *The Franklin's Tale*', *Studies in the Age of Chaucer* 34 (2012), 99–139 (p. 122). This reference to shame scripts is made once in passing, and Kao's article does not engage with McNamer's suggestion that literature can function as a script for emotion.
27 Ruth Leys provides an extensive overview and critique of the arguments of Silvan S. Tomkins, Paul Ekman, Brian Massumi, and other scholars of 'affect' in 'The Turn to Affect: A Critique', *Critical Inquiry* 37 (2011), 434–72. Holly Crocker makes a case for thinking in terms of medieval 'affect' in 'Medieval Affects Now', *Exemplaria* 29 (2017), 82–98 (see esp. pp. 83–5).
28 For an overview of the history of *emotion* as a scholarly term, see Thomas Dixon, '"Emotion": The History of a Keyword in Crisis', *Emotion Review* 4 (2012), 338–44. On medieval emotion theory, see, for example, Simo Knuuttila, *Emotions in Ancient and Medieval Philosophy* (Oxford: Clarendon Press, 2004); Piroska Nagy and Damien Boquet (eds), *Le Sujet des emotions au Moyen Âge* (Paris: Beauchesne, 2009); Peter King, 'Emotions in Medieval Thought', in Peter Goldie (ed.), *The Oxford Handbook of Philosophy of Emotion* (Oxford: Oxford University Press, 2010), pp. 167–88; and Damien Boquet and Piroska Nagy, *Sensible Moyen Âge: Une histoire des émotions dans l'Occident* (Paris: Seuil, 2015). Chapter 1 of Rosenwein, *Emotional Communities*, surveys emotion theory from Plato to Augustine.
29 Thomas Dixon, 'Revolting Passions', *Modern Theology* 27 (2011), 298–312 (p. 300); see also Thomas Dixon, *From Passions to Emotions: The Creation of a Secular Psychological Category* (Cambridge: Cambridge University Press, 2003), especially Chapter 2; and Knuuttila, *Emotions in Ancient and Medieval Philosophy*.
30 See Augustine, *The City of God Against the Pagans, Books XII–XV*, trans. Philip Levine, The Loeb Classical Library (Cambridge, MA: Harvard University Press, 1966), book XIV, chapter 6 (pp. 284–7).
31 See Thomas Aquinas, *Summa Theologiae*, I–II, quest. 22–48, edited and translated in Thomas Aquinas, *Summa Theologiae: Volume 19, The Emotions: 1a2ae. 22–30*, ed. Eric D'Arcy (Cambridge: Cambridge University Press, 2006); *Summa Theologiae: Volume 20, Pleasure: 1a2ae. 31–39*, ed. Eric D'Arcy (Cambridge: Cambridge University Press, 2006); and *Summa Theologiae: Volume 21, Fear and Anger: 1a2ae. 40–48*, ed. by J. P. Reid (Cambridge: Cambridge University Press, 2006). On Aquinas's discussions of the emotions, see Nicholas E. Lombardo, *The Logic of Desire: Aquinas on Emotion* (Washington, DC: Catholic University of America, 2011), and Peter King, 'Emotions', in Brian Davies and Eleonore Stump (eds), *The Oxford Handbook of Aquinas* (Oxford: Oxford University Press, 2011), pp. 209–26.
32 On emotion and action in medieval literature and culture, see, for example, Andrew Lynch, '"What Cheer?" Emotion and Action in the

Arthurian World', in Frank Brandsma, Carolyne Larrington, and Corinne Saunders (eds), *Emotions in Medieval Arthurian Literature: Body, Mind, Voice* (Woodbridge: D. S. Brewer, 2015), pp. 47–63.

33 Stephanie Trigg provides a useful survey of the distinctions between such terms as *affect, emotion, feeling, passion*, and *sentiment* in 'Introduction: Emotional Histories – Beyond the Personalization of the Past and the Abstraction of Affect Theory', *Exemplaria* 26 (2014), 3–15. Although she suggests that *affect* might be the best candidate for an 'umbrella term', she maintains that 'the phrase "the history of emotions" suggests a complex and productively layered sense of inquiry into historical change, historical emotions, and the history of the term and concept of the "emotions" themselves', and might thereby encourage 'dialogue and interchange across the network of terms such as feelings, passions, emotions, and affects' (p. 8).

34 Crocker, 'Medieval Affects Now', p. 94.

35 Claire Sponsler, *Drama and Resistance: Bodies, Goods, and Theatricality in Late Medieval England* (Minneapolis, MN: University of Minnesota Press, 1997), p. 73. A third problem identified by Sponsler is that readers of conduct literature might learn to imitate the wrong models; she goes on to discuss the problematic nature of imitation on pp. 75–103.

36 On the medieval concept of *habitus*, see Cary J. Nederman, 'Nature, Ethics, and the Doctrine of "Habitus": Aristototelian Moral Psychology in the Twelfth Century', *Traditio* 45 (1989–90), 87–110, as well as Breen, *Imagining an English Reading Public*, which traces the construction of an explicitly vernacular *habitus* in later medieval England.

37 Breen, *Imagining an English Reading Public*, p. 16.

38 *MED*, s. v. *habit*; also *OED*, s. v. *habit*. Breen argues that texts such as the Wycliffite Bible and Chaucer's *Boece* were 'early adopters of the word *habit* in part because they attach intrinsic value to Latin syntax and etymology – that is, to Latin grammar as a means of inculcating Christian ethics – and are willing to sacrifice English clarity to preserve it' (*Imagining an English Reading Public*, p. 24).

39 Breen, *Imagining an English Reading Public*, p. 23.

40 See *ibid.*, pp. 16–29.

41 *MED*, s. v. *habit*.

42 Pierre Bourdieu, *Outline of a Theory of Practice*, trans. R. Nice (Cambridge: Cambridge University Press, 1977; repr. 1987), p. 72, a translation of Bourdieu's *Esquisse d'une théorie de la pratique* (emphasis in original). Bourdieu offers an extended discussion of habitus in the second chapter of this book (pp. 72–95 in this translation).

43 *Ibid.*, p. 79 (emphasis in original).

44 Breen, *Imagining an English Reading Public*, p. 8.

45 *Ibid.*, p. 17. Breen argues that 'the meaning of *habit*, both as a garment and a newly-minted English term, goes straight to the heart of vernacular textuality and its ability to foster spiritual perfection' (p. 20).

46 Reginald Pecock, *The Folewer to the Donet*, ed. E. V. Hitchcock, EETS OS 164 (London: Oxford University Press, 1924), p. 79, lines 28–30. Pecock is here discussing the cultivation of moral virtues.
47 Breen, *Imagining an English Reading Public*, p. 27.
48 *Romaunt of the Rose*, in *The Riverside Chaucer*, C 6192. For other examples of the Middle English proverb that 'the habit does not make the monk', see Bartlett Jere Whiting, *Proverbs, Sentences, and Proverbial Phrases from English Writings Mainly Before 1500* (Cambridge, MA: The Belknap Press, 1968), H2. On the medieval Latin proverb, see Breen, *Imagining an English Reading Public*, p. 51.
49 For examples of the textual traditions that informed medieval misogynist writing, see *Woman Defamed and Woman Defended*, ed. Blamires, with Pratt and Marx.
50 1 Timothy 2: 9–10. Latin text taken from parallel-text edition of the Latin Vulgate and Douay-Rheims versions of the Bible, www.latinvulgate.com/lv/verse.aspx?t=1&b=15&c=2 [accessed 21 March 2017]. Middle English translation taken from John Wyclif, *Select English Works of John Wyclif*, ed. Thomas Arnold (Oxford: Clarendon Press, 1871), cap. III, p. 193.
51 *MED*, s. v. *ourning*. Elsewhere in *The Canterbury Tales*, Chaucer draws attention to the 'mixed signals' that a woman's appearance can put out when the Parson notes that, although the 'visages' of some women may seem 'ful chaast and debonaire', their clothing reveals their 'likerousnesse' and pride (*The Parson's Tale* 429–31).
52 *MED*, s. v. *habit*.
53 *MED*, s. v. *shulen* (v. 1).
54 See Ruth Evans, 'Virginities', in Carolyn Dinshaw and David Wallace (eds), *The Cambridge Companion to Medieval Women's Writing* (Cambridge: Cambridge University Press, 2003), pp. 21–39 (p. 25); Burger, *Conduct Becoming*, p. 39.
55 Among the many valuable studies of medieval virginity that have been produced in the last two decades are Kathleen C. Kelly and Marina Leslie (eds), *Menacing Virgins: Representing Virginity in the Middle Ages and Renaissance* (London: Associated University Presses, 1999); Anke Bernau, *Virgins: A Cultural History* (London: Granta, 2007); Sarah Salih, *Versions of Virginity in Late Medieval England* (Cambridge: D. S. Brewer, 2001); Kathleen C. Kelly, *Performing Virginity and Testing Chastity in the Middle Ages* (London: Routledge, 2000; repr. 2002); and Anke Bernau, Ruth Evans, and Sarah Salih (eds), *Medieval Virginities* (Toronto: University of Toronto Press, 2003).
56 See Evans, 'Virginities', p. 25; *Hali Meiðhad*, in *Medieval English Prose for Women: Selections from the Katherine Group and Ancrene Wisse*, ed. Bella Millett and Jocelyn Wogan-Browne (Oxford: Clarendon Press, 1990), p. 38, lines 20–4. *Hali Meiðhad* cites Jerome's mathematical ratio representing the respective heavenly rewards of wives, widows, and virgins at p. 20, lines 19–21.

57 See especially Burger, *Conduct Becoming*, but also Staley, *Languages of Power*, pp. 265–338; Sponsler, *Drama and Resistance*, pp. 50–74; and Felicity Riddy, 'Mother Knows Best: Reading Social Change in a Courtesy Text', *Speculum* 71 (1996), 66–86. On the evolution of medieval marriage symbolism, see David D'Avray, *Medieval Marriage: Symbolism and Society* (Oxford: Oxford University Press, 2005).
58 Burger, *Conduct Becoming*, pp. 5, 7.
59 *OED*, s. v. *shame* (under 'Etymology').
60 Sara Ahmed, *The Cultural Politics of Emotion* (Edinburgh: Edinburgh University Press, 2004; repr. 2010), p. 104.
61 David Watt, *The Making of Thomas Hoccleve's Series* (Liverpool: Liverpool University Press, 2013), p. 144. I am very grateful to Sebastian Sobecki for sharing his work concerning the dating of Hoccleve's *Series* (soon forthcoming from Oxford University Press in *Last Words: The Public Self and the Social Author in Late Medieval England*).
62 Watt, *Hoccleve's Series*, p. 145.
63 See especially Chapter 5 of Mary Carruthers, *The Book of Memory: A Study of Memory in Medieval Culture*, 2nd edn (Cambridge: Cambridge University Press, 2008; repr. 2011), as well as her book on *The Craft of Thought: Meditation, Rhetoric, and the Making of Images, 400–1200* (Cambridge: Cambridge University Press, 1998; repr. 2008), and *The Medieval Craft of Memory: An Anthology of Texts and Pictures*, ed. Mary Carruthers and Jan M. Ziolkowski (Philadelphia, PA: The University of Pennsylvania Press, 2002).
64 Carruthers, *The Craft of Thought*, pp. 5, 14. As she goes on to explain, 'The monks thought of *intentio* as concentration, "intensity" of memory, intellect, but also as an emotional attitude, what we now might call a "creative tension," willingly adopted, that enabled productive memory work to be carried on (or that thwarted it, if one's *intentio* were bad or one's will ineffectual)' (p. 15).
65 Carruthers, *The Book of Memory*, p. 85.
66 Frevert, *Emotions in History*, p. 10. William Ian Miller similarly defines honour as a disposition in his study of humiliation: 'Honor is above all the keen sensitivity to the experience of humiliation and shame, a sensitivity manifested by the desire to be envied by others and the propensity to envy the successes of others. To simplify greatly, honor is that disposition which makes one act to shame others who have shamed oneself, to humiliate others who have humiliated oneself' (*Humiliation and Other Essays on Honor, Social Discomfort, and Violence* (Ithaca, NY: Cornell University Press, 1993), p. 84. While sensitivity to shame is indeed a significant part of what makes up honour, Miller's definition would be more accurately applied to a masculine sense of honour as depicted in later medieval texts than to female honour, which does not rely on shaming others and is not a matter of desiring to be envied or of envying the 'successes' of others.

67 *The Holy Bible, Containing the Old and New Testaments with the Apocryphal Books, in the Earliest English Versions made from the Latin Vulgate by John Wycliffe and his Followers*, ed. Josiah Forshall and Frederic Madden (Oxford: Oxford University Press, 1850), Genesis 2: 25; see also Valerie Allen, 'Waxing Red: Shame and the Body, Shame and the Soul', in Lisa Perfetti (ed.), *The Representation of Women's Emotions in Medieval and Early Modern Culture* (Gainesville, FL: University Press of Florida, 2005), pp. 191–210.
68 Allen, 'Waxing Red', pp. 194–5.
69 Robert Mannyng, *Robert of Brunne's 'Handlyng Synne'*, ed. Frederick J. Furnivall, EETS OS 119 (London: Kegan Paul, Trench, Trübner & Co., Ltd., 1901), lines 1–6.
70 Walter Hilton, *The Scale of Perfection*, ed. Thomas H. Bestul, TEAMS (Kalamazoo, MI: Medieval Institute Publications, 2000), 89, fol. 80v.
71 This is not to say that shame was not sometimes viewed as an obstacle to such processes as confession. If felt too keenly, it might prevent a man or woman from confessing altogether. As Thomas N. Tentler has noted, the key was not to be coerced by shame, but to experience the appropriate amount while repenting of one's sins (*Sin and Confession on the Eve of the Reformation* (Princeton, NJ: Princeton University Press, 1977), p. 108). Similarly, as Robert Stanton points out, revelling in self-righteous shame could also lead to the sin of vainglory ('Lechery, Pride, and the Uses of Sin in *The Book of Margery Kempe*', *The Journal of Medieval Religious Cultures* 36 (2010), 169–204).
72 See, for example, Allen, 'Waxing Red'; Miller, *Humiliation*; J. A. Burrow, 'Honour and Shame in *Sir Gawain and the Green Knight*', in *Essays on Medieval Literature* (Oxford: Clarendon Press, 1984), pp. 117–31; Virginia Burrus, *Saving Shame: Martyrs, Saints, and Other Abject Subjects* (Philadelphia, PA: University of Pennsylvania Press, 2008); Mary C. Flannery, 'A Bloody Shame: Chaucer's Honourable Women', *The Review of English Studies* 62 (2011), 337–57, as well as 'The Shame of the *Rose*: A Paradox', in Jennifer Chamarette and Jennifer Higgins (eds), *Guilt and Shame: Essays in French Literature and Culture* (Oxford: Peter Lang, 2010), pp. 51–69, and 'The Concept of Shame in Late-Medieval English Literature', *Literature Compass* 9 (2012), 166–82; Robert L. Kindrick, 'Gawain's Ethics: Shame and Guilt in *Sir Gawain and the Green Knight*', *Annuale mediavale* 20 (1981), 5–32; Anne McTaggart, *Shame and Guilt in Chaucer* (New York, NY: Palgrave Macmillan, 2012); Stephanie Trigg, '"Shamed be …": Historicizing Shame in Medieval and Early Modern Courtly Ritual', *Exemplaria* 19 (2007), 67–89; and Loretta Wasserman, 'Honor and Shame in *Sir Gawain and the Green Knight*', in Larry D. Benson and John Leyerle (eds), *Chivalric Literature: Essays on Relations Between Literature and Life in the Later Middle Ages* (Kalamazoo, MI: Western Michigan University, 1980), 77–90. Shame and embarrassment have

also attracted the attention of several early modernists; see, for example, Brian Cummings, 'Animal Passions and Human Sciences: Shame, Blushing and Nakedness in Early Modern Europe and the New World', in Erica Fudge, Ruth Gilbert, and Susan Wiseman (eds), *At the Borders of the Human: Beasts, Bodies and Natural Philosophy in the Early Modern Period* (London: Macmillan Press, 1999), pp. 26–50; Ewan Fernie, *Shame in Shakespeare* (London: Routledge, 2002); Werner L. Gundersheimer, 'Renaissance Concepts of Shame and Pocaterra's *Dialoghi Della Vergogna*', *Renaissance Quarterly* 47 (1994), 34–56; and Paster, *The Body Embarrassed*.

73 Prominent among these are the discussions of shame in Ahmed, *The Cultural Politics of Emotion*, pp. 101–21; Eve Kosofsky Sedgwick, *Touching Feeling: Affect, Pedagogy, Performativity* (Durham, NC: Duke University Press, 2003), esp. p. 35–65; and Elspeth Probyn, *Blush: Faces of Shame* (Minneapolis, MN: University of Minnesota Press, 2005).

74 Allen, 'Waxing Red', p. 192.

75 Stearns, *Shame*, p. 10.

76 One exception is the work of early modernist Robert A. White on the distinction between *verecundia* and *pudicitia* in Spenser's *The Faerie Queene* ('Shamefastness as *Verecundia* and as *Pudicitia* in *The Faerie Queene*', *Studies in Philology* 78 (1981), 391–408).

77 Thomas Aquinas, *Summa Theologiae: Volume 43, Temperance: 2a2ae. 141–154*, ed. Thomas Gilby (Cambridge: Cambridge University Press, 2006), quest. 143.

78 Aquinas, *Summa Theologiae: Volume 43*, quest. 151, art. 4. White discusses Aquinas's distinction between *verecundia* (an 'integral part' of temperance) and *pudicitia* ('a circumstance of chastity' that is a 'subjective part' of temperance) in relation to the dual figures of Shamefastness in *The Faerie Queene*, the first of which he argue personifies *verecundia* and the second of which personifies *pudicitia* ('Shamefastness', esp. p. 398).

79 The multiple valences of shame are discussed in *Histoire de la vergogne*, a special issue of *Rives Méditerranéennes* edited by Damien Boquet (*Rives Méditerranéennes* 31 (2008)), as well as in White, 'Shamefastness'.

80 For the definitions of *verecundus* and *inpudens* contained in Worcester Cathedral Chapter Library MS F. 174, see *Anglo-Saxon and Old English Vocabularies, Vol. 1: Vocabularies*, ed. Thomas Wright and Richard Paul Wülcker (London: Trübner & Co., 1884), col. 553, lines 9–10 (included under 'Semi-Saxon Vocabulary (of the Twelfth Century)'). For the definition of *schamefast* contained in London, British Library MS Harley 221, see *Promptorium Parvulorum sive Clericorum, Dictionarius Anglo-Latinus Princeps*, ed. A. Way, Camden Society 25, 54, 89, 3 vols (London: Camden Society, 1843–65), vol. 3, p. 443, col. 2, line 27.

81 *MED*, s. v. *shame* (n.).

82 *MED*, s. v. *shamefastness*.

Introduction

83 Frevert, *Emotions in History*, p. 36.
84 Aristotle, *The Nicomachean Ethics*, trans. H. Rackham, The Loeb Classical Library (Cambridge, MA: Harvard University Press, 1926), pp. 248–51.
85 English from *Il Convivio (The Banquet)*, trans. R. H. Lansing (New York, NY: Garland, 1990), p. 205 (Book 4, chapter 19); Italian from *Dante Alighieri Convivio*, ed. F. B. Ageno, 3 vols (Florence: Le Lettere, 1995), vol. 3 (second volume of the text), p. 383.
86 Allen, 'Waxing Red', pp. 194–95.
87 See Allen, 'Waxing Red', p. 198; Aquinas, *Summa Theologiae: Volume 43*, quest. 144, art. 1.
88 Stearns observes that the general consensus among emotion scholars is that embarrassment 'is simply less intense and noticeably less durable than shame, and is more quickly forgotten by the same token. ... In contrast, shame often lasts longer – up to forty-eight hours – and its sensations can be revived through community pressure, again, in contrast to embarrassment' (although he also notes that this distinction does not explain why 'one person might be merely embarrassed by a miscue that would cause others even in the same culture and certainly between two cultures, to feel shame' (*Shame*, p. 3). For a study that suggests that embarrassment is essentially the contemporary equivalent of shame, see Thomas J. Scheff, 'Shame and the Social Bond: A Sociological Theory', *Sociological Theory* 18 (2000), 84–99). Although E. R. Dodds's distinction between 'shame cultures' and 'guilt cultures' (*The Greeks and the Irrational* (Berkeley, CA: University of California Press, 1951)) is now generally considered obsolete, scholars have frequently continued to put them in separate rather than overlapping categories of emotion. Thus, Helen Lynd has argued that shame was related to being, whereas guilt was related to doing and interacting with others (*On Shame and the Search for Identity* (London: Routledge, 1958), 49–56). Gabriele Taylor has argued that '[g]uilt, unlike shame, is a legal concept'; if one feels guilty, one feels responsible for a transgression, whereas if one feels ashamed, one has a damaged sense of self (*Pride, Shame, and Guilt: Emotions of Self-Assessment* (Oxford: University of Oxford Press, 1985), p. 85). Ewan Fernie, in his study of shame in Shakespeare, has argued that 'guilt is other-directed; shame comes from within' (*Shame in Shakespeare*, p. 14). Anne McTaggart, writing on shame and guilt in the works of Chaucer, also attempts to draw a clear distinction between the two emotions (*Shame and Guilt*, p. 6).
89 Flannery, 'A Bloody Shame'.
90 Ethan Knapp, 'Thomas Hoccleve', in Larry Scanlon (ed.), *The Cambridge Companion to Medieval English Literature 1100–1500* (Cambridge: Cambridge University Press, 2009), pp. 191–203 (p. 196).
91 I adapt this phrase from McNamer, *Affective Meditation*, esp. Chapter 4, 'Feeling Like a Woman' (pp. 119–49).

1
Show and tell: shame and the subject of women's bodies

> And yf hit fall any man to rede hit, I pray hym & scharge hym in ovre Lady be-halue þat he rede hit not in no dyspyte ne sclavndure of no woman ne for no cause but for þe hele & helpe of hem, dredynge þat vengavns myht fall to hym as hit hath do to oþer þat have schevyd here preuytees in sclauvndyr of hem, vndyrstondynge in certeyne þat þey have no oþer euylys þat nov be a-lyue than thoo women hade þat nov be seyntys in hevyn.
> (*The Knowing of Woman's Kind in Childing*, Douce Version, 24–31)[1]

To begin a book by threatening one's readers seems counterintuitive (not to mention rude). Yet this is precisely what the author of one fourteenth-century Middle English gynaecological treatise chose to do. In the prologue of a text now known as *The Knowing of Woman's Kind in Childing*, the passage above (which is not found in its sources) warns any men who might happen to read the treatise not to read it in a spirit of *dyspyte* (a desire to humiliate someone) or *sclavndure* (disrespect, contempt) towards women.[2] Instead, male readers should approach the text with caution, 'dredynge þat vengavns myht fall to hym as hit hath do to oþer þat have schevyd [women's] preuytees in sclauvndyr of hem'. These readers should not merely be careful – they should be *afraid*.

Precisely what vengeance might befall an insensitive male reader of this text remains unclear, as does the identity of those 'oþer' men foolish enough to expose women to shame and derision. Yet the passage is striking both because of its protective stance towards women and because of the vehemence of its warning to men, features that have made it perhaps the most oft-discussed part of the text in modern scholarship. Why should a gynaecological treatise necessitate such a warning? The answer seems to lie in the prologue's reference to women's *preuytees*, a term that encompasses both the 'secrets' of women's medicine (as they had come to be known by the time *Knowing* was written) and the secret places of women's bodies – their internal and external genital organs.[3] The author of the prologue anticipates that these private matters may well be *schevyd* – 'examined', but also 'exhibited' – by men with malicious motives.[4] As a consequence, at the very moment at which the text is about to embark on an extended project of 'showing' and telling about women's bodies, its prologue warns readers of the need for caution and concealment. Reading (and writing) about women's bodies is a risky activity: when it is undertaken out of *dyspyte* or *slavndure*, it puts women's reputations and emotions at risk. The fact that the author of this prologue presents the shaming of women as something deserving of vengeance hints at the gravity of these consequences for women. The prologue of *Knowing* demands that readers not only bear these consequences in mind, but also dread them in sympathy with women. When reading about women's *preuytees*, the prologue implies, men must be sure to keep those *preuytees* under cover.

Such gestures of concealing and revealing are characteristic not only of the medieval discourse surrounding the *preuytees* of women's bodies, but also of the discourse and imagery surrounding what the present book identifies as the medieval practice of female honour. As I will show over the course of this study, the practice of being an honourable woman entailed *feeling* like an honourable woman by developing a hypervigilance against the possibility of shame, most particularly the prospect of sexual shame. A strong sense of shame, often termed *shamefastness* in Middle English, was necessitated in part by the unsettlingly embodied nature of female honour, proof of which was thought to reside in those parts of women's bodies which usually remained safely hidden, but which were also most closely bound up with women's allegedly undisciplined, sinful natures. And while the medieval consensus was that a woman's honour was determined primarily by her sexual continence, the difficulty of ensuring or proving a woman's chastity rendered female honour elusive and uncertain. By practising shamefastness, women might practise habits of mind and body that, by interiorizing and exteriorizing a strong sense of shame, could both preserve their chastity and communicate it to others. As this chapter will begin to show, however, practising shamefastness involved women in a bizarre sort of gestural paradox whereby they were expected to make a spectacle of their shamefast concealment and withdrawal, ideally in a manner that seemed effortless and unpractised and which, by its apparent effortlessness, demonstrated their virtue. While the practice of shamefastness was a crucial support for female honour, it should never appear *practised*.

I begin by using the subject of women's *preuytees* (or *shamefuls*, as genitalia might also be termed in Middle English) as a gateway to examining the relationship between shame and the embodied nature of female honour in medieval English culture, focusing on the links between postlapsarian shame and the body in the medieval imagination. I then consider how postlapsarian shame contributed to medieval understandings of pain and shame as universal features of women's experience of childbirth. Finally, I explore how the prologue of one version of the mid-fifteenth-century gynaecological treatise now known as *The Sickness of Women*, as well as the prologue of *Knowing*, employ strategies to mitigate the social and emotional risks women faced in exposing their bodies even for the ostensibly innocent purposes of medical diagnosis and treatment. While they perhaps inevitably replicate the gestures of concealing and revealing that distinguish the practice of female honour, these prologues also present women's shamefastness as something deserving of sympathy, respect, and protection. My primary goal is not to make claims about the practice of women's medicine, or even about medieval writing on women's medicine more broadly (although I engage with both subjects), but rather to situate these two specific examples of gynaecological writing within a broader pattern of thinking about women's bodies and women's shame. The prologues of *Knowing* and *Sickness* explicitly acknowledge that 'showing' and 'telling' about women's *preuytees* potentially risked women's feelings and reputations, and they each make the case that this risk demanded sensitivity on the part of male readers. Both prologues implore their readers to approach the texts they preface with an awareness of how their reading might affect women's honour and women's emotions, a plea that points to some of the ways in which the maintenance of female honour was believed to depend upon a wide network of interlinked practices involving not only women's emotions, but those of men as well.

The matter of women's *shamefuls*

The idea that the subject of gynaecological ailments might be a cause for female shame or embarrassment is closely bound up with the links between shame and the human body in the medieval imagination. Biblical history reinforced the association between the uncovered male or female body and the experience of shame – although Adam and Eve had initially not felt shame at their nakedness (*non erubescant*; they 'were not ashamed'), their first act after their commission of original sin was to recognize their nakedness as something that should be covered.⁵ In his Anglo-Norman poem *Le Mirour de l'Omme* (c. 1376–79), John Gower cites this moment as an example that the 'shameless' prostitute should bear in mind:

> Responde, o pute, ne scies tu
> Queu part vergoigne est devenu?
> De tes parens essample toi,
> Q'en paradis se viront nu,
> Dont vergondous et esperdu,
> Tantost chascun endroit de soy
> D'un fueill covry le membre coy.
> Mais tu, putain, avoy, avoy!
> es tant aperte en chascun lieu,
> Sans honte avoir d'ascune loy,
> Que je dirray, ce poise moy,
> Tu as vergoigne trop perdu.

> (Answer, O whore, don't you know where shame [*vergoigne*] has fled? Look up to your forefathers, who saw themselves naked in Paradise, shameful and distressed, and so each on his own covered his privy member with a leaf. But you, whore, come on, you are exhibited in every corner, feeling neither shame [*honte*] nor bond with respect to any law; I'll say it, it bothers me, you utterly lost shame [*vergoigne*].)⁶

As Gower emphasizes, this moment in biblical history was the moment when mankind acquired a sense of shame (*vergoigne*) and learned to cover 'le membre coy' (the privy member). That the prostitute addressed by Gower's narrator exposes hers without feeling shame (*sans honte*) is a sign that she no longer possesses a sense of shame. As Guillemette Bolens points out in her discussion of this passage, just as a sense of shame was acquired, so too can it be lost, and with it the bodily gestures that demonstrate one's shamefastness.⁷ When this happens, women risk becoming like Gower's shameless prostitute by disregarding '[t]he imperative of covering and concealing' (which, Bolens notes, 'is also applied to speech'): '[t]he hymen must remain covered and the female must stay hidden'.⁸

This familiar narrative of shame's origins presented postlapsarian human nudity as inherently shameful, an idea already latent in the linguistic origins of Old English *scamu/sceamu/scomu* and Middle English *shame* in a Proto-Indo-European verb meaning 'to cover'.⁹ Both Old English and Middle English terms for genitalia bear witness to the longstanding belief that these were the parts of the human body that most urgently needed to be hidden. In Anglo-Saxon England, the word *sceamlim* ('shame-limb') was one of several Old English terms for genitalia.[10] Likewise, a number of later medieval English texts refer to genitalia as the 'shamefast' or 'shameful parts' or 'shameful things'. When referring to ulcers 'of þe wombe', one Middle English translation of Guy de Chauliac's *Grande Chirurgie* characterizes them as those ulcers which appear 'about þe pudende .i. shameful membre' (the translator's somewhat emphatic rendering of the Latin *circa totum pudendum*).[11] A lengthy diatribe against 'scantnesse of clothyng' in *The Parson's Tale* rails against those men's jackets that are cut so short that they 'ne covere nat the shameful membres of man, to wikked entente' (421). The Parson paints a graphic picture of men's 'horrible swollen membres', which are transformed by the snugness of tights into something resembling 'the maladie of hirnia' (422) or (when the tights in question are brightly coloured) to appendages that seem as though they were 'corrupt by the fir of Seint Antony, or by cancre, or by oother swich meschaunce' (426). These passages conjure up a horrifying image of man's most shameful parts, framing them as both abhorrent and a potential incitement to sin.[12]

While both male and female nakedness were linked to shame, the fact that female honour was so firmly rooted in sexual continence meant that the shame of female nakedness carried a stronger, more specific charge. Other virtues or vices aside, the most basic measure of a woman's honour in a given secular medieval text is her degree of sexual continence. As the fifteenth-century poet John Lydgate declares in his *Fall of Princes*, 'In womanheede, as auctours alle write, / Most thyng comendid is ther chast honeste'.[13] 'Chast honeste' was defined differently depending on whether a woman was unmarried, married, or a widow: strictly observed virginity was prized in unmarried women, whereas married women were expected to be sexually active within the bounds of their marriage, either for the purposes of procreation or in payment of the marriage debt; ideally, widowed women would only resume sexual activity if they married again.[14] The sexual continence that these three groups of 'honourable' women were expected to maintain was as much a product of mindful practice as it was a product of bodily practice; as Bella Millett and Jocelyn Wogan-Browne have pointed out in their discussion of medieval virginity, for example, early Christian writers depict a 'virginal habit of mind' as 'even more important than literal intactness (which can be rendered meaningless by the wrong interior disposition)'.[15] This observation highlights the medieval awareness of the potential for inconsistencies between mind and body, between one's true character and one's outward appearance. The most perfectly chaste woman would cultivate perfection in *both*, but must do so unceasingly in order to maintain and prove this chaste habit at all times and in all places. Such a strict interpretation of sexual continence demanded discipline over both mind and body.[16] Although this was a 'superlative form' of chastity rather than a reflection of historical fact – and although (as Glenn Burger has argued) the 'benefits of chastity' became 'available to a much wider group of women' in the later Middle Ages – *all* women, regardless of marital status, were expected to avoid arousing suspicion of sexual looseness.[17] This was particularly difficult given that the entire female gender was subject to suspicion, believed to be naturally undisciplined in both mind and body, or at least much less disciplined than men. This belief contributed to the idea of female honour as a precarious thing; in medieval writings 'female honor exists always under threat of slippage into shameful behavior'.[18] Writers of treatises on natural philosophy drew on ancient Greek authorities to support their claims that women were deformed – or not-fully-formed – men, creatures driven more by their bodily urges than by the reason characteristic of men.[19] Such beliefs rendered female honour unstable, difficult to maintain and perhaps impossible to prove.

Medieval expectations of and anxieties about female chastity were reinforced by the idealization of virginal maidenhood, which remained significant despite the increasing prominence of the good wife as an ethical subject. Marriageable women were expected to transition smoothly from the carefully preserved virginity of youth to sexual activity that would take place exclusively within marriage (if at all). As a consequence of these expectations, honourable female chastity became not only virtuous, but desirable. In her study of medieval maidenhood, Kim Phillips notes that models of idealized maidenly femininity would have been easily accessible and visible to girls and women in medieval Europe, and mingled depictions of virtue with depictions of desirability. Even virgin martyrs were presented as objects of desire:

> When they walked into a parish church, or (if they had access to books) opened an illuminated prayer book, [medieval women] would have been confronted with images not only of the enormously popular virgin martyrs including St Katherine and St Margaret but also of

the most holy saint herself, the Virgin Mary, which celebrated the appearance and qualities of the idealised maiden. Those images of teenaged girls with long blonde hair, garlands or crowns, and conventional beauty celebrated the unique combination of sexuality and virginity which most strongly defined maidenhood as a phase in the life cycle. Though the ideology and the lived reality by no means perfectly matched one another any more than the modern ideology of childhood innocence lines up precisely with the experience of actual children, the realms of ideas and experience did overlap in some ways. The lives of girls were partly defined and influenced by wider cultural ideas of what it meant to be a maiden.[20]

The pervasiveness of these ideals ensured that women were educated to view chastity as a supremely desirable quality to possess (and one that might render them more desirable in turn). Saints' lives, exempla, proverbs, church art and architecture, and the Virgin Mary herself were legible, visible, and audible reminders to women of virginity's value as a hallmark of female goodness. In the context of the household, the reasons for this were economical as well as spiritual, since 'within medieval systems of inheritance and land tenure, the woman's body [was] male property' and the purity of a family line was only guaranteed by the virginity and subsequent chastity of a man's wife.[21] As a consequence, virginity continued to be idealized, however much some, like Chaucer's Wife of Bath, might point out that, 'if ther were no seed ysowe, / Virginitee, thanne wherof sholde it growe?' (*The Wife of Bath's Prologue* 71–2).

Despite the postlapsarian shamefulness of the naked female body, therefore, the pre-eminence of sexual continence as a determinant of female honour rendered women's *shamefuls* the key locus for the testing, proving, and protection of female honour. At the same time that women's *shamefuls* were expected to remain concealed, their integrity was necessarily something that demanded disclosure and examination. By extension, this had the rather paradoxical effect of making both the physical site and even the subject of women's *shamefuls* matters that demanded the most careful concealment and, on occasion, the closest possible scrutiny, particularly when virginity was in question. In the Middle Ages (as now), some physicians acknowledged that a woman's first experience of intercourse could result in bleeding, and that such bleeding was one of many physiological signs that might help to confirm a woman's virginal state.[22] Yet, as Kathleen C. Kelly and others have noted, even medieval physicians seem to have noted that tests for female virginity were by no means foolproof: indeed, in a number of medieval texts, 'at the very moment it is asserted that virginity can be tested, it is recognized that virginity can be faked'. A woman seeking to feign virginity might be advised to resort to 'a dove's bladder filled with blood, inserted into the vagina, and designed to break at the climactic moment', or to take 'a warm bath infused with certain herbs (to tighten the muscles of the vagina) on the wedding night'.[23] Whether or not women resorted to such stratagems, such passages suggest the extent to which the very same bodily sites held to be the markers of a woman's honour were themselves thought to be potential sites of deception. As a result, some texts argued that a woman's manifest sense of shame should itself be held up as potential proof of a woman's virgin state; Esther Lastique and Helen Rodnite Lemay cite one later medieval gynaecological treatise that argues that

> Virginitatis ... signa sunt pudor et verecundia cum casto incessu loquale gestus, gressus cum despectu applicationis ad virum quodam torvo aspectu[.]
>
> the signs of virginity are shame and bashfulness with respect to manner of walking and manner of speaking, and with a downward glance in inclination when approaching men, and in such a way with sternness in manner of appearance[.][24]

In this instance, as Sarah Salih has observed, virginity is depicted as something that 'should be read from a woman's behaviour, rather than her genitalia'.[25]

If the private parts of both male *and* female postlapsarian bodies were associated with shame in the medieval imagination, that shame had greater social implications for women. As one of the key sites upon which chastity or its lack was believed to be determined, women's *shamefuls* were to be kept firmly under cover at all times. But the uncertain nature of female virginity made that site of the female body at once an important source of proof concerning a woman's honour and a site at which the basest forms of feminine deception might be practised. As I will show, postlapsarian associations affect the way that medieval writers refer to those moments when women needed to reveal their bodies in order to receive gynaecological or obstetrical treatment.

'Shamecraft'

As the epigraph to this chapter indicates, the prologue to the *Knowing of Woman's Kind in Childing* argues that men should be charitable towards women seeking gynaecological treatment because such women 'have no oþer euylys þat nov be a-lyue than thoo women hade þat nov be seyntys in hevyn'. Yet this claim glosses over the fact that the pain and shame of childbirth were believed to be direct consequences of original sin, and therefore part of women's post-lapsarian experience of their bodies. Thus, in the course of making its case for virginity, *Hali Meiðhad* discusses the unpleasant subject of pain in childbirth as follows:

> Hwen hit þenne þerto kimeþ, þet sore sorhfule angoise, þet stronge ant stikinde stiche, þet unroles uuel, þet pine ouer pine, þet wondrinde ȝeomerunge; hwil þu swenchest terwiþ, ant þine deaðes dute, scheome teke þet sar wið þe alde wifes scheome creft þe cunnen of þet wa-sið, hwas help þe bihoueð, ne beo hit neauer se uncumelich; and nede most hit þolien þet te þerin itimeð.[26]

A nearly unbearable consequence of man's fallen state, labour is depicted as a horrific ordeal that all women will be compelled to undergo if they do not choose to embrace a life of virginity. This, in the end, is what awaits all sexually active women. The variation of the passage's opening lines lays powerful emphasis on the 'sorhfule angoise' of childbirth, which is described with no fewer than five different phrases (e.g. 'þet unroles uuel, þet pine ouer pine'). Medieval awareness of the physical pain of childbirth is attested not only by references such as this, but by numerous prayers and charms that were believed to help ease this pain and ensure a safe delivery, and which are recorded in manuscripts, fragments, and other sources.[27] *Hali Meiðhad* stresses that childbirth is accompanied not only by physical anguish, however, but also by *emotional* anguish, as the author's reference to midwifery makes clear: labouring women will be forced to rely on the *scheome creft* of old women.

The author's choice of language here is telling. The *MED* defines *shamecraft* as 'skill in matters of a shameful nature, midwifery', and cites this passage from *Hali Meiðhad* as the only recorded example of its occurrence.[28] Given that other Middle English writings refer to male and female genitals as *shameful membres*, *shameful limbes*, or *shamful thingis*, it is unsurprising that a body of knowledge pertaining at least partially to the workings and maladies of female genitalia might be associated with shame.[29] But the above passage from *Hali Meiðhad* suggests that this lexical association of shame with midwifery might also be read as a reflection of the emotions a woman might feel upon having to expose her genitals to close scrutiny and handling. The text reminds female readers that they can expect to experience not only pain, but also shame at the moment of childbirth, a double threat that renders labour a doubly horrifying prospect. Female shame in relation to childbirth was proverbial enough that the twelfth-century author Marie de France made reference to it in a story concerning animal birth. In her fable *De lupo et sue* (*The Wolf and the Sow*), a wolf encounters a pregnant sow and promises to let her pass if she will give birth quickly, since he wants to eat her piglets. The sow claims to be too ashamed to do such a thing:

> Ele respunt par grant saveir:
> 'Sire, cument me hastereie?
> Tant cum si pres de mei vus veie,
> ne me puis jeo pas delivrer;
> tel hunte ai de vus esguarder.
> Ne savez mie que ceo munte?
> Tutes femeles unt grant hunte,
> se mains madle les deit tuchier
> a tel busuin ne aprismier.'

> She answered wisely, 'Sir, how would you hurry me? As near to me as I see you, I can't give birth, because I'm so ashamed to have you in my sight. Don't you know how important this is? All females are ashamed for male hands to touch them or come near them during such an event.'[30]

Even though the male and female characters concerned are not members of the same species (or, indeed, members of the human race), the proverbial knowledge on which the fable turns is depicted as so universally accepted as true that even a ravenous wolf cannot deny it. Flummoxed, the wolf leaves the sow in peace, and the fable concludes with the remark that '[a]ll women should listen to this fable and remember it. They should not let their children perish just to save their own skins' ('Cest essample deivent oïr / tutes femmes e retenir; / pur sulement lur cors guarir / ne laissent lur enfanz perir!').[31]

The 'rule' of women's pain and shame during childbirth might be said to be proved by the one woman who was believed to have experienced neither: the Virgin Mary. A variety of narratives concerning the birth of Jesus present that birth as miraculous not only because Mary's virginity remained intact, but also because she appeared not to have suffered during labour. As Alaya Swann has outlined, these narratives place emphasis on Mary's swift recovery and her claims not to have experienced pain, claims which, according to an apocryphal story in circulation from the second century onward, prompted at least one midwife named Salome to conduct a test of Mary's virginity.[32] Doubting that a virgin birth has in fact taken place, Salome insists on confirming Mary's virginity through visual and/or tactile examination, depending on the narrative in question. When her hand or arm withers during the attempt, she is advised to touch either the infant Christ or his clothing, whereupon she is miraculously healed. The story of the doubting midwife Salome circulated in several medieval English texts, which, as Swann has shown, lay particular emphasis on the proper or improper motives that midwives like Salome might have had for touching the Virgin's body. In the N-Town Nativity play, for example, Mary is visited by two midwives, Zelomy and Salomé; while the former touches the Virgin to see '[y]f ye have nede of medycyn' (offering to 'comforte and helpe ryght wele / As other women, yf ye have pyn' (219–21)), the latter touches the Virgin because of her doubt, declaring that she will never believe in Mary's virginity 'but I it preve, / with hand towchynge' (246–7).[33]

While the apocryphal tale of Salome and the Virgin should be read neither as evidence of medieval medical practice nor as a model for how midwifery *should* be practised, it is suggestive of the complex interplay of intentions, gestures, and emotional experiences believed to be involved in the medieval practice of women's medicine. The story of the Virgin's experience of pregnancy and childbirth is remarkable precisely because of its status as an exception to the human rules of reproduction and the shame and pain that normally accompanied labour: Mary experiences neither the loss of her virginity upon her conception of Jesus, nor the physical and emotional suffering other human women could expect to experience during labour. The figure of Salome is presented as a figure who approaches the Virgin's body with improper intentions (doubt, curiosity) or, at the very least, a lack of *proper* intentions. In the version recorded in Lydgate's *Life of Our Lady*, for example, Salome is described as venturing to touch the Virgin 'with-outen Reuerence, /Devoyded of drede or devocion' – these are emotions she *should* feel, but doesn't.[34] In these respects, the story touches on related beliefs and concerns that may also be found in writings on the subject of women's medicine from a very early date. One of the most widely circulated and influential gynaecological treatises of the Middle Ages, the *Liber de sinthomatibus mulierum* (more commonly known as one of the texts purportedly authored by the elusive 'Trotula'), opens by reflecting on the ways that both women's diseases and the practice of women's medicine are powerful sources of shame and suffering for female patients:

> Moreover, women, from the condition of their fragility, out of shame and embarrassment do not dare reveal their anguish over their diseases (which happen in such a private place) to a physician. Therefore, their misfortune, which ought to be pitied, and especially the influence of a certain woman stirring my heart, have impelled me to give a clear explanation regarding their diseases in caring for their health.

> Et ipse condicione sue fragilitatis propter uerecundiam et faciei ruborem egritudinum suarum, que in secreciori loco accidunt, angustias non audent medico reuelare. Earum igitur miseranda calamitas et maxime cuiusdam mulieris gratia animum meum sollicitans inpulit, ut circa egritudines earum euidentius explanarem earum sanitati prouidendo.[35]

This passage vividly invokes women's fear of shame as justification for the existence of the text that follows. The author's observation that, because of their shame, women 'do not dare' (*non audent*) to disclose their illnesses to a physician captures the fear that attends a sense of shame: the fear to 'reveal' something (*reuelare*) that should otherwise remain covered, and which might result in one's disgrace – or, at the very least, in the redness of one's face (*faciei ruborem*). Here, women's fear concerning the potential uncovering of their bodies – whether by word of mouth or by the lifting of clothing – is explicitly linked to their fear of shame. An understanding of their shamefuls as *shameful*, as best kept under wraps, inhibits these women's behaviour and prevents them from seeking medical aid. Read another way, their determination to keep their shamefuls covered becomes confirmation of their shamefastness. Unlike the prostitute addressed by Gower in *Le Mirour de l'Omme*, they have not lost *vergoigne*. But what is also noteworthy is the way that this passage expresses charitable intentions towards women, intentions motivated both by women's predicaments and by the alleged pleas of one woman in particular. In other words, the author of this passage presents himself and his text as shaped by an awareness of the link between women's bodies and women's potential shame, the same link that otherwise complicates the diagnosis and treatment of gynaecological illnesses.

In the rest of this chapter, I turn to two Middle English gynaecological texts – *The Sickness of Women* and the *Knowing of Woman's Kind in Childing* – whose prologues also address the potential shame of gynaecological diagnosis and treatment. I argue that these prologues use the prospect of women's potential shame to shape their readers' approach to and use of the practical material that follows. But as I will show, they also suggest that even textual encounters with the most private spaces of women's bodies for the purposes of medical diagnosis and treatment are encounters that put female honour at risk.

The Sickness of Women

The most widely disseminated Middle English text on women's medicine was a translation of Gilbertus Anglicus's *Compendium medicinae* (c. 1240) now referred to as *The Sickness of Women*, which circulated in two versions.[36] Version 1 (the most popular, extant in twelve manuscripts) translates fifteen of the *Compendium*'s twenty chapters, and Version 2 (extant in four manuscripts) includes all the material from Version 1 (rearranged) as well as several additions drawn from other texts.[37] The most striking addition made to the material contained in Version 2 of *The Sickness of Women* is its prologue, which proclaims the text to have been written specifically to help women avoid feeling shame at having to discuss their illnesses with 'vncurteys men'.[38] Although it is unclear whether this particular text was intended for or reached an extensive female readership (or any female readers whatsoever), the prologue to Version 2 of *The Sickness of Women* directly engages with the issue of what it means to talk, write, or read about women's *shamefuls*, and, more particularly, the impact of these activities on female emotions and on female honour.

The prologue appears in all four manuscripts in which Version 2 of *The Sickness of Women* survives.[39] Like the *Liber de sinthomatibus mulierum*, it opens with the claim that the guide has been produced partly in response to the shame women feel during medical examination:

> For as moche as ther bien many wymmen that han many diuers maladies and sikenessis nygh to the deth and they also bien shameful to shewen and to tellen their grevaunces to any wight, therfor I shal sumdel write to their maladie remedy, prayeng to God and to his blessid moder Marie ful of grace to sende me grace triewly to write to the pleasaunce of God and to al wymmens helping; for charite axith this, that every man shuld travaile for helpyng of his brethren and sustren after the grace of God that he hath vnderfong.
>
> (*The Sickness of Women* 1–8)

As this passage makes clear, the prologue begins by presenting the text that follows as a charitable solution for what appears to be a persistent problem: the fact that women's fear of shame can prevent them from seeking diagnosis and treatment for gynaecological ailments. The use of the word *wight* (individual, person) suggests that the gender of the person to whom women must disclose their illnesses may be irrelevant – the mere fact of showing and telling is enough for women to experience (or fear) shame.[40] And because women can be 'shameful to shewen and to tellen' what ails them, it is more difficult for them to be diagnosed and treated. Notably, the author of this prologue never suggests that women should *not* feel shame when discussing ailments linked to their shamefuls, nor is the text presented as a remedy for women's fear of shame; rather, it is a necessary workaround. The prologue introduces *The Sickness of Women* as a text written in response to the fact of female shamefastness out of *charite* (love, kindness).[41]

This statement of charitable intent is tied to an additional reason that women might feel shame when seeking treatment for gynaecological ailments: women are afraid of *who else* may be tempted to discuss their ailments, and of their motives:

> And though wymmen have divers evils and many grete grevaunces mo than al men knowen of, as I saide, hem shamen for drede of reprevyng in tymes comyng and of discuryng of vncurteys men that loven wymmen but for their lustis and for their foul likyng; and if wymmen bien in disease, suche men han hem in dispite and thynken nat how moche disease wymmen han or than thei han brought hem [i.e. men] furth into this world.
> And therfor in helpyng of wymmen I wil write of wymmen prevy sikenes the helpyng of, that oo womman may help another in hir sikenes and nat discure hir privitees to suche vncurteys men.
> (*The Sickness of Women* 8–18)

As this passage suggests, in addition to fearing 'reprevyng [disgrace, shame] in tymes comyng', women also fear 'discuryng' (exposure) at the hands of 'vncurteys men', men whose only interest in women stems from their own 'lustis' and 'foul likyng'.[42] These uncharitable motives are identified here not only as the reason why women dislike speaking about their gynaecological illnesses, but also, arguably, as the reason for their shamefastness *in general*. At the same time, the passage's reference to 'suche' men reads like an attempt to reassure readers that 'not all men' are so *vncurteys*; some men may be capable of sympathizing with female shamefastness, and, indeed, all men ought to be.

The prologue to Version 2 of *The Sickness of Women* has most frequently been read for what it seems to suggest about the status and/or gender of the text's intended readers. The prologue invites women to 'helpe another in her sykenesse', although it does not specify precisely how these women will come to possess the information contained in the text that follows, leaving room for imagining various possible kinds of female audiences (whether as audiences for the text being read aloud, or as direct readers themselves). Regardless of the form such a female audience might take, the prologue envisages a community of women who are able to share the medical expertise gained from *The Sickness of Women*, and who are not compelled to discuss their ailments with men. This opening up of gynaecological knowledge to an imagined female audience is a striking shift away from the practices of masculine secrecy that Karma Lochrie has identified as a characteristic of one of the most popular medieval texts concerning women's medicine, *De secretis mulierum* (*On the Secrets of Women*).[43] The prologue does not for a moment suggest that the treatise is not to be read by men, nor that it will not be read by men; but its fantasy of a closed community of women is presented as all the more important because of the danger a woman incurs when she must 'diskuren her previtees to suche vncurteys men'. Also significant is the way that women's fear of shame is presented here: not merely as an obstacle (although it *is* an issue to be addressed), but as the reason *The Sickness of Women* was written in the first place. Writing 'in helping of women', the author of this prologue identifies him-/herself as someone who understands and sympathizes with female emotions, and by offering a way for women to avoid exposing themselves and their troubles to 'vncurteys men', the author identifies the text as something intended for readers who share that understanding and sympathy. In other words, what matters most here is not gender or literacy, but rather one's intentions and, even more specifically, one's emotional disposition. Whether or not it was reflected in actual practice, the prologue's reassuring stance towards women is noteworthy. The text markets itself as the product of (and for) a mind that is not *vncurteys* to women, a mind that wishes to help them to avoid shame.

The prologue to Version 2 of *The Sickness of Women* suggests that women's medicine and, more broadly, women's 'shamefuls' might be subjects that demand an investment in female shamefastness – not on the part of female patients (who, as I will argue in subsequent chapters, would already be expected to practice it), but on the part of male readers and writers. Women's medicine was not only a practice that might call up the shame and pain of the postlapsarian female body; it was also a subject that might potentially affect women's reputations and emotions. With this in mind, in the final section of this chapter I return to the threatening prologue with which I began.

The Knowing of Woman's Kind in Childing

The translator of the earlier treatise now known as *The Knowing of Woman's Kind in Childing* similarly imagines its ideal readers in terms of their sympathy with women's fear of shame. The earliest manuscript to contain *Knowing* may be dated to the late fourteenth century.[44] Although it contains a number of structural and rhetorical similarities to *The Sickness of Women*, *The Knowing of Woman's Kind* derives from a separate textual tradition: it is the earliest Middle English translation of selections from the *Trotula* (which are included alongside passages drawn from other gynaecological and medical texts) via a French version of the material. Like Version 2 of *The Sickness of Women*, *Knowing* claims in its prologue to have been written for a female audience:

> And be-cause whomen of oure tonge cvnne bettyre rede & vndyrstande þys langage þan eny oþer & euery whoman lettyrde [may] rede hit to oþer vnlettyrd & help hem & conceyle hem in here maledyes with-owten schevynge here dysese to man, I have þys drawyn & wryttyn in Englysch.
> (*The Knowing of Woman's Kind in Childing*, Douce Version, 18–22)[45]

This passage imagines a female readership much more explicitly and fully than does the prologue of Version 2 of *The Sickness of Women*, justifying the text's translation into English on the grounds that English women can read and understand it more easily, and that 'euery whoman lettyrde' will be able to read the text aloud to illiterate women, who may therefore learn from the text's contents indirectly. This is presented as a covert exchange of information: women will be able to 'conceyle' their ailments and avoid 'shevynge' them to men. In this exchange, both the information and the women themselves are covered and concealed, kept safe from prying eyes and prurient interests. While the prologue to Version 2 of *Sickness* had also emphasized the female fear of exposure to and by 'vncurteys men', *Knowing*'s prologue goes further: its aim is to remove men from the informational transaction altogether. The Englishing of this text simultaneously opens it up to a new, female readership and seeks to close off that readership and its activities from men. Moreover, far more than in the case of *The Sickness of Women*, the content of the main text supports its prologue's claims that *Knowing* is directed at a female audience: unlike *Sickness*, it is written entirely in English, and some of its advice seems to be addressed directly to female patients (rather than to the midwife, as is the case in corresponding Latin passages).[46]

By composing a text that theoretically can be read by and shared among women, this author – like the author of the prologue to Version 2 of *The Sickness of Women* – seeks to insulate women from the potential shame of exposure to men. However, the lines immediately following these (which form the epigraph to this chapter) concede that men may indeed read this text, and consequently admonish any male readers to respect the 'preuytees' of women:

> And yf hit fall any man to rede hit, I pray hym & scharge hym in ovre Lady be-halue þat he rede hit not in no dyspyte ne sclavndure of no woman ne for no cause but for þe hele & helpe of hem, dredynge þat vengavns myht fall to hym as hit hath do to oþer þat have schevyd here preuytees in sclauvndyr of hem, vndyrstondynge in certeyne þat þey have no oþer euylys þat nov be a-lyue than thoo women hade þat nov be seyntys in hevyn.
>
> (*The Knowing of Woman's Kind in Childing*, Douce Version, 24–31)

The vehemence of this passage has moved Green to observe that 'it seems to reflect a sincere concern for women'.[47] The author of the passage claims the same mistrust of men's motives that would later be articulated in the prologue to Version 2 of *The Sickness of Women*, which laments the fact that some men only view women as a means of satisfying their 'lustis' and 'foul likyng'. Like the author of that prologue, *Knowing*'s translator 'foresaw that some might take a prurient interest in the contents, and he warns them off in no uncertain terms'.[48] This passage's references to 'ovre Lady' and other women 'þat nov be seyntys in hevyn' lend an aura of sanctity to women in general, incorporating them into a community defined by female saintliness. And although it is unclear what 'vengavns' might be experienced by the male reader who peruses the text out of 'dyspyte' or a desire to 'sclavndure' women, the author's claim to issue the warning 'in ovre Lady be-halue' suggests that the Virgin (that supreme celestial mediator between God and man) might be inclined to play the role of avenging angel in such a scenario.

As I noted at the beginning of this chapter, this prologue's protective stance towards women and its vehement warning to men render it remarkable to read even in the present day. But it is particularly remarkable for its solicitous attitude towards women's shamefastness; indeed, it is explicitly written in aid of this shamefastness, a text that will help women 'conceyle hem'. As a text that concerns the potentially shaming *preuytees* of women, *The Knowing of Woman's Kind* begins with a preface that functions as a gatekeeper to the delicate subject of women's medicine. The prologue acknowledges that men may indeed read the ensuing text – and it nowhere suggests that this is, in and of itself, a problem (although it recognizes that women may not want to discuss the text's subject with men).[49] What *is* a potential problem is the intent or disposition of those male readers.[50] The prologue seems to suggest that the solution lies in a kind of vicarious shamefastness: in order to approach and use this treatise correctly, male readers must, like the prologue's author, learn to be hypervigilant against women's shame on women's behalf.

The prologues to *The Knowing of Woman's Kind in Childing* and Version 2 of *The Sickness of Women* rely on what is explicitly conceived of as a required, shared sensibility to shame for their definition of good reading and use. They thus might be said to effect two translations: one from Latin or French into English, and one from a potentially *vncurteys* male perspective to a perspective that is sympathetic to women's honourable shamefastness. According to this new perspective, the ideal audience is defined in terms of what we might describe as its emotional intelligence: a shamefast mind is the only mind capable of writing, reading, and using these texts appropriately. Perhaps most remarkable of all is the fact that both prologues seem to suggest that, in relation to the showing and telling of women's *preuytees*, men are both the problem and the solution: if the texts are to be used properly, and if women are to avoid shame connected with the subject of these texts, men must learn to be courteous and charitable towards women. This is a striking counterpoint to the models of masculinity I will consider later in this study, and deserves to be born in mind.

At the same time, however, as a number of the texts cited above make clear, neither women nor female shamefastness are always perceived as reliable. If chastity was as much a habit of mind as it was a habit of body, then it was susceptible to whatever weaknesses mind or body might possess, and, morally speaking, women's minds and bodies were believed to be exceptionally weak. A woman might 'lose' her sense of shame, as Gower observes, or aim to exploit it like the pregnant sow of Marie de France's fable. Even the physical evidence of women's bodies might be faked in order to provide a false impression of sexual virtue. Such suspicion attends even texts on the subject of women's medicine; indeed, as Lochrie notes, if the female body can be said to have belonged 'to the domain of trickery, of seeming, of lies' in the Middle Ages, 'nowhere is this more true than in the *Secrets of Women*'.[51]

One of the problems to which this book will repeatedly return is that, in the literature of medieval England, female shamefastness and, by extension, female honour are always potentially suspect. This suspicion stems in large part from the fact that female chastity, as the foundation of female honour, necessarily entailed a pattern of concealing and revealing, interiorizing and exteriorizing. This same pattern informs the practice of shamefastness that I will outline in the next chapter, which considers how conduct literature for women sought to direct both the interiorization and exteriorization of hypervigilance against disgrace in order to safeguard their honour.

Notes

This chapter includes some material that was previously published in Mary C. Flannery, 'Emotion and the Ideal Reader in Middle English Gynecological Texts', in Rachel Falconer and Denis Renevey (eds), *Literature, Science and Medicine in the Medieval and Early Modern Periods* (Turnhout: Swiss Papers in English Language and Literature (SPELL), 2013), pp. 103–15. I am grateful to the editors of that volume, and to Lukas Erne, the general editor of SPELL, for permission to use this material here.

1 Unless otherwise noted, all citations from *Knowing* are taken from the Douce Version contained in *The Knowing of Woman's Kind in Childing: A Middle English Version of Material Derived from the Trotula and Other Sources*, ed. Alexandra Barratt (Turnhout: Brepols, 2001), and cited above by line number. The warning contained in this passage may also be found in a nearly identical form in the Cambridge Version of the text, which appears on the facing page of Barratt's edition (p. 43).

2 *MED*, s. v. *despit, sclaundre*. In the notes accompanying these lines in her edition, Barratt points out that this 'conventionally pious but

Shame and the subject of women's bodies 53

slightly sinister' passage is not in the Old French source text (*The Knowing of Woman's Kind in Childing*, p. 116).

3 As Monica H. Green has demonstrated, later medieval gynaecological literature undergoes a fundamental 'change in title': whereas earlier writings on women's medicine had referred to their subject as the 'conditions' or 'sufferings' of women, 'women's affairs', or 'the diseases of women', among similar titles, from the thirteenth century onward '[s]ome gynecological literature began to be called "Secrets of Women," an epithet which hitherto had never been used for these texts' ('From "Diseases of Women" to "Secrets of Women": The Transformation of Gynecological Literature in the Later Middle Ages', *Journal of Medieval and Early Modern Studies* 30 (2000), 5–39 (p. 5)). I draw on her arguments regarding the ramifications of this shift (and, indeed, on much of her research on medieval women's medicine) later in this chapter.

4 *MED*, s. v. *sheuen* (v. (1)).

5 Genesis 2: 25 (Latin and English taken from Douay-Rheims and Latin Vulgate versions of the Bible, http://drbo.org/drl/chapter/01002.htm [accessed 12 March 2018]); see also Genesis 3: 7.

6 John Gower, *Le Mirour de l'Omme*, in *The Complete Works of John Gower: The French Works*, ed. G. C. Macaulay, EETS ES 81 (Oxford: Clarendon Press, 1899), pp. 1–334, lines 9241–52; English translation adapted from that featured in the discussion of this passage in Guillemette Bolens, *The Style of Gestures: Embodiment and Cognition in Literary Narrative* (Baltimore, MA: The Johns Hopkins University Press, 2012), pp. 101–2 (the book is an English translation by Bolens of her earlier French book *Le style des gestes: Corporéité et kinésie dans le récit littéraire* (Lausanne: Bibliothèque d'histoire de la médecine et de la santé, 2008)).

7 Whereas Bolens characterizes *vergoigne* as an emotion (*The Style of Gestures*, p. 102), in equating it with shamefastness I am characterizing it as an emotional capacity or disposition: the sensibility and susceptibility to the experience of shame.

8 *Ibid.*, p. 103.

9 *OED*, s. v. *shame* (under 'Etymology'). Of course, linguistic associations between shame and the human body have an even longer history. Valerie Allen notes that both Latin (*pudenda*) and Greek (*aidoia*) terms for genitals are linguistically connected to shame (*pudor* in Latin, *aidōs* in Greek) ('Waxing Red', p. 191). See also Green, 'From "Diseases of Women" to "Secrets of Women"' (esp. pp. 8–10 and 16), which discusses some of the 'rhetoric' and 'terminology' of shame in late antique and medieval gynaecological texts (although she observes that the topic and vocabulary of shame are absent from most gynaecological texts 'in Europe up through the eleventh century' (p. 9)).

10 *An Anglo-Saxon Dictionary*, s. v. *sceamlim*.

11 Guy de Chauliac, *The Middle English Translation of Guy de Chauliac's Treatise on Ulcers, Part I, Text: Book IV of the Great Surgery*, ed. by Björn Wallner (Stockholm: Almqvist & Wiksell International, 1982), p. 66; Latin from Guy de Chauliac, *Inventarium Sive Chirurgia Magna, Volume One: Text*, ed. by Michael R. McVaugh (Leiden: Brill, 1997), p. 239, line 38.
12 I make reference to this passage in Flannery, 'The Concept of Shame', pp. 174–5. *Peter Idley's Instructions to His Son* likewise suggests that women might find these short jackets pleasing to the eye and imagination, claiming that, while in church, some women 'set þeir myndes galantes to asspye, / Beyoldyng þe schort garmentes round all abouȝt / And how þe stuffyng off þe codpece berys ouȝt' (*Peter Idley's Instructions to His Son*, ed. Charlotte d'Evelyn (Boston, MA: D. C. Heath and Co., 1935; repr. 1975), 2C. 418–20). As I mention in my introduction (p. 29, n. 51), Chaucer's Parson does not let women off the hook: he goes on to note that, 'as of the outrageous array of wommen, God woot that though the visages of somme of hem seme ful chaast and debonaire, yet notifie they in hire array of atyr likerousnesse and pride. I sey nat that honestitee in clothynge of man or womman is unconvenable, but certes the superfluitee or disordinat scantitee of clothynge is reprevable' (*The Parson's Tale* 429–30).
13 John Lydgate, *Lydgate's Fall of Princes*, ed. by Henry Bergen, EETS ES, 121, 122, 123, 124, 4 vols (London: Oxford University Press, 1924–27), II, Book IV, lines 2374–75.
14 See 'Introduction', p. 12 for discussion.
15 Bella Millett and Jocelyn Wogan-Browne, 'Introduction', *Medieval English Prose for Women: Selections from the Katherine Group and Ancrene Wisse*, ed. Bella Millett and Jocelyn Wogan-Browne (Oxford: Clarendon Press, 1990), pp. xi–xxxviii (p. xv). R. Howard Bloch surveys the most rigid interpretations of virginity in 'Chaucer's Maiden's Head: "The Physician's Tale" and the Poetics of Virginity', *Representations* 28 (1989), 113–34. Although I am primarily concerned with the implications of female chastity throughout this study, valuable work has also been undertaken in recent years on expectations surrounding, and interpretations of, male chastity and virginity in the Middle Ages; see, for example, John H. Arnold, 'The Labour of Continence: Masculinity and Clerical Virginity', in Bernau, Evans, and Salih (eds), *Medieval Virginities*, pp. 102–18.
16 I discuss how Middle English conduct texts encouraged women to cultivate such a habit in Chapter 2.
17 Millett and Wogan-Browne, 'Introduction', p. xv; Burger, *Conduct Becoming*, p. 5.
18 Kao, 'Conduct Shameful and Unshameful', p. 127.
19 See Kim M. Phillips, *Medieval Maidens: Young Women and Gender in England, 1270 – 1540* (Manchester: Manchester University Press,

2003), p. 11, as well as the extracts from Scripture, treatises on natural philosophy, and theological writings included in *Woman Defamed and Woman Defended*, ed. Blamires with Pratt and Marx.
20 Phillips, *Medieval Maidens*, pp. 3–4.
21 Evans, 'Virginities', pp. 22–3. See also *The Book of the Knight of La Tour Landry*, pp. 75–6, which warns of the negative economical consequences of adultery: 'For the children that ben not of trewe maryage, they be they by whome the grete herytages and Auncestri ben loste ... Therfor, doughtres, be ware for brekinge of youre mariage, and of getinge of false heires, the whiche may putte alle a londe in tribulacion. And the moder shall be dampned perpetuelly, as long as thaire chyldren kepithe awey the londe that they haue no right to from the rightfull heyres, that is to saie, her moderis husbondes londes. And therfor be ware, doughtres, of this auouutry, and that ye take no man saue hym that ys ordeined you by sacrement of mariage, and kepithe and holdithe hym to you truly.'
22 Kathleen Coyne Kelly, 'Menaced Masculinity and Imperiled Virginity in the *Morte Darthur*', in Kelly and Leslie (eds), *Menacing Virgins*, pp. 97–114 (p. 104), which also points out that '[t]here are no virginity tests or prescriptions for faking virginity for men in these medical treatises'.
23 Kelly, 'Menaced Masculinity', p. 104; on virginity tests and their flaws, see also Salih, *Versions of Virginity*, pp. 20–1; and Kelly, *Performing Virginity*.
24 Esther Lastique and Helen Rodnite Lemay, 'A Medieval Physician's Guide to Virginity', in Joyce E. Salisbury (ed.), *Sex in the Middle Ages: A Book of Essays* (New York, NY: Garland, 1991), pp. 56–82 (p. 77 n. 78, p. 66). My thanks to Daniel DiCenso for his assistance with my English translation of this passage.
25 Salih, *Versions of Virginity*, p. 21.
26 *Hali Meiðhad*, p. 32 (lines 8–13).
27 On these prayers and charms for safe and (relatively) painless birth, see Marianne Elsakkers, 'In Pain You Shall Bear Children (Gen 3:16): Medieval Prayers for a Safe Delivery', in Anne-Marie Korte (ed.), *Women and Miracle Stories: A Multidisciplinary Exploration* (Leiden: Brill, 2001), pp. 179–209.
28 *MED*, s. v. *shame* (under 3a).
29 See *MED*, s. v. *shameful* (under d).
30 In *The Fables of Marie de France: An English Translation*, ed. and trans. Mary Lou Martin (Birmingham, AL: Summa Publications, Inc., 1984), pp. 78–80 (facing-page translation). I am very grateful to Emma O'Loughlin Bérat for bringing this example to my attention. Although extended consideration of the Anglo-Norman vocabulary linked to women's medicine lies beyond the scope of this study, pursuit of this line of inquiry might well compare such references to shame

in childbirth as that cited above with the language of Anglo-Norman treatises on women's medicine. Monica H. Green has noted that '[m]edical precepts for women were also commonly found in Anglo-Norman texts, and at least one Anglo-Norman translation of *Trotula* had been made by the mid-thirteenth century' ('Obstetrical and Gynecological Texts in Middle English', *Studies in the Age of Chaucer* 14 (1992), 53–88 (p. 55).

31 *The Fables of Marie de France*, pp. 79–80.

32 On representations of Salome in medieval England, see Alaya Swann, '"By Expresse Experiment": The Doubting Midwife Salome in Late Medieval England', *Bulletin of the History of Medicine* 89.1 (2015), 1–24.

33 *Play 15, Nativity*, in *The N-Town Plays*, ed. Douglas Sugano, TEAMS (Kalamazoo, MI: The Medieval Institute, 2007), http://d.lib.rochester.edu/teams/text/sugano-n-town-plays-play-15-nativity [accessed 17 November 2016], cited above by line number.

34 John Lydgate, *A Critical Edition of John Lydgate's Life of Our Lady*, ed. Joseph A. Lauritis (Pittsburgh, PA: Duquesne University, 1961), Book III, lines 387–8. As Swann puts it, 'touching the body of the virgin mother is not prohibited; instead, it is the mind-set with which the touch is approached that is important. ... Salome's transgression is not her touch but her doubt' ('"By Expresse Experiment"', p. 19).

35 English and Latin text taken from *The Trotula: A Medieval Compendium of Women's Medicine*, ed. and trans. Monica H. Green (Philadelphia, PA: The University of Pennsylvania Press, 2001), pp. 70–2 (facing-page translation). The Latin title of this text is most frequently translated as *Conditions of Women*. In medieval tradition, the text was later known as the *Trotula Major* (*The Trotula*, p. 3). On the complicated textual history of the compendium commonly known as the *Trotula*, see Monica H. Green, 'The Development of the *Trotula*', *Revue d'histoire des textes* 26 (1996), 119–203. As the *Liber sinthomatibus mulierum* suggests, shame and women's medicine have gone hand in hand for millennia. Writing in the fifth and fourth centuries BC, the author(s) of the ancient Greek Hippocratic text *Diseases of Women* observed that complications could arise in the diagnosis and treatment of female maladies because 'women are ashamed to tell even if they know [what ails them], and they suppose that it is a disgrace, because of their inexperience and lack of knowledge' (Ann Ellis Hanson, 'Hippocrates: *Diseases of Women 1*', *Signs: Journal of Women in Culture and Society* 1 (1975), 567–84 (p. 582)). A few centuries later, the Roman author Hyginus (ca. 64 BC–AD 17) recorded the remarkable story of Agnodice, who disguised herself as a man in order to learn about gynaecology and obstetrics and to treat women, but who was herself compelled to expose her body in order to prove her true sex when she was accused of seducing her patients. See Hyginus, *Fabulae*, ed. Peter

K. Marshall (Stuttgart: Teubner, 1993), Fable CLXXIV (pp. 196–7); for an English translation, see *Apollodorus' Library and Hyginus' Fabulae: Two Handbooks of Greek Mythology*, trans. R. Scott Smith and Stephen M. Trzaskoma (Indianapolis, IN: Hackett Publishing Company, 2007), p. 180.
36 Thanks largely to the work of Monica Green, our knowledge of Middle English texts on women's medicine has expanded significantly over the past few decades. While Rossell Hope Robbins was able to identify ten manuscripts 'containing material of obstetric and/or gynecological content' in 1970, by 1992 Green was able to identify thirty manuscripts containing such material, some of which had already begun to appear in scholarly editions (see Green, 'Obstetrical and Gynecological Texts', pp. 53–4; Rossell Hope Robbins, 'Medical Manuscripts in Middle English', *Speculum* 45 (1970), 393–415 (especially pp. 395, 406, and 410); and Green's introduction to *The Trotula*). Green and Linne R. Mooney note that *The Sickness of Women* likely originated out of a selective English translation of the *Compendium* made earlier in the fifteenth century (Monica H. Green and Linne R. Mooney, 'The Sickness of Women', in M. Teresa Tavormina (ed.), *Sex, Aging, and Death in a Medieval Medical Compendium: Trinity College Cambridge MS R.14.52, Its Texts, Language, and Scribe*, 2 vols (Tempe, AZ: Arizona Center for Medical and Renaissance Studies, 2006), pp. 455–83 (pp. 456–7)).
37 See Green and Mooney, 'The Sickness of Women', pp. 457–8; and Green, 'Obstetrical and Gynecological Texts', pp. 73–7.
38 *The Sickness of Women*, ed. Monica H. Green and Linne R. Mooney, in Tavormina (ed.), *Sex, Aging, and Death*, pp. 485–568. All citations from this text are taken from this edition and cited above by line number. As Green points out, the prologue's claim that the text has been written for women 'needs to be taken with a grain of salt: it fails to find any support in the substance of the text, which has no stylistic or grammatical alterations to gear it specifically to a female audience[,]... a discrepancy further underscored by the extended Latin text ... which would be useless to an unlatinate female audience'. By contrast, 'some of the scribes of Version 1 of "The Sekenesse of Wymmen" – which has no prologue declaring its intended audience – felt a need to clarify to whom they were speaking by adding the direct address "Sirs"' (Green, 'Obstetrical and Gynecological Texts', pp. 77, 58); Green cites three manuscripts – London, British Library, MS Sloane 5; Cambridge, Trinity College MS O.9.37, and Longleat House, MS Longleat 174 – as examples (p. 58, n. 20). Indeed, in the introduction to their edition of *The Sickness of Women*, Green and Mooney argue that in the case of at least one manuscript (Cambridge, Trinity College MS R.14.52), the text was included 'not because it was meant to be used by women, but because it was of interest to the codex's (male) compilers, who correctly assessed that the text had always been meant for male as

well as female readers' (Green and Mooney, 'The Sickness of Women', p. 455).
39 Version 2 is preserved in the following four manuscripts: London, British Library, Sloane MSS 249 (fols 180v–205v) and 2463 (fols 194r–232r); London, Royal College of Surgeons, MS 129 (fols 1r–45v); and Cambridge, Trinity College MS R.14.52 (fols 107r–135v).
40 *MED*, s. v. *wight*.
41 *MED*, s. v. *charite*.
42 *MED*. s. v. *repreving(e, discoveren*.
43 Karma Lochrie, *Covert Operations: The Medieval Uses of Secrecy* (Philadelphia, PA: University of Pennsylvania Press, 1999), pp. 118–34. Lochrie argues that *De secretis mulierum* participates in a wider discourse common to medieval 'secrets' literature, which 'make[s] visible the gendered interests of these dialogic acts of secrecy that always take place between two men' (p. 97).
44 Monica H. Green, 'A Handlist of Latin and Vernacular Manuscripts of the So-Called *Trotula* Texts', *Revue Internationale des Études Relatives aux Manuscrits* 51 (1997), 80–103 (pp. 84–6, which also discusses the sources of *Knowing*). As Green and Mooney note in their introduction to *The Sickness of Women*, although '*Sickness* owes no direct textual debt to *Knowing*', 'their structural similarities are unlikely to have been merely coincidental' (p. 463). Indeed, they suggest that it seems 'quite likely, then, that the author of *Sickness 2* was aware of the existence and the rhetorical posture of *Knowing* even if s/he didn't employ it as a direct model. Both texts see male involvement with women's diseases as potentially threatening to women, and both claim to wish to empower women to "help one another" by reading (and using) their text, thereby allowing them to bypass any dependence on males' (p. 466).
45 Different manuscripts of *The Knowing of Woman's Kind in Childing* tell different stories of textual transmission: three of the five manuscripts claim to be translated only from Latin sources, while the remaining two manuscripts specify that they were translated from French and Latin sources (p. 1 of Barratt's general introduction to her edition of *Knowing*; see also Green, 'A Handlist of Latin and Vernacular Manuscripts', pp. 84–6).
46 See Barratt's discussion of the text's intended readership on pp. 2–6 of her general introduction to *Knowing*. As she points out, although it seems clear that 'the author and/or translator intended this text to be read primarily by, and secondarily to, women', there is little evidence that would enable us to determine 'whether the text was in fact used by a woman' (p. 4).
47 Green, 'Obstetrical and Gynecological Texts', p. 65.
48 Barratt, p. 4 of her general introduction to *Knowing*.
49 Elizabeth Dearnley has read the prologue to *The Knowing of Woman's Kind in Childing* as 'vehemently defending women against the possibility

of male reading (regarded as intrusive or prurient) and censure' (*Translators and Their Prologues in Medieval England* (Cambridge: D. S. Brewer, 2016), p. 203). I would argue, however, that it is not the mere idea of male reading that is regarded as dangerous, but only male reading undertaken with the wrong motives.
50 Green makes a similar point regarding the contents of gynaecological treatises: 'What is at issue is not so much what the texts contain as *how* they are read' (*Making Women's Medicine Masculine: The Rise of Male Authority in Pre-Modern Gynaecology* (Oxford: Oxford University Press, 2008), p. 201).
51 Lochrie, *Covert Operations*, p. 129 (here citing Marie-Christine Pouchelle on the trickery of women's bodies: *The Body and Surgery in the Middle Ages*, trans. Rosemary Morris (Cambridge: Polity Press, 1990), p. 191).

2
Lessons in shame

In 1371, a knight sat down in his garden in Anjou and reflected on the companions of his youth. Many of them had deceived and seduced women with false promises of fidelity and love, exposing these women to 'mainte honte et maint villain diffame' ('gret defames and sclaundres') in the process.[1] Still reminiscing, the knight looked up to see his three young daughters approaching him across the garden. He resolved to write a book that would educate them in knowledge of the virtues and vices and in the ways of the world so that they might avoid being similarly 'blasmées, et honteuses et diffamées' ('blamed, dishonoured, and shamed').[2] His primary objective was not to help his daughters avoid heartbreak and grief, but instead to help them turn 'à bien et à honneur ... sur toutes riens' ('turne to good and worshipe aboue all ertheli thinges').[3] By learning how to recognize and resist seduction, these young women would safeguard both their chastity and their reputations.

This account opens the prologue to Sir Geoffrey de la Tour Landry's book of advice for his daughters, now known as the *Le livre du Chevalier de la Tour Landry pour l'enseignement de ses filles* (1371–72) or, in its Middle English form, *The Book of the Knight of La Tour Landry*. As Geoffrey's prologue makes clear, his aim is to teach his daughters how to grow up into good and honourable women. He declares himself to be speaking to 'none other women but to myn propre doughtres and seruantis of myn howse' ('à mes propres filles et à mes femmes servantes').[4] However, *Le livre* circulated widely in the later Middle Ages in both manuscripts and print editions, and was translated into English (twice) and into German. Its Middle English versions survive as part of the conduct literature for women that circulated in medieval England and, for the most part, closely follow their source.[5]

As its name suggests, 'conduct literature' is chiefly concerned with proper comportment in social situations. Those examples of the genre that are addressed to women advocated behaviour that would enable women to remain free from any vice and retain spotless reputations (as much a matter of concern for women's families as it was for women themselves).[6] Consequently, much of the advice contained in these texts is directed towards the problem of how to preserve one's chastity and how to avoid arousing even the slightest suspicion of sexual incontinence. In other words, the conduct literature of medieval England presents female honour as essentially a matter of learnable shamefastness – one can learn how and when and why one ought to be ashamed, and to what degree. These lessons are particularly important for women who want to secure their honour by maintaining their sexual continence, and conduct literature outlines programmes of behaviour designed to achieve that goal. In this chapter, I will show that medieval English conduct texts exhort women to be invested in being hypervigilant against the possibility of shame, and that they function as guides for practising that shamefastness, advocating and describing 'manipulations of body and mind' that are intended to intensify and communicate a woman's sense of shame.[7] A sense of shame is a matter of mental and behavioural practice in these texts: learning to develop watchfulness against shame is how women can construct an honourable habit for themselves.

I begin by situating conduct literature in relation to the education of girls and young women in medieval England, and in relation to the chaste ideals to which medieval women were expected to adhere. As I will show, the lessons of medieval conduct literature for women are both reinforced and complicated by surrounding discourses concerning the nature of women, the pliability of youth, and the desirability of virginal maidenhood. I then turn to the conduct texts themselves, focusing primarily on four examples of conduct literature in Middle English and Middle Scots: the Middle English translation of *Le livre du Chevalier de la Tour Landry pour l'enseignement de ses filles*, and the poems *How the Good Wife Taught Her Daughter*, *The Good Wife Would a Pilgrimage*, and the Middle Scots *Thewis of Good Women*. These texts present shamefastness as a practice demanding conscious effort of mind and body. Enjoining their readers to '[l]oke what woman þou wolt be, and theron set thy thowȝt' (in the words of *The Good Wife Would a Pilgrimage* (61)), medieval conduct texts for women outline a rigorous embodied programme of self-surveillance, which women must make a matter of daily habit if they are to secure their honour. In the final section of the chapter, I return to the *Book of the Knight* to demonstrate how it situates its advice regarding how to secure womanly 'honoure and goodnesse' within a recognizably literary frame, one that describes the pursuit of female honour in heroic terms. By likening female hypervigilance against shame to the chivalric quests and battles of medieval romance, the *Book of the Knight* shows how the motifs of imaginative literature might be used to motivate and guide emotional practices.

Chaste ideals and conduct literature

'Schamfast schuld maydons be.' This assured statement appears early on in *The Good Wife Would a Pilgrimage* (34), a poem addressed by a fictitious 'Good Wife' to her daughter describing how she ought to behave in her mother's absence.[8] We do not know who authored the poem, which is extant in only one mid-fifteenth-century manuscript, although its editor, Tauno Mustanoja, suggests that the author may have been acquainted with the slightly earlier and now better-known conduct poem *How the Good Wife Taught Her Daughter*.[9] As I will discuss later in this chapter, both poems employ a discourse of female virtue that is common to medieval English conduct literature for women, a genre that aims to teach women how to develop virtuous habits by presenting them with examples of good (and bad) behaviour – or, as the Middle Scots *The Thewis of Good Women* puts it, 'the thewis' of both 'a gud woman' and of 'ful women and schrewis' (C 1–6; J 1–6).[10]

Although conduct literature may not be evidence of either educational or behavioural practice in medieval England, its descriptions of good and bad 'thewis' and habits provide valuable evidence regarding the kinds of idealized standards to which medieval women from what we might call 'bourgeois classes' were held.[11] As Anna Dronzek has noted, these texts concern 'the transmission of ideals of proper behavior rather than any formal intellectual program. They are texts not of the classroom, but of the household, for the household provides the setting in which proper behavior takes places.'[12] The meagre information that we have concerning the authorship and readership of medieval conduct texts for women and the relative scarcity of surviving examples of the genre make it difficult to make claims concerning how these texts were used, or how they fit into the education of young women in medieval England. Our knowledge concerning the education of women and girls in medieval England is similarly limited; Alexandra Barratt notes that 'most of the evidence is anecdotal, impressionistic, can be gleaned only incidentally and must be treated with caution'.[13]

But however little access medieval English women might have had to a classroom or to formal instruction, certainly girls and women from the middle and upper classes would have been instructed in proper conduct either at home or at the homes of others.[14]

Those medieval conduct texts for women that survive express the view that such instruction was best begun at a young age, when maidens were most biddable. When discussing diet, for example, *The Book of the Knight* urges women to begin practising moderation in their diets from as young an age as possible, 'for suche lyff as ye will contynue, use you to in youre youthe, ye shal be by youre flesshe constreined to kepe in youre age' ('car telle vie, comme vous voudrez tenir et user en vostre jonnesce, tenir et user la vouldrez en vostre vieillesce').[15] Similarly, in a later discussion regarding the importance of developing good eating habits at a young age, *The Book of the Knight* argues that 'vsaunce and custume' in one's youth is the key to good behaviour as an adult:

> alle comithe but of vsaunce and custume; for right as ye custume youre self in youre youthe in etinge and drinking, and in alle youre other disposicion, right so ye shalle desire euer more for to continue in youre age. And therfor it behouithe and it is right necessarie, faire doughters, that ye putte remedie euermore contrarie to the flesshely appetite, that vertu and worship gouerne you euer more[.]

> tout chiet par coustume et par usaige, car de telle vie, soit de boire ou de mengier, comme vous vouldrés acoustumer en vostre jeunesse, vous le vouldrez maintenir en vostre viellesse, et pour ce ne chiet que en vostre voulenté à y mettre remède à heure.[16]

Both the process outlined here and the language Geoffrey uses to describe it point to an informal but clear concept of virtuous discipline at work in the text. One must 'custume' oneself in one's behaviour in order to be a good woman. This behaviour pertains not only to eating and drinking but to 'alle youre other disposicion' (here, the Middle English translator expands on the original French quoted above). The Middle English word *disposicioun* is particularly close to the emerging vernacular understanding of *habit* as both 'mental or moral condition' and 'customary practice', encompassing *both* the processes of planning, ordering, and governing *and* one's frame of mind or constitution, the product of those conscious processes.[17] By consciously cultivating good behaviour in one's youth, one ensures that one will naturally continue that good behaviour in adulthood. Like virginal maidenhood, this good behaviour is presented not only as a desirable habit to cultivate, but as a way of enhancing female desirability.[18] In a similar vein, *The Thewis of Good Women* argues that it is particularly important to watch over maidens while they are young, and therefore both most at risk and most capable of forming good habits; just as recalcitrant medical patients should be made to endure treatments they may not enjoy,

> ȝhit weil mar suld madenis ȝhinge
> Be stratly kepit, with gret awinge,
> In teching with a gud maistress,
> Quhilk knawis gud thewis, mar and less.
> And chaiste thaim quhill thai are child,
> Quhill wysdome cum throw wyt or eild.
> For ȝouthed ay inclynis to wyce,
> For selding find we barnis wyss.
> Folk may in ȝouthed tist a child,
> That fore na gold wald do in eild.
> (*The Thewis of Good Women* C 203–12; J 243–52)

The Thewis of Good Women differs from the other conduct poems examined in this chapter in that, although it describes its contents as the wisdom of a 'gud wyf' (C 1; J 1), it is not presented as advice given from a parent to a daughter. Nevertheless, it stresses that the guidance of a 'gud maistress' is key to ensuring that a young woman does not go astray.[19] In this passage, the poet sets up a play upon the homonymic link between *chaiste* ('chastise', 'discipline', 'teach') and *chaist* ('chaste' – C 225; J 261) in order to emphasize the importance of both education and vigilance in raising honourable women. Only if young maidens are 'stratly kepit', watched closely and chastised firmly, can they learn chaste habits.

But one of the chief complications related to chastity-centred constructions of female honour was that medieval reverence for chastity went hand in hand with a sense of delectation in it, particularly in discussions of maidenhood, that ideal stage in the female life cycle.[20] This dynamic is apparent in John of Trevisa's fourteenth-century English translation of Bartholomaeus Anglicus's *De proprietatibus rerum*, which in turn cites Isidore of Seville's etymological definition of *puella*:

> A maiden childe and a wenche hatte *puella*, as it were clene and pure as þe blake of þe yȝe, as seiþ Isidre. For among alle þat is iloued in a wenche chastite and clennes is iloued most. Men schal take hede of wenches for þey ben hote and moist of complexioun; and tendre, smal, pliaunt, and faire of disposicioun of body; schamefast, fereful, and mury, touchinge þe affeccioun; delicat in

Lessons in shame

clothinge. For as Senec seiþ, semelich cloþinge bysemeþ hem wel þat beþ chast wenchis [*et cetera*]. *Puella* is a name of age of soundenes wiþoute wem, and also of honeste. So seiþ Isidre. For comounliche we vsen to clepe maydenes wenchis. And a maide hatte *virgo* and haþ þat name of grene age, as *virga* 'a ȝerde' is iseide as it were *viridis* 'grene'. Oþir a maide haþ þat name *virgo* of clennes and incorrupcioun as it were *virago*, for sche knowiþ not þe verrey passion of wommen.

Puella dicitur quasi pura ut pupilla, ut dicit Isidorus. Super omnia enim que diliguntur in puella maxime diligitur pudicitia. Sunt autem puelle considerande quia secundum complexionem sunt calide, et humide, et tenelle, secundum corporis dispositionem graciles, flexibiles atque pulcre, secundum mentis affectionem verecunde, timide, et iocunde, quoad exteriorem compositionem moribus disciplinate, in sermonibus caute et tacite, in vestibus delicate. Nam, ut dicit Seneca, vestis decentia pudicas decet, etc.

Est autem puella nomen etatis integritatis et etiam honestatis, ut dicit Isidorus. Nam virgines puellas usualiter appellamus. Dicitur autem virgo ab etate viridiori, sicut et virga. Vel dicitur virgo ab incorruptione quasi virago, eo quod ignorat femineam passionem[.][21]

While maidenhood 'was not merely an age which was looked upon with alarm or anxiety', the tension inherent in maidenhood subjected young women 'both to protection and display, anxiety and appreciation'.[22] Thus, although Bartholomaeus here states that 'chastite and clennes' are 'iloued most' in young maidens, he also pays particular attention to the pleasures given by these maidens' appearance to those looking at them. The passage above stresses the flawlessness of maidenhood while lingering hungrily over the complexion, tenderness, pliability, and delicacy of young women. This dynamic reflects the instability and sense of flux that accompanied not only medieval conceptions of female nature, but also medieval conceptions of female honour. A maiden characterized by 'chastite and clennes' was, by virtue of those very characteristics, worthy of both admiration and desire. Bartholomaeus's observation that such maidens are *pliaunt* suggests that they are not only tractable in terms of disposition, but also in terms of their bodies (a suggestion that is equally inescapable in Chaucer's description of the old knight January's desire for a young wife who can be moulded '[r]ight as men may warm wex with handes plye' (*The Merchant's Tale* 1430)). Even during an academic discussion of chaste maidenhood such as Bartholomaeus's, chastity's status is precarious. It is in the context of this precariousness that shamefastness is cited alongside fearfulness and merriment as one of the key emotional attributes of virginal maidens – an unstable combination of those traits that can preserve female chastity and those traits that can jeopardize it. On the one hand, this dispositional makeup might be read as deriving from medieval notions of women as inconstant creatures; on the other hand, it contributes to a sense that womanly chastity itself is unstable and at risk.

Conduct literature for women describes the development of female virtue in terms of shamefast chastity, and as something to be practised from youth. But if shamefast chastity is envisioned as a habit in these texts, it is as a habit that must be maintained in the face of challenges presented by women's nature, the temptations of youth, and even the desirability of chastity itself. Under these circumstances, how could women develop or maintain such a habit? How could they definitively prove that they were chaste in body and mind? In the next section, I explore the ways that conduct texts for women seek to guide the practice of shamefast chastity.

Conduct unbecoming

Given the glorification of female sexual continence in medieval culture, it is no surprise that maintaining and (even more importantly) demonstrating one's sexual continence is the dominant theme in the Middle English conduct texts for women that survive. The advice contained in these texts tends to be proscriptive rather than prescriptive – it lays particular emphasis on what must be avoided, what must not be done, lest a woman become infamous within her community. Above all, according to these texts, a woman must avoid anything that might be interpreted as the behaviour of a *strumpet* or *giglot* (a loose woman, courtesan, harlot).[23] At the same time, conduct texts offer this guidance on shame avoidance in terms that are intended to help women develop a shamefast practice that is both mindful and embodied.

The variety and number of prohibited behaviours listed in medieval conduct poems indicate how easily a woman's honour might be called into question. A particularly suggestive list may be found in one version of *How the Good Wife Taught Her Daughter*, a poem that survives in different forms in five manuscripts dating from the fourteenth and fifteenth centuries, as well as in a 1597 print collection of *Certaine Worthye Manuscript Poems of Great Antiquitie*.[24] The version of the poem contained in Oxford, Bodleian

Library MS Ashmole 61 provides a fairly comprehensive list of behaviours associated with *giglotrie*:

> Change not thi countenans with grete laughter,
> And wyse of maneres loke thou be gode.
> Ne for no tayle change thi mode,
> Ne fare not as thou a gyglot were,
> Ne laughe thou not lowd, be thou therof sore.
> Luke thou also gape not to wyde,
> For anything that may betyde.
> Suete of speche loke that thow be,
> Trow in worde and dede – lerne this of me.
> Loke thou fle synne, vilony, and blame,
> And se ther be no man that seys thee any schame.[25]

Looseness of sexual mores is here tied to looseness of expression – a woman must exercise strict control over her face, mouth, and speech at all times. To do otherwise would be to risk being taken for a *gyglot*, a bad woman. The passage places remarkable emphasis on the necessity of controlling one's facial muscles, calibrating the volume of one's laughter and the openness of one's mouth, and modulating one's emotional responses. 'Grete laughter', changing 'mode', and gaping 'to wyde' here function as thumbnail sketches of an overly accessible or even inviting female body as it engages with the surrounding world.

This excerpt from *How the Good Wife Taught Her Daughter* exemplifies the proscriptive advice found in medieval conduct literature for women, its emphasis on what to avoid. It also presents this avoidance as a form of mindful, embodied practice. The 'Good Wife' urges her daughter to be attentive ('loke thou', 'se') to her behaviour – more specifically, she urges her daughter to pay attention to how her body moves, feels, and sounds, enlisting her mind and her senses to monitor how she is feeling and how she appears to those around her. The daughter is to search her own body – sensibly and imaginatively, both from her own perspective and as if through the eyes and ears of others – for any way it might be acting like that of a *gyglot*: is it too mobile? too loud? too open and accessible? The focal point of these processes of evaluation should always be mental and physical self-discipline and self-restraint that is aimed at shame-avoidance. While making her case for the relevance of kinesic intelligence to literary analysis, Guillemette Bolens proposes that '[a] literary study of *verecundia* and *vergoigne* reveals that these concepts refer to a category of emotions related to the act of inhibiting impulses that are deemed detrimental to social ties'.[26] Taking the narrative of Lucretia as her key example, Bolens unpacks the ways that various redactors of that narrative play upon a shared understanding of what physical movements are associated with shame – Lucretia's physical gestures testify to how much she values her good name and how much she fears losing it. What we see in medieval English conduct texts like *How the Good Wife Taught Her Daughter*, however, is a concerted effort to *teach and guide* the kinesic intelligence at the heart of Bolens's argument. In effect, the passage above outlines what Bolens identifies as 'inhibition of motor impulses' associated with the physical performance of *vergoigne*; by exercising constraint over their facial expressions and voices, women do not simply exhibit the socially recognizable gestures of shamefastness: they feel shamefastness itself.[27] Consequently, in addition to fleeing 'synne, vilony, and blame', they must be careful to physically, visibly, and aurally *perform* this shamefastness in order to ensure that 'no man ... seys [them] any schame'.

As *How the Good Wife Taught Her Daughter* later warns, the sensorimotor practice of shamefastness extends beyond the body and what it is doing to the spaces within which it is situated. One must also pay attention to the company one keeps, and where one keeps it:

> Ne go thou nought to the taverne,
> Thy godnes for to selle therinne.
> Forsake thou hym that taverne hanteth,
> And all the vices that therinne bethe.
> Wherever thou come at ale or wyne,
> Take not to myche, and leve be tyme,
> For mesure therinne, it is no herme,
> And drounke to be, it is thi schame.
> Ne go thou to no wrastlyng,
> Ne yit to no coke schetyng,
> As it were a strumpet or a gyglote,
> Or as a woman that lyst to dote.[28]

This passage calls attention to the way that certain spaces and entertainments might call a woman's honour into question. As it is depicted here, the tavern is a place where both appetites and appetitive vices are indulged; when those appetites are indulged beyond measure, the tavern becomes a particularly dangerous place for a woman eager to safeguard her chastity and good name. The opening lines of this passage suggest that the *godnes* a woman might *selle* ('give away', 'offer for sale', but also 'betray') in a tavern could be either her reputation or her chastity and sexual favours.[29] By spending too much time in a tavern, a woman might be viewed as signalling her willingness to exchange her reputation for dangerous pleasures, or even her willingness to whore herself out. The poem tasks its imagined female readers with strictly controlling their exposure to temptation (and, perhaps, the likelihood that they might tempt others) – they should not imbibe or consume too much of what the tavern offers, and they should limit the time they spend on the premises. Other low-class public entertainments, such as wrestling and cock shooting, are similarly risky attractions: the only kind of woman who attends these entertainments (or who attends them without following the disciplines required to maintain her shamefastness) is either a *strumpet* (prostitute, whore, loose woman), a *gyglote*, or very foolish: in short, most assuredly not a good woman.[30] Like a woman who 'gapes' too widely, the tavern-going woman imagined in these lines is one whose bodily borders are not as closed as they ought to be, and one whose bodily borders demand careful surveillance. The slightly later poem, *The Good Wife Would a Pilgrimage*, likewise discourages over-indulgence in food and drink: 'Revle þe well in met and drende, doȝttor, it is nede. / Lechery, sclandorynge, and gret dyssese commythe of dronken hede' (73). The phrase *revle þe well* aptly signals the self-governance that women should employ in order to safeguard their chastity and reputation, a discipline that should be easily evident to onlookers, and which can also be conspicuous by its absence.

Even if a woman chose not to frequent taverns, the mere fact of being visible in public posed risks to her reputation, as *The Good Wife* makes clear. The poem warns women not to be too sociable while out and about:

> When I am out of þe toun, loke that þou be wyse,
> And rene þou not from hous to hous lyke an Antyny gryce;
> For þo yonge men cheres the, they wyll sey þou art nyce,
> And euery boy wyll wex bold to ster þe to lovd wysse.
> (*The Good Wife Would a Pilgrimage* 7–10)[31]

This passage warns women to be careful to inhibit their movement in and through communal spaces. Being too mobile outside of the home could give men the impression that one is open to 'lovd wysse' (foolish or wicked ways), and could encourage boys and young men to lead a young woman astray.[32] The passage does not specify what other activities the daughter might be engaged in on these errands; indeed, they are irrelevant to the poem's warning. Simply running 'from hous to hous', circulating too actively and too visibly within the community, could be enough to embolden young men to take advantage of a young woman, and to speak ill of her behind her back. *The Thewis of Good Women* similarly discourages women from 'wauerand' ('wavering', wandering, moving back and forth) outside of the home, 'For wauerynge betaknis wylsumnes, / Wanwyt, welth, ore wantonness' (C 110–12; J 148–50). Likewise, *How the Good Wife Taught Her Daughter* urges women to be careful not to spend too much time speaking to men in public, and not to be too easily persuaded by men's fair speech:

> Aquyente thee not with every man.
> That inne the stret thou metys than;
> Thof he wold be aqueynted with thee,
> Grete hym curtasly, and late hym be.
> Loke by hym not longe thou stond,
> That thorow no vylony thi hert fond
> All the men be not trew
> That fare spech to thee can schew.[33]

These lines highlight the many and various dangers that every social interaction presents. Speaking too long with a man in a street risks inviting 'vylony' into a woman's heart, already so easily inclined to sin. Even 'fare spech' may conceal sinful ulterior motives, and cannot be trusted. Here, the uncertain nature of *men*'s motives is used to teach women the importance of demonstrating their own virtue as clearly as possible through physical self-restraint and withdrawal.

Like overindulgence in a tavern, being overly mobile in public is presented as a sign that one lacks discipline over one's body and morals; as Gail Kern Paster has noted in her work on shame and gender in early modern drama, 'a woman who leaves her house is a woman who talks is a woman who drinks is a woman who leaks'.[34] This 'leakage' may take the form of anything crossing a woman's borders, or of a woman herself crossing borders and thresholds that ought to remain closed to her. A woman seen to be overindulging in ale, wine, or public entertainments is a woman who may well be indulging her other bodily appetites with equal enthusiasm – thus, '[a]ny point in the leakage may imply or abridge the rest'.[35] The bodily restraint women are urged to practice also extends to how they cover or adorn their bodies, as *The Thewis of Good Women* makes clear. Both copies of the poem warn women against using 'colouris' or 'payntry' to beautify themselves on holy days: 'syk thing is bot gyglotry' (C 87–92; J 127–30). But in addition to condemning such deliberate *gyglotry*, the copy of *The Thewis* held in St John's College, Cambridge (J), warns that being even slightly overdressed can give men the wrong idea; in a passage that does not appear in the other surviving version of the poem, this version of *The Thewis* points out that when women 'cled ar our-statly, / Men will presoyme na gud, treuly, / But þat at scho dois it for paramour, / And þus-gat faid sal hir honour' (J 63–66). The promise of the instantaneous loss of 'hir honour' is offered up as proof that a woman's reputation might rest on the smallest detail of her appearance – one accessory too many, a dress or kerchief judged to be too beautiful or too intricate. Too little clothing can have the same effect: *The Good Wife Would a Pilgrimage* warns young women not to expose their 'legys whyte' or their 'stret hossyn, to make men have delytt' because 'men wyll sey of þi body þou carst but lytt' (25–28). The image of pale skin normally not exposed to sunlight is particularly striking; it reads like an invitation to imagine what such an intimate moment of exposure might feel like, and to cringe at the thought. Although, as I noted in the previous chapter, medieval texts also warn men to cover their bodies (particularly their *shamefuls*) in order not to inspire lust in others, a woman's exposed body poses additional risks to her honour because it is taken as evidence of her motives, almost as a sartorial statement of sexual consent-in-advance. Such passages are strikingly resonant with the kind of warnings women continue to receive today, warnings that make women responsible for performing their shamefastness (or, in contemporary terms, their lack of consent) via word, gesture, and appearance. Looking like a woman who wants to provoke male desire is equated with looking like a woman who has no sense of shame; that is, like a *giglot*. Like drinking too much in a tavern, over-exposing her body to the male gaze renders a woman more vulnerable to disgrace, according to *The Good Wife*, because it gives men the impression that she does not care what happens to it, and even that she has deliberately made it more accessible to them. This passage explicitly links *caring* (and appearing to care) about one's chastity with *preserving* one's chastity: if a woman cares enough about maintaining her sexual continence, she must broadcast that sentiment. *Not* taking pains to demonstrate one's hypervigilance against shame is interpreted as asking for trouble.

The proscriptive advice offered by medieval conduct literature for women bespeaks an underyling anxiety about the instability and haziness of the boundary between 'good' women and *giglots*. Women must practise constant vigilance concerning the propriety of their behaviour because, even if one *is* an honourable, chaste woman, the slightest miscalculation in one's behaviour or appearance might lead one to be taken for a strumpet. These texts suggest that women are forever at risk of slipping from one category to the other, or at risk of being mistaken for the wrong kind of woman. Yet conduct literature for women is founded on the premise that *giglots* and shameless women have certain recognizable habits and dispositions, which honourable women should learn to avoid. As we have already seen, these habits can include being too sociable or too mobile in public, frequenting taverns and public entertainments too often, or seeming to put too much effort into appearing attractive. That these texts aim to educate women in the habits that distinguish good women from bad is clear in the opening lines of *The Thewis of Good Women*, which outline the poem's purpose:

> Þe gud wiff schawis, fore best scho can,
> Quhilkis ar the thewis of a gud woman,
> Quhilkis gar women be haldin deir,
> And pouer women princis peir;
> With sum ill maneris and thewis
> That folowis ful women and schrewis.
>
> (C 1–6; J 1–6)

This passage unequivocally states that the poem aims to make clear what distinguishes the *thewis* (deportment, habit, practice) of a good woman from those of a bad woman.[36] Like the word *habit*, the word *thewis* slips between referring to one's customary behaviour and referring to one's moral character, which, given the poem's interest in outlining a social and emotional programme of honourable behaviour, is particularly apt. A woman's *thewis* and *maneris* demonstrate whether she is 'a gud woman' or a foul shrew. Notably, here the *thewis* of a good woman are not dependent on class: a 'pouer' woman who conducts herself appropriately may be considered a 'princis peir'.[37] Moreover, the poem's opening lines suggest that it will also educate men as well as women in how to distinguish good women from bad:

> men suld considyr
> That womenis honore is tendyr and slyddyr,
> And raithar brekis be mekil thinge,
> As farest ross takis sonest faidinge.
> A woman suld ay have radour
> Of thinge that gref mycht hir honoure[.]
>
> (C 7–12; J 7–12)

With this passage, the poem's introduction highlights the need for its counsel as well as introducing the advice that follows. It is precisely because female honour is so open to question – so 'tendyr and slyddyr' – that it can only be secured and proven by means of hypervigilance and discipline. At the same time, the Middle English word *slyddyr* (slippery, uncertain, but also treacherous, deceitful) suggests that there is something in femininity itself that renders female honour a difficult, dangerous thing, an unreliable marker of goodness.[38] Like the 'fairist ross', it is precious, and supremely vulnerable. Consequently, any woman aspiring to goodness must 'have radour' (rigour and strictness, but also fear) when it comes to anything that might threaten her honour.[39]

This emphasis on the need for hypervigilance against the possibility of disgrace is what enables medieval conduct literature to shape women's practice of shamefastness. These texts aim to cultivate a hypervigilance against shame in their female audiences (in addition to reinforcing male vigilance concerning women's propensity to go astray), a shamefastness that is presented as a product of mindful and embodied effort, something that women must practise in order to perfect and in order to protect their chastity. In so doing, medieval conduct texts contribute to the cultivation and promotion of an informal yet cohesive system of habits intended to secure female honour in the face of ever-present threats. They persistently warn their readers that a woman's speech, behaviour, and appearance are constantly subjected to the scrutiny of others, and that women must modulate their activity accordingly. Thus, *How the Good Wife Taught Her Daughter* warns,

> Loke thou chyd no wordes bolde,
> To myssey nother yonge ne olde
> For and thou any chyder be,
> Thy neyghbors wylle speke thee vylony.
> Be thou not to envyos,
> For dred thi neyghbors wyll thee curse[.][40]

The lesson is clear: someone is always watching, and judging. But in addition to warning readers that they are being observed, these texts repeatedly invite women to observe themselves, and to be alert to any possibility of misbehaviour. It is in women's best interest to bear the fragility of their reputations in mind when going about their daily business.

The guidance offered for the cultivation of shamefastness by conduct literature is framed within a broader discourse of vigilance found throughout these texts, which are filled with admonitions to observe one's own actions with a critical eye – to be ware. In *How the Good Wife Taught Her Daughter* (whose opening words are 'Lyst and lythe', 'listen and be attentive'), the author uses the phrase 'loke thou' ('see to it that you …') more than a dozen times when issuing warnings and advice, a call to alertness that is expressed in the language of observation.[41] Similarly, in *The Good Wife Would a Pilgrimage*, the 'mother' repeatedly employs the language of 'looking' in her admonitions to the 'daughter' ('loke that þou be wyse' (7); '[l]oke what woman þou wolt be' (61)), in addition to reminding her that others will be watching as well (the text warns that fidgeting 'ys not a goodly sy3t' (33)). If conduct literature teaches women how to view themselves and their behaviour, it is most especially as objects of constant surveillance. This is apparent in *The Good Wife*'s warning that women should not be 'of low3ttor ly3t, nor of contenance ly3t' (31), an admonition that echoes *How the Good Wife Taught Her Daughter*'s remarks regarding gaping too widely or laughing too much. The first things mentioned by *The Thewis* as giving potential *gref* to a woman's honour are loud speech and loud laughter; women must be '[f]ul of piete and humylitee, / And lytill of langage … / Nocht loud of lange na lauchtyr crouss' (C 13–15; J 13–15). A good woman may be seen, but she should not be too easily heard.

As Claire Sponsler has pointed out, this sense of a need for self-surveillance is one characteristic that distinguishes conduct literature addressed to women from that addressed to men. In her discussion of the late-medieval conduct poem *How the Wise Man Taught His Son* (which appears alongside *How the Good Wife Taught Her Daughter* in Oxford, Bodleian Library, MS Ashmole 61), Sponsler notes that the poem begins with the assumption that the man 'is pre-scripted into the realm of the already disciplined', and presents the male body 'as an agent of discipline'; by contrast, *How the Good Wife Taught Her Daughter* suggests that women and their bodies are in much more need of disciplining:[42]

> the daughter is presented as by nature unruly, possessed of and by a transgressive body. As a consequence of her innate unruliness, she has to be ordered to be 'meke and myld' (20) and to be 'of gode berynge and of gode tonge' (24), unlike the son who is by nature predisposed to bodily restraint … The social space is here envisioned as highly theatrical, requiring a nuanced, self-aware, and highly

guarded performance. In this performance the natural female body has to be constantly monitored and regulated, its basic impulses restrained and reshaped in socially acceptable ways so as to hem in its potential transgressiveness.[43]

Sponsler points out that the discourse of *How the Good Wife Taught Her Daughter* teaches female readers that 'continual self-vigilance' is necessary in order to maintain proper behaviour, to behave like a 'good woman'.[44] This simultaneously trains women to look at and listen to themselves as if through the eyes of others *and* to remember that others are always looking and listening. But as I hope I have shown, within the medieval English conduct texts examined above, this self-surveillance and bodily discipline has an emotional goal. These texts exhort women to control their bodies in social spaces not only because of how this will look to those around them, but also because of how it will make them *feel*. It is precisely through the regular inhibition of motor impulses that women will generate an authentic, mindful, and embodied experience of shamefastness within themselves. As McNamer demonstrates in her study of medieval compassion, the authors of medieval texts insist on the fact that these feelings do not spring up out of nowhere, but are in fact the product of conscious effort. It is precisely the constant, conscious effort detailed in medieval conduct literature for women that eventually makes shamefastness 'true': that makes it a habit.

Medieval English conduct literature teaches women that, in order to generate shamefastness that is both genuinely felt and manifestly obvious to others, they must continuously exert themselves, returning over and over to the meditations and gestures outlined in conduct texts. When *The Good Wife Would a Pilgrimage* argues that '[s]chamfast schuld maydons be, and stronge witt all ther myȝt' (34), the declaration conveys the steadfastness and fortitude required for such a feat. Only a strong woman can be disciplined enough to make a habit of shamefastness, which is why it is so striking when Chaucer's Physician remarks of Virginia that '[s]hamefast she was in maydens shamefastnesse' (*The Physician's Tale* 55): the double reference to her shamefast nature – once at the beginning, and once at the end of the verse – functions as a symbol of her steadfastly chaste conduct and safely encases her maidenly identity within a shamefast epanalepsis.[45] When *The Thewis* claims that women should 'ay be dredand to have blame' (C 144; J 186), the adverb *ay* (continuously, eternally) insists that women maintain steadfast attention to the prospect of shame if they wish to safeguard their honour.[46] Women must never forget (or be allowed to forget) to fear disgrace – hence the necessity of repeatedly warning women to 'loke' and 'se' that they are behaving correctly. The looking and seeing of self-surveillance is also a reminder to set one's mind to the task: goodness will not happen without persistent effort and attention.

Conduct literature's lessons in good and bad female behaviour are, in fact, lessons in female shame. They explain when and why women should fear shame for particular behaviours, and they explain how a woman's conduct affects her sexual continence and her reputation for chastity, both of which are key components of her honour. They offer guidance regarding how to cultivate an interiorized sense of shame that will also be recognizable to others. In the final section of this chapter, I will return to the *Book of the Knight of La Tour Landry* in order to show how, in addition to outlining a mindful and embodied practice of female shamefastness, it employs a literary trope in order to transform this emotional practice into a heroic undertaking.

Heroic shamefastness in *The Book of the Knight of La Tour Landry*

Two Middle English translations of *Le livre du Chevalier de la Tour Landry* survive as the text now known as *The Book of the Knight of La Tour Landry*: one anonymous translation in London, British Library, MS Harley 1764 (which dates from the middle of the fifteenth century), and a translation by William Caxton printed in 1484. (Since Caxton sticks so literally to the French that the sense of the text is sometimes completely lost in his translation, the following discussion will centre on the slightly earlier manuscript version of the text.) The twin themes of 'honoure and goodnesse' surface repeatedly throughout the *Book of the Knight*, which closely links these qualities to medieval expectations of female chastity and defines a 'good woman' as follows:

> this is saide be a woman that is not wedded, and she lyuithe in uirginite, clennesse, and chastite; or ellys bi a woman that is wedded, and she kepithe truly and honestly the sacrement of mariage, & also by them that worshipfully and perfitly kepe thaire wedwhode, that lyuen in chastite and in sobriete. These be the .iij. manere of women the whiche God praisithe, and likenithe hem vnto the precious margarite, that is alle faire withoute ani foule tache or ani foulenesse[.]

> c'est-à-dire celle qui n'est pas mariée et se tient vierge ou chaste, et aussi celle qui est mariée et se tient nettement ou saint sacrement de mariaige, sans souffrir estre avillée que de son époux que Dieu lui a destiné et donné, et aussy celle qui nettement tient son vefvage, cestes-cy sont celles, si comme dit la glose, de qui Dieu parla en sa sainte Euvangile. Ce sont celles qui en ces iij. estas se tiennent nettement et chastement. Elles sont comparagiées, si comme dist nostre seigneur Jhesuchrist, à la precieuse marguerite, qui est clère et nette, sans nulle taiche.[47]

In a clear departure from the earlier medieval hierarchy of female virtue (within which virginity reigned supreme), the above enumeration of the three categories of honourable women – virgins, wives, and widows – distinguishes no single group as most deserving of either spiritual or social honour. Although the precise definition of sexual continence differs for wives, unmarried maidens, and widows, chastity remains a universal hallmark of female honour. Regardless of marital status, a woman's goodness and honour were determined in the eyes of others by her perceived chastity. Anything that might appear to deviate from these ideals left a woman open to accusations of lasciviousness; an honourable woman should be free from even the slightest suspicion of such a thing.[48]

While the *Book*'s advice suggests that women are capable of the discipline required to maintain this degree of inner and outer virtue, its emphasis on the labour required to secure female chastity also bespeaks the pervasive perception of women as fundamentally undisciplined creatures. Thus the *Book* remarks that women who succeed in exercising control over their bodies in order to preserve their chastity deserve even more praise than a man who achieves the same goal for himself:

> And by cause and raisone that woman is of more light courage thanne man, that is for asmoche as the woman is ycome and was drawe oute of the man, and in asmoche as she is more feble to withstonde the temptaciones of the flesshe, whanne she withstondithe and ouercomithe the flesshe in so moche she is worthi to haue the more merite and thanke before the man.

> Nulle chose n'est si noble que de bonne femme, et playst à Dieu et aux angels en partie plus que l'omme, et doit avoir plus de merite, selon rayson, pour ce que elles sont de plus foible et legier couraige que n'est l'homme, c'est-à-dire que la femme feust traitte de l'omme, et, de tant comme elle feust plus foible et elle puet bien resister aux tamptacions de l'ennemy et de la chair, et, en l'aventure, de tant doit-elle avoir plus grant merite que l'omme.[49]

It is in part because of the widely asserted moral weakness of women that that the *Book of the Knight* warns against regularly attending events such as jousts, or even regularly going on pilgrimages: 'it is gret perile a woman to acustume her or to desire to goo to suche festis ther she might abide atte home with her worshippe saued, vndefamed of her good name; for atte suche places mani women takith moche blame withoute cause'.[50] As this prohibition notes, attending social events outside the home should be the exception rather than the rule of a woman's behaviour – a woman should not *acustume* herself (become habituated) to such entertainments.[51] This warning suggests that the home is perhaps the only place where a woman can be sure not to put her reputation at risk, whether through her own actions of those of others. The *Book of the Knight* goes on to warn women to keep friends around them at social events

> not for no ferde of none euell that ye wolde do, but for ferde of euell tonges that gladlyer wolle saie harme than good, and more thanne thei knew. And it is good that ye do so for the suerte of youre good name, that thei that stondithe bi you may saie, yef that thei here a false iangeler or a lyer saie aught on you that is not true, that thei may be sure to saye that it ys false.

> non pas pour nulle doubtance de nul mal, maiz pour le peril de mauvais yeulx et de mauvaises langues, qui tousjours espient et disent plus de mal qu'il n'y a, et aussy pour plus seurement garder son honnour contre les jangleurs, qui voulentiers disent le mal et taisent le bien.[52]

This warning points to the double danger incurred in women's social interactions: the danger lies not only in one's own behaviour, but also in what others may think or say about it. This makes securing the *suerte* of one's good name increasingly difficult, and increasingly crucial. The situation is further complicated by the fact that even if a man may seem to speak well of a woman who is generous with her favour, the tune changes once she has departed:

> 'Loo! suche a gentille woman, she is right curteys and kynde, for she wille suffre you to do with her alle youre plesaunce, and mani a good felaw hathe had his parte.' And thus saithe one to another of suche women. And in this wyse, he that spekithe right fayre and makithe her reuerence as his lady before her, whanne they be departed he spekithe suche worshippe of her as she hathe deserued. But such women as be foles aperceiue it not, but they seme that no man coude knowe nor aspie thaire fauute, for they be so bolde in thaire synne and wille not vnderstonde nor knowe thaire shame, so that the tyme

is chaunged. But it were moche beter forto shewe hem thaire blame and thaire synne, as the auncyen knightes sheued vnto women thaire foly in that tyme, as here before y haue tolde you.

'Vées cy une telle; elle est trop bien courtoise de son corps; tel et tel se esbat avecques elle', et la racontent et la nombrent avecques les mauvaises. Et ainsi tel lui fait honneur et belle chière par devant, qui lui trait la langue par derrière. Mais les folles ne s'en apperçoivent mie, ains se esbaudissent en leur folie, et leur semble que nul ne scet leur honte ne leur faulte. Sy est le temps changé comme il souloit, et je pense que c'est mal fait, et que il vaulsist mieulx devant touz monstrer leurs faultes et leurs folies, comme ilz faisoient en cellui temps dont je vous ay compté.[53]

This passage describes how some women who are too sociable with men remain ignorant of how those men speak of them behind their backs: 'they be so bolde in thaire synne and wille not vnderstonde nor knowe thaire shame'. In this example, shame*less*ness is a fatal form of ignorance – women must know when they *should* be ashamed if they are to behave honourably. Consequently, *The Book of the Knight* insists that a woman most ought to 'be displeased and hate herself' if she fails to maintain herself 'withoute ani foule tache or ani foulenesse' and removes herself from 'the nombre and memorie of alle good women'.[54] Blameworthy women – particularly women too foolish to know they have attracted blame in the first place – need a lesson in shame in order to understand how they may avoid it. The root of the problem is a kind of ignorance or blindness; if a woman is not aware of her behaviour and her reputation, and acutely alert to how they may be interpreted (or misinterpreted) by others, she will not know when she ought to be ashamed, and, the *Book* implies, she will not know how to avoid shameful behaviour in the first place.

This need for self-awareness is also emphasized elsewhere in *The Book of the Knight of La Tour Landry*, as when Geoffrey de la Tour Landry explains to his daughters that if they wish to avoid the sin of lechery, they must approach shamefast behaviour via a series of constant reflections and remembrances:

And this shall helpe to kepe you, that is to loue and drede God and youre husbonde, and *bethenke you* what sorw, harme, and worldes shame hathe and may falle therof, and ye do amisse; and how ye lese the loue of God, and of youre husbonde, kyn, frendes, and of all the worlde that knouithe you and heres therof; and therfor, doughters, yef temptacion assailethe you, *haue mynde* day and night to make recistens ageynes hem, to kepe you clene and ferme in goodnesse. And *bethenke what ye are, and whennes ye come, and what shame and dishonour may falle you yef ye do euell.*

Or vous dy, mes belles filles, qu'il n'y a que faire qui se vieult garder nettement, c'est amer Dieu et craindre de bon cuer et penser quel mal, quelle honte, quelle doleur et aviltance en vient à Dieu et au monde, et comment on y pert l'amour de Dieu, et l'ame, et l'amour de ses parens et l'amour du monde. Sy vous pry moult doulcement comme mes très chières filles que vous y pensez jour et nuit quant mauvaises temptacions vous assauldront, et que soiés vaillans et seures et resistez fort encontre, et regardez du lieu dont vous estes e quel mal et deshonneur vous en pourroit venir.[55]

What *The Book of the Knight* is outlining here is effectively a short meditation that is intended to arouse and intensify a fear of disgrace. These reflections are intended to form a regular pattern of thinking that will deter lascivious behaviour by instilling a strong fear of shame in the female reader. Geoffrey repeatedly urges his daughters to reflect on what is at stake when they conduct themselves, to 'haue mynde day and night' to resist temptation, and to remember all they stand to lose if they give in to temptation. The instructions to *reflect, remember, be mindful (haue mynde)* read very much like a set of instructions for a series of mental exercises directed towards a specific end: to remain 'clene and ferme in goodnesse' – that is, chaste. At the same time, the passage makes clear that these are meant to be *regular* exercises, repeated 'day and night to make recistens' against fleshly temptation. The consequences he mentions are both spiritual and social, since lechery will cause his daughters not only to 'lese the loue of God' but also to lose the love of 'youre husbonde, kyn, frendes, and of alle the worlde that knouithe you and heres therof'. Piling up the variety of consequences that his daughters will suffer if they lose their names, Geoffrey seeks to intensify his daughters' fear of such an eventuality.

Passages such as these are one reason why historians of emotion have gravitated to texts like conduct books as some of the 'least dishonest' forms of literary evidence that might be employed in service of emotion history.[56] Even if they do not constitute evidence of lived emotional experience, they may be used as evidence of the emotional standards to which individuals were held within a particular period, as well as the practical methods individuals may have used to meet these standards. But the final passage that I will consider in this chapter also reveals a distinctly literary sensibility at work in *The Book of the Knight*. When describing the efforts that women must make to secure their honour, the text asks its readers to imagine a knight who 'desirithe worshippe and vaillaunce, the whiche he wynnithe by gret payne and laboure in hete and colde', and describes how such a knight would travel on many 'straunge viages', enduring great suffering and having many 'aduentures' and fighting 'diuerse gret batailes' before winning himself a good name.[57] The *Book* then compares an undefiled woman to this hero:

> Right so it is of a good woman, that in all places berithe a goode name of honoure and goodnesse, as she that hathe atte al tymes putte her payne in trauaile to kepe her body vndefouled and in clennesse, and refused the delytes of youthe and of foule plesaunces, wherby she hath wonne good name and moche worshipe, for euermore to be putte in the nombre of good ladyes and of all good women, wherby she hathe also wonne the loue of God, and of her husbonde, and of the worlde, and the saluacion of the sowle, the whiche is the worthiest and the beste of all.
>
> Et tout aussi est-il de la bonne femme et de la bonne dame qui en tous lieuz est renommée en honneur et en bien, c'est la preude femme qui met paine et travail à tenir nettement son corps et son honneur, et refuse sa juennesce les faulx delis et folles plaisances dont elle puet recouvrer et recevoir blasme. Comme j'ay dit du bon chevalier qui telle peine sueffre pour estre mis ou nombre des bons, ainsi le doit faire toute bonne femme et bonne dame et y penser, et comme elle en acquiert l'amour de Dieu et de son seigneur et du monde et aussy de ses amis, et le sauvement de son ame, qui est le plus digne[.][58]

This passage frames the female practice of shamefastness in recognizably literary terms. Although one might argue that the knight described here could be any knight, the way that the *Book of the Knight* presents him as an idealized hero venturing off on 'aduentures' and 'straunge viages' invites us to read this as a romance-in-miniature. This is a knight that female readers might know in their imaginations, or from their books, but would probably not know in real life. Here, the everyday risks of a woman's social interactions are *also* the very same 'adventures' that can prove their honour. In this passage, female honour is something that can be won, not just something that can be lost. That a knight writing for his daughters might draw on a genre like romance should not strike us as all that surprising. Nor is the idea of chastity as a kind of battle unique to this passage; similar remarks concerning the effort required to resist fleshly temptation may be found elsewhere in medieval English literature (for example, in the late thirteenth-century *Proverbs of Hendyng*, which warns its readers, 'Yef thou wolt fleyshe-lust overcome, / Thou most fiht ant fle ylome / With eye ant with huerte. / Of fleysh-lust cometh shame').[59] And as I will show in the next chapter, medieval texts featuring personifications of female shamefastness often depict it as literally under siege by masculine desire. But what is remarkable here is the recourse to imaginative literature, specifically, rather than to exempla or anecdotes (the bulk of the narratives we find elsewhere in his book), or even simply to the kind of direct advice found throughout medieval English conduct literature for women.

The *Book of the Knight* invites women to envision themselves as the chivalric heroes of romance narratives in order to encourage them to practise shamefastness and secure their honour. By rendering women's shamefast practice analogous to a knight's voyages and adventures, the text uses romance to reframe that emotional practice as gloriously heroic, a reframing that may be directed at all of the text's originally envisioned female audiences, whether Geoffrey's 'propre doughtres' or the female 'seruantis' of his house: for if his daughters are invited to imagine themselves as the knights of romance, so, too, are his servants invited to imagine themselves as aspiring to the same behaviour practised by the noble classes that so often feature in romance. In performing the cultural work of teaching women constant vigilance against disgrace, this passage turns to literary culture, and to a literary genre that is ideally suited to the text's presentation of shamefastness as something to which all good women should aspire.

***

Despite the uncertainty of their origins and the varied contexts in which the above medieval conduct texts for women survive, they have much in common. They all define an honourable woman as one who safeguards both her chastity and her reputation for sexual continence, and they describe mindful, embodied techniques aimed at achieving both goals. Although they cannot be taken as evidence of social practice, they provide us with evidence of the ideologies that would have shaped social and emotional practice in medieval England, as well as representations of good and bad behaviour intended to educate women about what conduct should be imitated and what should be avoided.[60] As I have shown, they all depict the practice of shamefastness as one of the most reliable safeguards of a woman's honour. This practice is a combination of inward reflection (what kind of woman do you want to be? what will you lose if you are disgraced? what will people think?) and outward comportment that involves women in a virtuous cycle of concealing and revealing. By these means, medieval conduct literature for women both encourages physical concealment and warns of the extent to which women and their characters are constantly revealed to the eyes of others. On those occasions, women must reveal themselves to be chaste *by means of* concealment, withdrawal, and visible motor inhibition: they must make their shamefastness conspicuous. In so doing, they will be generating shamefast chastity within themselves, and manifesting outward signs of it to others.

Under ideal circumstances, this practice of shamefastness will result in a self-sustaining hypervigilance against disgrace, one that will be instantly recognizable to others. However, the strategies employed by the texts I have considered here suggest that this may be an unfinishable and perhaps impossible project. If women's honour is 'tendyr and slyddyr' in these texts, so, too, are women themselves, always threatening to slide away from being 'good' women towards becoming *giglots*. After all, as the *Book of the Knight* contends, a woman is 'of more light courage thanne man', and 'more feble to withstonde the temptaciones of the flesshe'. Geoffrey de la Tour Landry maintains that, for these reasons, women deserve more praise than men when they practise chastity; however, this presumption of moral debility also left women open to suspicion. Medieval conduct literature's frequent instructions to 'look', 'think', 'beware', and 'reflect' are intended as a guide to develop the vigilance against shame that will reinforce a woman's sexual continence. But in drawing women's attention to the way their conduct is perceived, these texts also offer a blueprint for constructing the *appearance* of shamefastness, a means of regulating their behaviour in such a way as to convince others of a virtue that they may or may not possess. Indeed, the belief that women were capable of (and inclined to) such dissembling was a standard trope of medieval anti-feminist writing, much of which presented women as slippery and cunning enough to hide their natural lustfulness under the guise of chaste virtue. In the next chapter, I examine the effects of this perspective on literary depictions of the relationship between masculine desire and female shamefastness. As I will show, in these texts, female shamefastness is not merely suspected, but besieged.

Notes

1. French quotation taken from *Le livre du Chevalier de la Tour Landry pour l'enseignement de ses filles*, ed. Anatole de Montaiglon (Paris: P. Jannet, 1854), p. 3; English quotation taken from *The Book of the Knight*, p. 2. All citations from the English and French versions of these texts will be taken from these editions and cited by page number.
2. *Le livre du Chevalier*, p. 3; *The Book of the Knight*, p. 3.
3. *Le livre du Chevalier*, p. 2; *The Book of the Knight*, p. 2.
4. *The Book of the Knight*, p. 32; *Le livre du Chevalier*, p. 49.
5. I note some particularly significant instances of deviation from the French source text in my discussion below. The term 'conduct literature', which I adopt throughout this chapter, is often taken to be more inclusive and more neutral than 'courtesy texts', a term more commonly used to refer to texts concerning court etiquette (although this material can also have strong religious overtones). See Anna Dronzek, 'Gendered Theories of Education in Fifteenth-Century Conduct Books', in Kathleen Ashley and Robert L. A. Clark (eds), *Medieval Conduct* (Minneapolis, MN: University of Minnesota Press, 2001), pp. 135–59 (p. 137), as well as the introduction to the same volume (Kathleen Ashley and Robert L. A. Clark, 'Introduction: Medieval Conduct: Texts, Theories, Practices', pp. ix–xx (esp. pp. ix–x)).
6. In her examination of one manuscript of the *Miroir des Bonnes Femmes* (a French text that provided many of the examples of good and bad women cited in *Le livre du Chevalier*), Kathleen Ashley correctly points out that, although most readings of conduct literature's passages concerning female chastity focus on their implications for female sexuality, these passages should also be read as evidence of 'the social constructions of family honor in aspirants to higher class status' ('The *Miroir des Bonnes Femmes*: Not for Women Only?', in Ashley and Clark (eds), *Medieval Conduct*, pp. 86–105 (p. 99)). On the relationship between the *Miroir des Bonnes Femmes* and *Le livre du Chevalier*, see John Grigsby, 'A New Source for the *Livre du Chevalier de la Tour Landry*', *Romania* 84 (1963), 171–208.
7. See Scheer, 'Are Emotions a Kind of Practice', p. 209.
8. Quotations from *The Good Wife Would a Pilgrimage* are taken from the edition provided by Tauno Mustanoja in *The Good Wife Taught Her Daughter*, pp. 173–5, and are cited above by line number.
9. See *The Good Wife Taught Her Daughter*, p. 130. *The Good Wife Would a Pilgrimage* is recorded in Aberystwyth, National Library of Wales, Brogyntyn MS II.1 (formerly Porkington MS 10), f. 135v.
10. Except where I refer specifically to J, whenever citing from *Thewis* I will cite from C by line number, but I will also give the line numbers for corresponding passages in J where relevant.

11 These texts also provide evidence of how women might be encouraged to see themselves as well-behaved members of particularly privileged classes; for example, *The Book of the Knight* makes distinctions between how lower-class and upper-class women can and should be disciplined: 'pore men canne chaste her wyues with fere and strokes, but a gentile woman shulde chastise her self with fairenesse, for other wise thei shulde not be taught' (p. 28; 'gens voitturiers sy chastient leurs femmes par signes de cops; et aussy toute gentil femme de son droit mesmes doit l'en chastier et par bel, et par courtoisie, car autrement ne leur doit l'en faire' (*Le livre du Chevalier*, p. 43)). As Claire Sponsler notes, this kind of perspective enabled the authors of conduct texts to pitch their works 'as a source of financial and social profit for their readers. Part of the success of conduct books as commodities is in fact attributable precisely to their ability to *market* conduct' (Sponsler, *Drama and Resistance*, pp. 54–5, original emphasis).
12 Dronzek, 'Gendered Theories of Education', p. 138.
13 Alexandra Barratt, 'Introduction to the First Edition (1992)', in *Women's Writing in Middle English: An Annotated Anthology*, ed. Alexandra Barratt, 2nd edn (London: Routledge, 2006), pp. 1–19 (p. 2).
14 Dronzek notes that 'Girls of any class, like lower-class boys, were likely to receive their only education at home', although she also notes that both boys and girls from the nobility and gentry were often sent to other households for their education ('Gendered Theories of Education', pp. 136, 142). See also Nicholas Orme, *From Childhood to Chivalry: The Education of the English Kings and Aristocracy, 1066–1530* (London: Methuen, 1984), pp. 58–60.
15 *The Book of the Knight*, p. 9; *Le livre du Chevalier*, p. 14.
16 *The Book of the Knight*, p. 116; *Le livre du Chevalier*, p. 176.
17 Breen, *Imagining an English Reading Public*, pp. 23–4; *MED*, s. v. *habit*.
18 Kao has noted that good female conduct is presented as desirable in conduct literature: 'conduct literature, aiming at bourgeois readers, seeks to redefine women's desirability through their comportment' ('Conduct Shameful and Unshameful', p. 117).
19 A similar view is expressed by the Physician in Chaucer's *Canterbury Tales*: the Physician addresses governesses in an aside during his retelling of the story of Virginia in order to remind them that they have 'lordes doghtres … in governaunce' to offer wisdom and guidance on the basis of their own sexual continence (or lack thereof): 'Outher for ye han kept youre honestee, / Or elles ye han falle in freletee, / And knowen wel ynough the olde daunce, / And han forsaken fully swich meschaunce / For everemo' (*The Physician's Tale* 77–81).
20 Phillips, *Medieval Maidens*, p. 7.
21 John Trevisa, *On the Properties of Things: John Trevisa's Translation of Bartholomaeus Anglicus De proprietatibus rerum. A Critical Text*, ed. M. C. Seymour *et al.*, 3 vols (Oxford: Oxford University Press,

1975), vol. 1, lib. 6, cap. 6; Latin text taken from the appendix to Juris Lidaka, 'Glossing Conception, Infancy, Childhood, and Adolescence in Book VI of *De proprietatibus rerum*', in Baudouin Van den Apeele and Heinz Meyer (eds), *Bartholomaeus Anglicus, De Proprietatibus Rerum: Texte latin et réception vernaculaire* (Turnhout: Brepols, 2005), pp. 117–36 (appendix at pp. 127–36; passage at pp. 135–6).

22 Phillips, *Medieval Maidens*, p. 7.
23 *MED*, s. v. *giglot*.
24 The poem appears in the mid fourteenth-century manuscript Cambridge, Emmanuel College, MS 106 (I.4.31); London, Lambeth Palace Library, MS 853 (dated to around 1400); the early fifteenth-century manuscript San Marino, CA, Huntington Library MS HM 128; the late fifteenth-century copy in Cambridge, Trinity College, MS R.3.19; and Oxford, Bodleian Library MS Ashmole 61 (late fifteenth century), which Felicity Riddy describes as 'fairly corrupt' ('Mother Knows Best', 70, n. 16). A version of it is also included in *Certaine Worthye Manuscript Poems of Great Antiquitie*, ed. J. S[tow?] (London: R. Robinson f. R. D[exter]), 1597, Short Title Catalogue (STC) 21499. Riddy notes that the poem appears in two manuscripts whose other contents lie at 'the interface between clerical and lay cultures', whereas the other manuscripts in which it appears are 'vernacular household books' (70). While she points out that the earliest version of the poem appears in a friar's handbook compiled around 1350, she also notes that it was not necessarily composed by a friar (although she suggests that the author may have been some kind of cleric); see Riddy, 'Mother Knows Best', 73. The possibility of a clerical author for this poem chimes with Roberta L. Krueger's suggestion that, 'Despite emphasis on women's spiritual well-being and their positive roles in the family, conduct works addressed to women may reflect clerical attitudes about women's submission and obedience to their husbands' ('Introduction: Teach Your Children Well: Medieval Conduct Guides for Youths', in *Medieval Conduct Literature: An Anthology of Vernacular Guides to Behaviour for Youths, with English Translations*, ed. Mark D. Johnston and Kathleen M. Ashley (Toronto: University of Toronto Press, 2009), pp. ix–xxxiii (p. xvii).
25 *How the Good Wife Taught Her Daughter*, in *Codex Ashmole 61: A Compilation of Popular Middle English Verse*, ed. George Shuffelton, TEAMS (Kalamazoo, MI: The Medieval Institute, 2008), http://d.lib.rochester.edu/teams/text/shuffelton-codex-ashmole-61-how-the-good-wife-taught-her-daughter [accessed 26 March 2018], lines 46–56.
26 Bolens, *The Style of Gestures*, p. 100.
27 *Ibid.*, p. 48.
28 *How the Good Wife Taught Her Daughter*, in *Ashmole 61*, lines 65–76.
29 *MED*, s. v. *sellen*.
30 *MED*, s. v. *strumpet*. See Shuffelton's note to line 74 in his edition of *How the Good Wife Taught Her Daughter* (in *Codex Ashmole 61*), and

Mustanoja's related note in *The Good Wife Taught Her Daughter*, pp. 226–8.
31 On the obscure reference to 'Antyny gryce', see pp. 231–2 of Mustanoja's edition.
32 In his French poem the *Mirour de l'Omme*, John Gower suggested that a woman's virginity was best preserved when the woman remained hidden away at home, citing the biblical example of Dinah, daughter of Jacob and Leah, who was raped upon leaving home (*Mirour de l'Omme*, in *The Complete Works of John Gower: The French Works*, lines 16931–68; discussed in Bolens, *The Style of Gestures*, p. 103).
33 *How the Good Wife Taught Her Daughter*, in *Codex Ashmole 61*, lines 83–90.
34 Paster, *The Body Embarrassed*, p. 46.
35 *Ibid.*
36 *MED*, s. v. *theu*.
37 Geoffrey de La Tour Landry notes that it used to be the practice to confront blameworthy women of higher classes with their bad reputation by placing lower-class, but more honourable, women ahead of them at court; this served as a warning to blameworthy women, so that 'they douted and dradden forto do ani thinge other wise but welle' (*The Book of the Knight*, p. 161; 'elles doutoient et craingnoient à faire le mal'; *Le livre du Chevalier*, p. 230).
38 *MED*, s. v. *slider*.
39 *MED*, s. v. *reddoure* (n. (1)) and (n. (2)).
40 *How the Good Wife Taught Her Daughter*, in *Codex Ashmole 61*, lines 103–8. Another poem in MS Ashmole 61, *How the Wise Man Taught His Son*, admonishes the male reader not to defame his own wife, which would risk ruining his own name, too: 'Sone, thi wyfe thou schall not chyde, / Ne caule her by no vylons name; / For sche that schall ly by thy syde, / To calle hyr wykyd, it is thy schame. / When thou schall thy wyfe defame, / Welle may another man do so; / Bot sofer, and a man may tame / Hert and hynd and the wyld ro' (*How the Wise Man Taught His Son*, in *Codex Ashmole 61*, http://d.lib.rochester.edu/teams/text/shuffelton-codex-ashmole-61-how-the-wise-man-taught-his-son [accessed 27 March 2018], lines 45–52). For a comparative reading of the different teaching methods employed by each of these two poems, see Sponsler, *Drama and Resistance*, pp. 57–72.
41 See *How the Good Wife Taught Her Daughter*, in *Codex Ashmole 61*, lines 11, 12, 20, 34, 37, 47, etc. The poem includes many linguistic variations on this theme of self-surveillance, such as 'Loke, daughter' (179) and 'Byware, my doughter' (60).
42 Sponsler, *Drama and Resistance*, pp. 59, 61.
43 *Ibid.*, pp. 62, 63.
44 *Ibid.*, p. 63.
45 I discuss Chaucer's tale of Virginia in more detail in Chapter 4.
46 *MED*, s. v. *ai*.

47 *The Book of the Knight*, p. 163; *Le livre du Chevalier*, pp. 233–4.
48 At one point, Geoffrey tells his daughters that he himself chose not to marry a certain woman simply because she was too lightly spoken, and warns them that this is one reason young ladies should take particular care concerning their behaviour: 'alle gentilwomen and nobille maydenes comen of good kyn ought to be goodli, meke, wele tached, ferme in estate, behauing, and maners, litelle softe and esy in speche, and in ansuere curteys & gentile, and not light in lokinge. For mani haue lost her marriage bi to moche discouering hem self, and to haue mani wordes; and by to gret semblauntis making, of the whiche diuerse tymes is trowed in hem that thei neuer thought ne dede' (*The Book of the Knight*, pp. 18–19; 'toutes gentilz femmes de bon lieu venues doivent estre de doulces manières, humbles et fermes d'estat et de manières, poy emparlées, et respondre courtoisement et n'estre pas trop enresnées, ne surseillies, ne regarder trop legierement. Car, pour en faire moins, n'en vient se bien non; car maintes en ont perdu leur mariage pour trop grans semblans, dont par maintes foiz l'en esperoit en elles autres choses qu'elles ne pensoient'; *Le livre du Chevalier*, p. 29). Geoffrey's anecdote is a reminder of what is at stake in these matters: not only an abstract idea of honour, but also very concrete social consequences (a point he returns to in *The Book of the Knight*, p. 162; *Le livre du Chevalier*, pp. 231–2).
49 *The Book of the Knight*, p. 163; *Le livre du Chevalier*, p. 234.
50 *The Book of the Knight*, p. 36 (the discussion of jousts and pilgrimages begins on p. 35); 'et pour ce a grant peril à toutes bonnes dames de trop avoir le cuer au siècle, ne d'estre trop désirables d'aler à telles festes, qui s'en pourroit garder honnourablement ; car c'est un fait où moult de bonnes dames reçoivent moult de blasmes sans cause' (*Le livre du Chevalier*, p. 57).
51 *MED*, s. v. *accustomen*.
52 *The Book of the Knight*, p. 36; *Le livre du Chevalier*, p. 57.
53 *The Book of the Knight*, p. 161; *Le livre du Chevalier*, p. 230.
54 *The Book of the Knight*, p. 164. The Middle English elaborates on the comparatively simple statement made in the original French text: 'tant la femme se doit bien haïr et maudire sa mauvaise vie, quant elle n'est plus ou nombre des bonnes dont Dieu parla ainsi à ses appostres et au pueple' (*Le livre du Chevalier*, p. 235).
55 *The Book of the Knight*, p. 83 (my emphasis); *Le livre du Chevalier*, pp. 131–2.
56 McNamer, 'Feeling', p. 243.
57 *The Book of the Knight*, p. 157; 'Mes belles filles, si vous scavés le grant honneur et le grant bien qui yst de la bonne renommée, qui tant est noble vertus, vous mettrés cuer et peine de y entendre, tout aussi comme fait le bon chevalier d'onneur qui tire à venir à vaillance, qui tant en trait de paine et de grans chaux et de frois, et met son corps en tant d'aventure de mourir ou de vivre pour avoir honneur et bonne

renommée, et en laisse son corps en mains véages, en maintes battailles, et en maints assaulx, et en maintes armées et en maints grans perilz. Et quant il a assez souffert paine et endurée, il est trait avant et mis en grans honneurs et servis, et lui donne l'en grans dons et prouffis assez. Mais nul ne se apparrage à la grant honneur que l'en li porte, ne à la grant renommée' (*Le livre du Chevalier*, p. 225).
58 *The Book of the Knight*, p. 157; *Le livre du Chevalier*, pp. 225–6.
59 *Proverbs of Hendyng*, ed. Susanna Greer Fein, in *The Complete Harley 2253 Manuscript, Volume 3*, ed. and trans. Susanna Greer Fein, trans. David Raybin and Jan Ziolkowski, TEAMS (Kalamazoo, MI: The Medieval Institute, 2015), http://d.lib.rochester.edu/teams/text/fein-harley2253-volume-3-article-89 [accessed 27 March 2018], lines 79–82.
60 As Krueger notes, 'It is important not to read didactic treatises as snapshots or accurate reflections of medieval society or to assume that their prescriptions for ideal behaviour were faithfully enacted by readers. The books convey how their moralist narrators *wished* social life might be organized and ordered; they portray fantasies of domestic order and fears of shame and failure. The works provide precious testimony of attitudes towards marriage, education, sexuality, dress, domestic life, social justice, age, class, economic resources, and a host of other issues' ('Introduction', p. xxviii). Similarly, Ashley and Clark argue that, '[d]espite the fact that conduct books offer a set of didactic prescriptions, they can be seen as products to be consumed in a variety of ways, and so they may perform different functions socially' (Ashley and Clark, 'Introduction', p. xv).

3
Shame under suspicion, shame under siege

If good habits can be learned, can they not also be counterfeited? This is precisely the quandary articulated by the Middle English saying that claimed '[a]bit ne makith neither monk ne frere' – or, as the proverb ran in medieval Latin, 'habitus non facit monachum'. After all, appearances can be deceiving: a person's appearance and behaviour are no guarantee of his or her inner virtue. Even external signs like religious habits were ultimately unreliable signifiers of virtue and discipline – some who wore the habits were 'wolves in sheeps' clothing'.[1]

The possibility that women might counterfeit shamefastness did not escape medieval authors. In his *Troy Book* (completed in 1420), John Lydgate claims that women know best how shame deters lovers because, if Shame did not exist, they would abandon 'daunger' (resistance, reluctance), 'straungeness' (aloofness, haughtiness), and 'feyned fals disdeyne' (I. 2216–17).[2] While Lydgate credits a sense of shame with restraining female behaviour, he depicts that restraint as artificial and affected. Personified Shamefastness seems to be tarred with the same brush: Lydgate argues that, 'ne were Schame plainly þe wardeyne / Of þis wommen', they would yield their 'castel' up immediately without any further resistance (I. 2218–20). Shamefastness is not women's natural impulse, he suggests; rather, 'of nature', women are so easily won that no 'assaut' or 'sege' is necessary (I. 2218–19). Lydgate simultaneously implies that the necessity for the 'assaut' and 'sege' of women lies in shamefastness itself, and characterizes that shamefastness as suspect.

This passage is part of a longer episode in which Lydgate expands significantly upon his source text by playing upon the literary tropes of courtly erotic desire, which would have love ultimately triumph over obstacles such as jealousy, fear, or, in this case, shamefastness. According to these conventions, qualities like shamefastness are a (male) lover's worst enemies, and the worst enemies of love itself, an idea that is reinforced by the adversarial relationship between personifications of Shame and Love in texts such as the *Roman de la rose* and its successors. At the same time, the picture that Lydgate paints of reluctant and affected female shamefastness taps into an Ovidian strain of anti-feminist satire reaching back to the *Ars Amatoria*.[3] Such misogynist views of women presume that what might seem to be an honourable habit is in fact nothing more than 'feyned fals disdeyne' and 'straungenes', a flimsy cover for unbridled female desire.

This chapter explores how anxieties regarding women's ability to 'feyn' virtue contribute to the idea of female shamefastness is an enemy to be besieged and conquered by desiring men. As I will demonstrate in this chapter, this adversarial dynamic emerges clearly in personification allegories of varying scale and complexity.[4] These narratives present Shame as a stubborn adversary who must be defeated by Love by any means necessary, including force. As I will show, the latter tactic occasionally receives further justification from longstanding anti-feminist contentions that any form of female resistance to male seduction is an empty performance intended only to conceal women's lustful natures, intensify male desire, or even provoke male violence. I begin by considering the origins of the enmity between desire and shamefastness in the nature of personification allegory, focusing in particular on Prudentius's treatment of lust (*Sodomita Libido*) and modesty (*Pudicitia*) in his *Psychomachia*. I then examine how personification allegories such as the medieval French *Roman de la rose* and its Middle English translation draw on anti-feminist tradition in order to explicitly establish female shamefastness as an obstacle or opponent to be overcome by male desire. This in turn renders shamefastness both a necessary practice for honourable women, and an inevitable target of masculine aggression. In my final section, I return to Lydgate's discussion of female shamefastness in the *Troy Book*, and demonstrate how his depiction of Medea's 'staged' shamefastness and his allegorization of her subsequent emotional turmoil articulate the anti-feminist logic that put female honour at risk. It is not my intention to argue here that the misogynist rhetoric employed in these passages is necessarily representative of Lydgate's attitude towards women in general, or even within the rest of the *Troy Book*. Rather, I wish to show how the discourse and imagery he uses in this specific instance are participating in a long satirical tradition that discredits the very practices that conduct literature teaches women to protect their honour. The anti-feminist logic at work in this part of the *Troy Book*, I maintain, endangers women and their honour not only by depicting shamefastness as something to be attacked, but also by suggesting that even the most steadfastly shamefast woman might merely be putting up a front, pretending to chastity while secretly longing to succumb to male force.

Shamefastness personified

As we have already seen, it is not unheard of for non-allegorical texts to present a woman's struggle to remain chaste in martial or chivalric terms. *The Book of the Knight of La Tour Landry*, for example, compares a woman's quest for honour to a knight's pursuit of renown in 'diuerse gret batailes'.[5] But in personification allegory, emotions and other abstract concepts are often themselves depicted as the combatants.[6] In these contexts, shamefastness is transformed into a personified character who must take up literal arms against lust or desire.

Because personification allegory is often populated by characters that embody divergent or incompatible abstractions, it also often depicts disputes between these figures, disputes that offer writers and readers the opportunity to imagine how conflicting emotions might work within and upon individuals.[7] In allegorical narratives, jostling for influence can escalate into open warfare between different personifications, a phenomenon perhaps most clearly illustrated by the archetypal personification allegory of the early Middle Ages: Prudentius's *Psychomachia*. Written by the Christian Latin poet in the early fifth century, the poem depicts the eternal battle of the Virtues against the Vices for dominance over the soul of man, and for the unity of body and soul.[8] Over the course of the poem, pairs of contrasting Virtues and Vices face off in single combat until the Virtues eventually claim victory. These opponents are described not only as *Virtus* ('Virtues') and *Vitiis* ('Vices'), however, but also as *Sensus* ('Sentiments', 'Senses') and *Furores* ('Passions'), respectively, a distinction that defines not only the battle but also the warring emotions themselves in moral terms.[9] The poem depicts the virtuous *Sensus* forcibly subduing the vicious *Furores* – maddened, rebellious figures who rage across the battlefield until they are brought under control. This allegorical battle depicts emotion as neither universally good nor universally bad; instead, it depicts different emotional categories as capable of serving virtue or vice respectively.

A number of virtuous personifications in *Psychomachia* are linked to the concept of shame, including *Mens Humilis* ('Humble Mind', or 'Lowliness') and *Pudor* (another Latin word for shame, translated in one modern edition as 'Purity').[10] But *Pudicitia* is the personification most directly related to the shamefastness believed to determine a woman's sexual continence during the medieval period. As Rebecca Langlands has shown, while *pudicitia* may be loosely translated as 'sexual virtue', the term stands apart from other Latin words related to shame and shamefastness because it always refers to sexual behaviour (although it can pertain to both male and female behaviour). In its specific emphasis on sexual continence, *pudicitia* may be distinguished from the other shame-related word from which it derives: *pudor*, a general sense of shame.[11]

In *Psychomachia*, the *virgo Pudicitia* ('the maiden Chastity') is the second Virtue to do battle against the Vices, confronting *Sodomita Libido* ('Lust the Sodomite').[12] *Pudicitia* is given few personalizing details; the poem notes only that she is a maiden 'shining in beauteous armour' ('speciosis fulget in armis').[13] After *Fides* ('Faith') dispatches *Fidem Veterum Cultura Deorum* ('Worship-of-the-Old-Gods'), *Pudicitia* takes the field against *Sodomita Libido*:

> quam patrias succincta faces Sodomita Libido
> adgreditur piceamque ardenti sulpure pinum
> ingerit in faciem pudibundaque lumina flammis
> adpetit, et taetro temptat subfundere fumo.
> sed dextram furiae flagrantis et ignea dirae
> tela lupae saxo ferit inperterrita virgo,
> excussasque sacro taedas depellit ab ore.
> tunc exarmatae iugulum meretricis adacto
> transfigit gladio; calidos vomit illa vapores
> sanguine concretos caenoso; spiritus inde
> sordidus exhalans vicinas polluit auras.

> On her falls Lust the Sodomite, girt with the fire-brands of her country, and thrusts into her face a torch of pinewood blazing murkily with pitch and burning sulphur, attacking her modest eyes with the flames and seeking to cover them with the foul smoke. But the maiden undismayed smites with a stone the flamed fiend's hand and the cursed whore's burning weapon, striking the brand away from her holy face. Then with a sword-thrust she pierces the disarmed harlot's throat, and she spews out hot fumes with clots of foul blood, and the unclean breath defiles the air near by.[14]

Prudentius's language and imagery are remarkable for their violence. The heat and stench of *Libido*'s torch, the impact of *Pudicitia*'s stone, and the spectacle of *Libido*'s violent and stinking death are nothing if not memorable, which Mary Carruthers has argued is precisely the point: '[t]hese pictures stick in the mind, not as "concepts" or "objects" but *as an inventory* of synaesthetic, syncretic memory cues, to be drawn upon, drawn out from, and *used* for constructing new work'.[15] The work in question is both ethical and emotional: the text uses personification to stir its readers to resist their own lust by embracing a kind of militant sexual modesty. Because of the way in which a personified emotion is for all intents and purposes here an embodied emotion, it has the capacity both to represent embodied emotional practice and to put emotion *into* practice. This particular scene encourages the reader to imagine this emotional practice in combative terms – that is, not as disciplined conduct learned through careful repetition, but rather as an internal struggle between virtuous shamefastness and libidinous desire.[16] The scene suggests that the dynamic between shamefastness and desire is inevitably infused with violence; any confrontation between these two impulses must necessarily end in the violent death of one or the other.[17] Notably, however, although she is personified as female, the concept represented by *Pudicitia* is not gendered one way or the other; instead, the figure of *Pudicitia* is situated within an explicitly gender-neutral Christian framework: she links herself to the defence of both 'God's man-servants' (*famulos*) and his 'maid-servants' (*famulas*), aligning herself with neither sex over the other.[18] As she herself explains, she is a god-given character trait of the postlapsarian human soul:

> post partum virginis, ex quo
> corporis humani naturam pristina origo
> deseruit carnemque novam vis ardua sevit,
> atque innupta Deum concepit femina Christum,
> mortali de matre hominem, sed cum Patre numen.
> (...)
> dona haec sunt, quod victa iaces, lutulenta Libido,
> nec mea post Mariam potis es perfringere iura.
>
> Well, since a virgin immaculate has borne a child, hast thou any claim remaining – since a virgin bore a child, since the day when man's body lost its primeval nature, and power from on high created a new flesh, and a woman unwedded conceived the God Christ, who is man in virtue of his mortal mother but God along with the Father? ... It is his gift that thou liest conquered, filthy Lust, and canst not, since Mary, violate my authority.[19]

Pudicitia's words recast sexual continence as the starting point for a more general rehabilitation of human flesh made possible by the figure of Christ.

In the figure of *Pudicitia*, *Psychomachia* offers a striking example of how personified shamefastness could be depicted as a combatant against lust in the battle for human chastity. But this conflict between desire and shamefastness would later be presented in a more cynical light by texts that drew on anti-feminist satire in their depiction of courtly erotic desire. As I will show, the most influential example of this shift, the *Roman de la rose*, simultaneously depicts shamefastness as the adversary of masculine desire and insinuates that the blush of female honour might be nothing more than a red herring.

Shamefastness, the enemy

In the thirteenth-century dream poem *Le Roman de la rose*, readers encounter one personification of shamefastness constructed by two authors. Guillaume de Lorris, who began the poem in 1225 and is responsible for the first 4058 lines, crafted the *Roman*'s first glimpses of *Honte* ('Shame'), as well as the figure's origin story. Jean de Meun, who added nearly 18,000 lines to the poem forty years later, depicts *Honte*'s ultimately unsuccessful battle to defend the rose against the attack of Venus and her army. The poem as a whole recounts a dream in which the dreamer enters a garden where he sees and falls in love with a beautiful rosebud. Most of the *Roman* describes the dreamer/lover's lengthy quest to obtain the rose, in which he encounters personified abstractions who either help or hinder him before he manages to 'cut' the rose at the conclusion of the poem in a scene that bawdily symbolizes a sexual encounter.[20] Rather than a text that focuses solely on personifications of the dreamer's emotions, the *Roman de la rose* is a personification allegory of the responses of the rose and its guardians to the dreamer's advances and impulses (and vice versa). In other words, the poem's narrative is also concerned with interpersonal emotional interactions, rather than only with an individual's solitary emotional struggles.

Honte is prominent among the characters who seek to obstruct the dreamer's progress. She is the personification of one of the various terms available in medieval French dialects that referred to shame and the capacity to feel it.[21] The word *honte* could refer to disgrace, or to the sense of shame, but could also describe 'that which is shameful'.[22] In the *Roman de la rose*, however, the personification of *Honte* seems to embody the shamefastness that aids the preservation of chastity. This is made clear in the figure's origin story, recounted in Guillaume de Lorris's portion of the poem. When Guillaume introduces *Honte*, she is accompanying *Dangiers* ('Resistance'), *Male Bouche* ('Foul Mouth'), and *Peor* ('Fear'), but Guillaume singles out *Honte* as the most 'worthy' ('li mieuz vaillanz') of the group and digresses for a few lines on the subject of her ancestry. The result is a passage in which the lineage of personified *Honte* illuminates the relationship of shamefastness to female sexual continence:

> Li mieuz vaillanz d'aus si fu Honte,
> et sachiez que, qui a droit conte
> son parenté et son lignage,
> el fu fille Resson la sage,
> et ses peres ot non Maufez,
> qui est si hideus et si lez
> c'onques a lui Reson ne jut,
> mes dou veoir Honte conçut.
> Quant Dex ot Honte fete nestre,
> Chasteez, qui dame doit estre
> et des roses et des boutons,
> ert asaillie de glotons
> si qu'ele avoit mestier d'aïe;
> et Venus l'avoit envaïe,
> qui nuit et jor sovent li emble
> boutons et roses tot ensemble.
> Lors requist a Reson sa fille
> Chasteez que Venus essille;
> por ce que desconseillie ere,
> vost Resson fere sa priere
> et li presta a sa resqueste
> Honte, qui est simple et honeste[.]
>
> (*Roman de la Rose*, lines 2821–42)

The most worthy among them was Shame. If one tells her parentage and ancestry correctly, she was the daughter of Reason the wise, and her father's name was Misdeeds, a man so hideous and ugly that Reason never lay with him but conceived Shame just upon seeing him. When God had caused Shame to be born, Chastity, who should be the lady of roses and buds, was attacked by scoundrels of unbridled appetite so that she needed help, for it was Venus who had attacked her. Venus often steals from her, night and day, both roses and buds together. Chastity then asked Reason for her daughter. Since Chastity was the disheartened victim of Venus's persecution, Reason wanted to grant her her prayer and, in accordance with her request, loaned her her daughter Shame, a simple, honest girl.

(*Romance of the Rose*, p. 70)[23]

Honte is here numbered among mankind's more virtuous emotional operations, and is clearly envisaged as curbing the lower appetites (described as *glotons* working in the service of Venus). Even more strikingly, *Honte* is the emotional result of a cognitive process: the offspring of *Reson*'s sighting of *Maufez*. Like Prudentius's figure of *Pudicitia*, *Honte* is also described as a direct product of God's will: 'Dex ot Honte fete nestre' ('God had caused Shame to be born'); this casts shamefastness as a divinely conceived human emotion linked to reason. The passage also places *Honte* in a position analogous to that of *Pudicitia*: her divine purpose is to defend chastity against *glotons* (translated by Charles Dahlberg as 'scoundrels of unbridled appetite'). Significantly, Guillaume describes the birth of shame as the result of constant attacks on chastity (*Chasteez*); in this context, *Honte* is presented as a figure whose power overshadows that of *Dangiers*, *Male Bouche*, and *Peor* (none of whom are given much of an introduction, let alone an extensive backstory).

If we read the rose as symbolizing a female object of masculine desire, then the consequence of *Honte*'s failure to protect it would be the defeat of female chastity. Guillaume's section of the *Roman* depicts the 'rose' of female chastity as closely guarded against the advances of would-be male lovers. His contribution to the *Roman* concludes with *Jalousie*'s ('Jealousy') decision to enclose the rose's *Bel Acueil* ('Fair Welcoming') within a strong tower.[24] What occurs in Jean de Meun's continuation of the poem is a subtle but significant shift in terms of *Honte*'s role: no longer simply a formidable guardian to be circumvented, *Honte* becomes an opponent that must be assaulted and overcome by force. This shift is apparent in the advice given by *Ami* regarding how the lover should deal with *Dangier*, *Honte*, and *Peor* if *Bel Acueil* is able to escape his imprisonment:

> [...] lors devez la rose cuillir,
> tout vaiez von neïs Dangier
> qui vos acuelle a ledangier,
> ou que Honte et Poor en grocent,
> mes que feintement s'en corrocent
> et que laschement se deffendent,
> qu'an deffendant vaincu se rendent,
> si con lors vos porra sembler.
> Tout voiez vos Poor trembler,
> Honte rogir, Dangier fremir,
> ou tretoz .III. pleindre et gemir,
> ne prisiez tretout une escorce,

> *cuillez la rose tout a force*
> *et moutrez que vos estes hon,*
> quant leus iert et tens et seson,
> car riens ne leur porroit tant plere
> con tel force, qui la set fere[.]
> (*Roman de la Rose*, lines 7648–64, my emphasis)

> [...] you should cut the rose, even though you see Resistance himself, who receives you only to abuse you, or even though Shame and Fear grumble at your deed. They only pretend to get angry, and they defend themselves lazily, since in their very defense they give themselves up conquered, as it will then seem to you. Although you see Fear and Shame blush, and Resistance become agitated, or all three lament and groan, count the whole thing as not worth a husk. When place and time and season occur, *cut the rose by force and show that you are a man*, for, as long as someone knows how to exercise it, nothing could please them so much as such force.
> (*Romance of the Rose*, pp. 144–5, my emphasis)

Ami seems to be encouraging the lover to imitate the *glotons* who attacked *Chasteez* upon the birth of *Honte*. Although the extent to which we should take *Ami*'s advice at face value is unclear, what *is* clear is that force is being described as an appropriate tool to satisfy male desire. The guardians of the rose have now become opponents who must be overcome by manly violence, and in the act of overcoming them in this way, the lover will achieve two things: he will be able to cut the rose he has so long desired, and *he will show that he is a man*. At the same time, *Ami*'s suggestion that force is something that *Honte, Dangier,* and *Peor* in fact secretly desire ('riens ne leur porroit tant plere / con tel force') takes to extremes the satirical misogynist advice given by texts such as Ovid's *Ars Amatoria*, which not only urges the male reader to employ forcefulness during seduction, but even suggests that this is attractive or desirable to apparently unwilling women (although it also cautions against outright boorish behaviour).[25] The scenario imagined here presents female shamefastness and masculine forcefulness in terms that are both adversarial and mutually defining: *Honte* is defined by her inevitable subjection to (and possibly even desire for) manly force, while force is proof of manliness when it overcomes female *honte*. In this formulation, womanly shamefastness and manly force require one another to exist and to be proven.[26]

It is of course possible to read such passages as satire (the whole of Jean's contribution to the poem lends itself more to a satirical reading than does Guillaume's). And yet even such satirically misogynist writing might have an impact on the actions and experiences of medieval men and woman, as Christine de Pizan pointed out in the letters she contributed to what has now become known as the *Querelle de la Rose*.[27] Between 1401 and 1403, Christine participated in an epistolary debate involving Jean Gerson, Pierre and Gontier Col, and Jean de Montreuil concerning the merits (or lack thereof) of the *Roman de la rose*. Christine's critique of Jean de Meun's contribution to the *Roman* makes clear that she was aware of its indebtedness to Ovidian satire; in one passage, she excoriates the stratagems presented by the *Ars Amatoria* as the surest ways of seducing women:

> Lisez donc l'*Art*: aprenés a fere engins! Prenés les fort! Decevés les! Vituperés les! Assallés ce chastel! Gardés que nulles n'eschappent entre vous, hommes, et que tout soit livré a honte! Et par Dieu, si sont elles vos meres, vos suers, vos filles, vos fammes et vos amies; elles sont vous mesmes et vous mesmes elles. Or les decevés assés, car 'il vaut trop mieulx, biaue maistre', etc.
>
> Read then the *Art*. Learn then how to make traps, capture the forts, deceive them, condemn them, attack this castle, take care that no woman escape from you men, and let everything be given over to shame! And, by God! these are your mothers, your sisters, your daughters, your wives, and your sweethearts: they are you yourselves and you yourselves are they. Now deceive them fully, for it is 'much better, dear master, to deceive ...' etc.[28]

By echoing the *Roman*'s bellicose discourse, Christine's ironic encouragement of men to 'attack this castle' ('Assallés ce chastel!') points to the disturbing ways in which such discourse might be transformed into action, with men employing literal force in their efforts to overcome female chastity. This passage bears witness to the concerns that lay behind Christine's critique of the *Roman*'s treatment of violence towards women, particularly domestic abuse. As Marilynn Desmond has shown, for Christine, 'the most troubling aspect of the allegory of the *Rose* is the violent nature of erotic desire, and the potential for this violence to materialize as wife abuse'.[29] The *Roman*'s language of force also echoes euphemistic terms used in earnest to refer to rape in Old French law and literature. As Kathryn Gravdal has noted, there is no Old French equivalent for the modern French term for 'rape' (*viol*); instead, by the late twelfth century, the more euphemistic idea of 'force' came into use.[30] Once she turns her attention to the imagery and language of the *Roman de la rose*, Gravdal remarks that '[t]he "seduction" of Rose – the courtly lady – is depicted blatantly as the rape of a virgin [... which] asserts the violence at the heart of male seduction and courtly love'.³¹

Whether earnest misogynist advice or misogynist satire, *Ami*'s advice suggests the possibility of an untenable impasse between male desire and female shamefastness (or, as I will suggest in the next chapter, between aggressive masculinity and shamefast femininity). The role of *Honte* as something to be adhered to by chaste women, but overcome (in women) by the men who desire them, places women in an impossible situation: expected to remain shamefast and chaste, they are also subjected to pursuit by men whose ultimate masculine goal is to vanquish precisely those virtues. Just as troublingly, *Ami*'s advice seems to be laying discursive groundwork for discrediting the emotional practices that later English conduct texts exhort women to emulate.

The *Roman de la rose* goes beyond merely recommending the forcible overthrow of female shame, however: it actually depicts it. When the councillors of the God of Love gather to present their plan for attacking the rose's prison to him, they outline a strategy that pits *Faus Semblant* ('False Seeming'), *Attenance* ('Abstinence'), *Cortoisie* ('Courtesy'), *Largece* ('Generosity'), *Deliz* ('Delight'), and *Bien Celer* ('Skillful Concealment') against *Honte* and her allies.³² Here, *Honte* is depicted as something that must be slain in order for the quest for the rose to succeed.³³ The seduction of the rose must now be accomplished through force, and female shamefastness must be defended or vanquished in violent encounters. This opposes male emotionality to female emotionality in disturbingly – and explicitly – violent ways: through the terms in which these personifications are represented, the pursuit of erotic desire is here rendered a battle between the sexes, a battle which, the poem's conclusion suggests, must inevitably be won by the masculine opponent.

Honte is the last of the personified guardians of chastity to speak individually, when she tells Venus that the goddess and her army have no hope of entering the castle. Venus's reply is steeped in violent language and imagery, as she threatens *Honte* not just with defeat, but with rapine:

> Quant le deesse antandi Honte:
> <<Vie! orde garce, a vos que monte,
> dist ele, de moi contrester?
> Vos verrez ja tout tampester

Shame under suspicion, shame under siege

se li chasteaus ne m'est randuz.
Par vos n'iert il ja deffanduz.
Ancontre nos le deffandreiz!
Par la char Dieu! vos le randreiz,
ou je vos ardré toutes vives
conme doulereuses chetives.
Tout le porpris veill anbraser,
tours et tourneles arraser.
Ja vos eschauferé les naches,
j'ardré pilers, murs, et estaches[.]
[...] Et Bel Acueill lera tout prandre,
boutons et roses a bandon,
une heure en vante, autre heure an don.
Ne vos ne seroiz ja si fiere
que touz li mondes ne s'i fiere.
Tuit iront a procession,
san fere i point d'excepcion,
par les rosiers et par les roses,
quant j'avrai les lices descloses.>>
        (*Roman de la Rose*, lines 20689–716)

When the goddess had heard Shame, she said, 'Get out, you filthy slut. Where will it get you to resist me? You will see everything in a whirlwind if the castle is not surrendered to me. It will never be defended by you. You would defend it against us! By God's flesh, you will give it up or I will burn you alive like miserable prisoners. I will set fire to the whole enclosure and raze the towers and turrets. I'll warm up your rump; I'll burn the pillars, walls, and posts. [...] And Fair Welcoming will let the rosebuds and roses be taken at will, one hour by sale, another hour by gift. No matter how proud you are, all will strike in there. Everyone, with no exception whatever, will be able to go in procession among the rosebushes and the roses when I have opened up the enclosures.'
        (*Romance of the Rose*, p. 339)

Venus's threats to *Honte* fulfil all the violence of *Ami*'s advice earlier in the poem: discarding the idea of careful seduction and persuasion altogether, Venus threatens to use force to obtain the rose despite *Honte*'s objections. Even worse than the threats of fire and rape is Venus's declaration that the roses and rosebuds will be available to all comers 'une heure en vante, autre heure an don' ('one hour by sale, another hour by gift'). Venus threatens not just to violate the 'roses', but to reduce them to the level of prostitutes or war-prizes by allowing sexual appetite to be indulged unchecked. Taken at face value, this is a terrifying scene that suggests that even the most genuine, disciplined practice of female shamefastness might be viewed as something to be overcome by force. Read as satire, it still puts forward the disturbing possibility that force is the unbeatable weapon of last resort to be wielded by male desire. Ultimately, Venus wins the castle in a blaze of fire:

> Fuit s'an Poor, Honte s'eslesse,
> tout anbrasé le chastel lesse,
> n'onc puis ne vost riens metre a pris
> que Reson li eüst apris.
> (*Roman de la Rose*, lines 21243–6)

> Fear fled, and Shame shot forth; flaming, all left the castle. From that moment no one wanted to put to the test what Reason had taught them.
> (*Romance of the Rose*, p. 347)

The poem that concludes with the winning of the rose necessarily culminates first with the defeat of *Honte*. Built up in Guillaume's text as the best defender of honourable female chastity, she is then violently torn down in Jean's depiction of Venus's assault upon the castle.

By the end of the *Roman*, *Honte* is not only dismissed as a potentially counterfeit guardian of female chastity, but also depicted as a quality that, perhaps inevitably, is forcibly defeated by masculine desire. The Middle English afterlife of *Honte* takes the character's undoing still further. For while much of the fragmentary Middle English *Romaunt of the Rose* remains painstakingly faithful to its French source, its adaptation of the personified figure of *Honte* suggests that the translator(s) – consciously or unconsciously – discarded the slippery tone of the French text in favour of a more consistently negative characterization of female shamefastness. As in the *Roman*, womanly shamefastness plays an important role in the context of the *Romaunt*'s treatment of desire. But whereas in the *Roman de la rose* shamefastness is a 'worthy' (*vaillanz*) opponent, in the Middle English *Romaunt* the very same figure is worthy of vilification or even disgust.[34]

As it survives, the *Romaunt* is an incomplete close translation of the *Roman de la rose*, covering all of Guillaume de Lorris's portion of the poem and only fragments of Jean de Meun's continuation.[35] *Ami*'s 'rose-cutting' advice does not appear in the extant text of the Middle English translation, nor does the French poem's concluding battle scene depicting the defeat of *Honte* and her allies. Initially attributed to Chaucer by William Thynne in his 1532 edition of Chaucer's works, what survives today of the Middle English *Romaunt* is made up of three fragments (usually referred to as A, B, and C) that appear to derive from different authors working in different parts of late-medieval England.[36] Because the episodes I will be comparing with the *Roman* occur in Fragment B, my discussion will focus on that fragment of the *Romaunt of the Rose*. While early scholarship followed Thynne in attributing all or some of the *Romaunt* to Chaucer, the current consensus is that the second and third fragments are most likely not by him; with regard to the first fragment, the most that can be said is that 'there is no persuasive evidence that the author … is *not* Chaucer'.[37] Certainly Chaucer was very familiar with the French poem: as well as drawing on the motifs of the *Roman de la rose* in his own dream-poetry and elsewhere, he makes several direct references to the French poem and its authors throughout his works, and a furious Cupid accuses him of having translated the *Roman* in the Prologue to the *Legend of Good Women*.[38]

While the *Romaunt* translates *Honte* as 'Shame', it seems clear that, as in the case of the earlier personification allegories considered in this chapter, this figure is not meant to function as the personification of actual disgrace or the emotions associated with it, but rather as the personification of the capacity for shame typically referred to as shamefastness. Shame's latest appearance in the *Romaunt* is from the latter part of Guillaume's contribution to the *Roman*, when Shame takes up her position outside of the south gate of a tower imprisoning *Bialacoil* ('Fair Welcoming') (B 4212–16). What survives of the *Romaunt* follows its source text in casting Shame as one of the lover's chief obstacles in his quest to obtain the rose. In fact, from the moment that Shame is introduced into the poem, the *Romaunt* seems to take an even stronger line than its source by establishing her as one of the villains of the piece. Describing her as one of two allegorical figures (the other being Wicked Tongue) who are '[o]f wikkid maners and yvel fame' (B 3025), the *Romaunt* immediately establishes a much more antagonistic relationship between the lover and the allegorical forces who would hinder him. Whereas at this point in the *Roman* Guillaume had introduced *Honte* in ennobling terms as the most 'worthy' ('li mieuz vaillanz') of the rose's guardians, the author of the Middle English translation omits this characterization altogether and instead simply recounts the allegorical origins of Shame in a close translation from the *Roman*:

> Ther was a womman eke that hight
> Shame, that, who can reken right,
> Trespas was hir fadir name,
> Hir moder Resoun; and thus was Shame
> Brought of these ilke twoo.
> And yitt hadde Trespas never adoo
> With Resoun, ne never ley hir by,
> He was so hidous and so ugly,
> I mene this that Trespas highte;
> But Resoun conceyveth of a sighte
> Shame, of that I spak aforn.
>
> (*Romaunt of the Rose* B 3031–41)

As in the *Roman de la rose*, Shame is here described as the offspring of Reason, who conceived Shame at the mere sight of Trespass (sin, wrong). Although Trespass is named as Shame's father, the narrator is quick to emphasize that '[a]nd yitt hadde Trespas never adoo / With Resoun', a phrase that might either be read as an additional assertion that Trespass never 'ley' with Reason, or as a broader declaration that the two never had dealings of any kind with each other.[39] In either case, it constitutes a slight deviation from the *Roman* that seems to emphasize the distance between the two personifications, as well as Shame's prophylactic role within the poem. The personification of Shame is the result of the anticipation or contemplation of wrongdoing; once brought into being, she works to prevent actual wrongdoing. The *Romaunt*'s allegory depicts Shame as a virtuous emotional habit, one that can counteract the lower sexual appetites. So conceived, she is the perfect metaphorical guardian of chastity, a quality deemed both physical and spiritual:

> To Resoun thanne praieth Chastite,
> Whom Venus hath flemed over the see,
> That she hir doughter wolde hir lene,
> To kepe the roser fresh and grene.
> Anoon Resoun to Chastite
> Is fully assented that it be,
> And grauntide hir, at hir request,
> That Shame, by cause she [is] honest,
> Shall keper of the roser be.
>
> (*Romaunt of the Rose* B 3051–9)

While this explanation of Shame's role as a guardian of the roses closely follows the account provided in the *Roman*, it omits the *Roman*'s brief reference to Shame as the result of God's *causing* her to be born ('Dex ot Honte fete nestre'; 'God had caused Shame to be born').[40] It is a small detail to leave out, but its absence erases any association with the kind of salvific postlapsarian shamefastness embodied by Prudentius's *Pudicitia*, or the divine origins attributed to *Honte* by Guillaume de Lorris. In light of the earlier omission of the *Roman*'s characterization of *Honte* as the most 'worthy' ('li mieuz vaillanz') of rose's guardians, and coupled with the *Romaunt*'s added description of Shame as '[o]f wikkid maners and yvel fame' (B 3025), this second omission seems significant. It reinforces the lover's strongly antagonistic tone when speaking of Shame and her allies, and suggests that, in the *Romaunt*, Shame is not a worthy opponent, but a repulsive enemy that deserves to be dealt with by force.

With only fragments of the Middle English translation of the *Roman* surviving, it is of course impossible to know how any of the translators might have engaged with the figure of Shame in the rest of the poem. But the adjustments made to the original source material for Fragment B suggest an effort to cast Shame as even more of an enemy of male desire, one who deserves to be overcome by the end of the poem. Just as we cannot be sure of whether or not this was a sustained effort throughout the Middle English translation of the *Roman*, we cannot be sure why it was undertaken in the first place; but it is not inconceivable that, in its movement from thirteenth-century France to later medieval England, the depiction of *Honte* might have been affected by its importation into a culture that was experiencing a 'crisis of habit', and was therefore predisposed to viewing the appearance of virtue with suspicion. If habits could not be trusted to 'make' monks, neither could shamefast behaviour be accepted as sure proof of female virtue. By removing the *Roman*'s initial deference towards *Honte* and its description of shamefastness as a god-given quality, the *Romaunt of the Rose* places a target on female shamefastness at which desiring men are encouraged to aim. Although *Bel Ami* had suggested that this shamefastness might in fact be nothing more than a pretence of resistance, neither *Honte* nor Shame seem to be characters merely concerned with keeping up appearances; however, the vilification to which both figures are subjected reinforces the idea that female shamefastness should be *treated* as counterfeit.

The composite portrait of *Honte* that emerges from the two parts of the *Roman de la rose* presents shamefastness as a powerful defender of female chastity, but one whose potentially suspect nature invites, or even demands, a violent response from men. Shamefastness must be besieged because it hinders male desire, and because (if *Bel Ami* is to be believed) it is merely a pretence of resistance by women who long to be overcome. In the final part of this chapter, I turn to an episode from Lydgate's *Troy Book* in which Lydgate expands upon his source text's depiction of Medea's shamefastness by drawing on the type of anti-feminist discourses exemplified by the *Roman* and its successors. As I will show, Lydgate's portrayal of Medea's initially 'staged' shamefastness, and the subsequent defeat of her genuine shamefastness by her desire for Jason, cast doubt on both the reliability of conduct as a sign of inner virtue and the efficacy of shamefastness as a guardian of female chastity.

Medea's practised shamefastness

An expanded translation of Guido delle Colonne's Latin prose *Historia destructionis Troiae* (composed 1287), the *Troy Book* is a lengthy account of the Trojan War and the fall of Troy that amplifies Guido's original text by drawing on a number of outside sources.[41] Commissioned by Prince Henry in 1412, the poem was completed in 1420, and survives in twenty-three manuscripts and fragments. It stands apart from the other texts considered in this chapter in that it is neither a text that is primarily concerned with erotic desire nor an allegorical work. As I will show, however, Lydgate draws on the allegorical discourses of courtly erotic desire outlined above in his additions to Guido's account of Medea and Jason, in which he reflects at length on the nature of women, and on the qualities associated with 'femyn[yn]yte' (I. 1860), including shamefastness.

Medea is introduced in Book I of the *Troy Book*. Her father orders her to appear at a feast to honour his guest Jason and his companions, and when she appears Lydgate follows Guido in describing her at length, focusing in particular on her beauty ('Þis world þoruȝout, I do ȝou plein assure, / Men myȝt haue founde no fairer creature' (I. 1569–70)) and her learnedness, especially in the arts of necromancy. Like Guido, Lydgate argues that it was extremely imprudent of Medea's father to have invited her to join them at a dinner, 'Wher sche myȝt by casuel mocioun / Ful liȝtly cacche or han occasioun / To don amys' (I. 1837–9), a concern that would have been shared by the authors of medieval English conduct texts for women. Precisely how Medea might 'don amys' is not clear, although Lydgate's use of the word 'mocioun' (meaning 'impulse', 'inner prompting', or 'desire', and derived from Guido's Latin *motu*) describes in almost Thomistic terms the sudden internal movements of will that govern young women like Medea:[42]

> For vn-to hem it longeth of nature,
> From her birth to hauen alliaunce
> With doubilnes and with variaunce.
> Her hertes ben so freel and vnstable,
> Namly in ȝouthe, so mevynge and mutable,
> Þat so as clerkis of hem liste endite
> (Al-be þat I am sori it to write)
> Þei seyn þat chawng and mutabilite
> Appropred ben to femyn[yn]yte—
> Þis is affermed of hem þat were ful sage.
>
> (I. 1852–61)

The anxiety that Lydgate expresses in this passage concerning the possibility that Medea might 'don amys' echoes the warnings of medieval conduct literature for women concerning the dangers of social encounters and public entertainments: these are moments when female reputations hang in the balance, and when women's behaviour is most subject to scrutiny.[43] Lydgate presents this moment as particularly dangerous because of the nature of femininity: citing anonymous 'clerkis' as his authorities, he reminds readers that women are known for their 'doubilnes', 'variaunce', 'chawng and mutabilite'. As we have already seen, female pliability and mutability are often cited by medieval conduct texts as precisely the reason why women need to cultivate disciplined habits of shamefastness, particularly at a young age. Here, however, Lydgate explicitly links women's changeable nature to *duplicity* ('doubilnes') and the possibility of deliberate deceit and treachery, rather than simple waywardness. The passage leaves its readers in doubt as to whether women are at all capable of cultivating a stable virtuous disposition, or whether anything in their behaviour that resembles such a disposition might in fact be mere window-dressing.

Lydgate elaborates on how Medea exemplifies this kind of feminine doubleness in her demeanour: when she first sees Jason, although she rapidly changes colour from red to white (I.1951–3), she offers no other outward sign of her sudden interest in him. Lydgate attributes this to a conscious effort on Medea's part:

> Sche cast[e] rather þat men schulde wene
> Þat þenchesoun of hir abstinence,
> And why þat sche satte so in silence—
> How þat it was only of wommanhede,
> Of honest schame, and of chaste drede,
> Þat to-gidre in hir hert[e] mette;
> Þe whiche tweyn so þis maide lette
> Fro mete and drink, as it wolde seme.
> Þus of wisdam sche made hem for to deme,
> And so to cast in hir opinioun;
> And þus sche blent hem by discrecioun;
> For hir chere koude euery þing excuse.
> Sche ȝaf no mater folis for to muse,
> No cher vnbridled þat tyme hir asterte;
> For þer was oon enclosed in hir herte,
> And another in her chere declared.
>
> (I. 2006–21)

In this passage, Lydgate expands considerably upon his source text in order to detail the ways in which a woman like Medea might *fake* the appearance of shamefastness. Guido only remarks briefly that Medea is keen to conceal her desire from others, and that she tries to excuse it in herself.[44] By contrast, Lydgate primarily attributes Medea's behaviour to her deliberate efforts to deceive ('blent') onlookers 'by discrecioun': she 'cast[e]' (calculated, arranged) that those around her would interpret her behaviour in a certain way.[45] Medea's shamefast behaviour is thus, in Lydgate's text, a performance that is calculated and carefully calibrated, but ultimately misleading. Although medieval conduct texts suggest that women should aim to cultivate behavioural and bodily self-control in their practice of shamefastness, here those same tools are used to create a false impression of maidenly virtue that will blind onlookers to Medea's true feelings. Lydgate paints a complex picture of Medea's apparent control over her outward appearance in the wake of an involuntary emotional and physiological response to seeing Jason: she remains silent, in the hope that her companions will attribute her silence to 'wommanhede', 'honest schame', and 'chaste drede'. Lydgate's description of how '[n]o cher vnbridled þat tyme hir asterte' suggests Medea's mastery over her outward appearance, a mastery Lydgate (following Guido) uncharitably attributes to her womanly ability to dissemble. At the same time, Medea's external appearance conceals and even contradicts what is 'enclosed in hir herte', and which is apparently beyond her control. Although Lydgate echoes Guido's description of Medea's alternate blushing and blenching, he alters the tone of these descriptions. In Guido, Medea is seeking to cover the sin (*crimen*) she carries in her heart, and hopes 'to turn by excuses what might possibly be a wrong in a young girl into a right action' ('etiam a seipsa probabilis excusationis argumenta producit quibus illud quod esse posset nefas in virgine excusabile convertat in fas').[46]

Like the Middle English translator of the *Roman de la rose*, Lydgate makes adjustments to his source text that discredit female shamefastness, adjustments which, I propose, are facilitated by developments in the lay, vernacular discourse of habit in later medieval England. The importation of ideas related to Latinate *habitus* into new contexts enabled Middle English writers to conceive of emotional practices like shamefastness in terms of cultivated virtue, as we see in conduct literature from the period. But it also brought anxieties and questions concerning the authenticity of such virtue to the surface of vernacular discourse. Consequently, even while the cultivation of social and spiritual excellence was being made accessible to a wider portion of the population, the genuineness of that excellence was under constant scrutiny, particularly in the case of groups who – like women – were conventionally associated with 'doubilnes'. As we see in the *Troy Book*, Lydgate does not depict Medea's desire as inherently sinful or criminal, but her efforts to conceal her true state of mind are presented as a reminder of how deceptive virtuous appearances can be. The fact that Medea's outward performance diverges so sharply from her inward feelings proves that her shamefastness is only skin-deep. In the final lines of this passage, Lydgate plays upon the various meanings of the Middle English word *chere*, which can describe expressions of the human face, one's manner or bearing, or one's mood or state of feeling.[47] Medea does not permit any 'cher vnbridled' to escape her control: there is 'oon' thing in her heart, but 'another in her chere declared'. The control that she exercises over her *cher* recalls the way that *How the Good Wife Taught Her Daughter* urged women to practise visible motor inhibition, controlling their facial muscles so that they would 'gape not to wyde' like a 'gyglot' or a strumpet; in Lydgate's poem, however, Medea exploits this control in order to misrepresent what is in her heart.[48] Lydgate's Medea is clearly aware of the emotional performances and practices that are expected of honourable 'wommanhede', and exploits those expectations in order to maintain the outward appearance of perfect shamefastness.

That Medea's counterfeit shamefastness is meant to be viewed in a negative light is evident immediately following Lydgate's account of it:

> Loo, ay þe maner and condicioun
> Of þis wommen, þat so wel can feyne,
> And schewen on, þouȝ þe[i] þink[e] tweyne;
> And couertly, þat no þing be seyn,
> With humble chere and with face pleyn,
> Enclose her lustis by swyche sotilte,
> Vnder [þe] bowndis of al honeste
> Of hir entent, þouȝ þe trecherie
> With al þe surplus vnder be y-wrye.
> [...] But, trust me wel, al is but apparence.
>
> (I. 2072–88)

These lines extrapolate from Medea's carefully modest performance a condemnation of women in general, all of whom, it is suggested, are capable of such trickery; any woman well versed in the conventional gestures of shamefastness would be able to fake them at will, manipulating them to conceal her lust. This kind of duplicity would be child's play to a figure like Medea, whom classical and medieval accounts describe as employing cunning and specialized knowledge (sometimes characterized as witchcraft) in her efforts to aid Jason in his quest.[49]

Lydgate ascribes these anti-feminist sentiments to Guido, and they certainly follow Guido's assertion that 'omnium enim mulierum semper est moris vt cum inhonesto desiderio virum aliquem appetunt, sub alicuius honestatis uelamine suas excusationes intendant' ('For it is always the custom of women, that when they yearn for some man with immodest desire, they veil their excuses under some sort of modesty').[50] By contrast, Lydgate insists, he himself considers women to be 'so gode and parfyte euerechon, / To rekne alle, I trowe þer be nat on, / But þat þei ben in wille and hert[e] trewe' (I. 2105–7).[51] But in his depiction of the conflict between desire and shamefastness that Medea experiences when she retires for the evening – his greatest deviation from Guido's version of Medea's story – Lydgate makes use of decidedly misogynist tropes concerning the role of female shamefastness in the context of erotic desire that belie his claims to be women's friend. In the *Historia*, Guido describes this conflict in a spare three sentences;

Lydgate develops this description into an allegorized account of a battle between the personified figures of Love and Shame.[52] Lydgate describes Love in the language of forceful masculine desire: he is Cupid's '[c]hefe champioun' (2172), as 'bolde and hardy, liche a fers lyoun, / ... nat ferful of spere, swerde, nor knyf, / But hoot and hasty for to awnter his lif, / Eke surquedous, stout, and ful of pride' (I. 2168–71). His 'enmy' Shame, on the other hand, is portrayed

> Liche a coward, feynt and hert[e]les,
> As he þat neuer dar put hym self in pres,
> For lak of manhod drawiþ hym euer a-bak;
> He is so dredful and ferful of þe wrak,
> Lyche a childe, ʒong and tender of age;
> For he hath nouther herte nor corage
> For to assaille, he is so feble of myʒte;
> And ʒit ful ofte he hath stonde in þe siʒte
> Of many louer, to let hym for to spede,
> Þoruʒ fals conspiring of his broþer Drede.
>
> (I. 2180–90)

The picture of personified Shame that we see here is an object of disdain and disgust characterized by his utter 'lak of manhod'. The qualities earlier described as marks 'of wommanhede' – 'honest schame' and 'chaste drede' – are presented in craven terms as the forces that jointly 'unman' the love Medea feels for Jason.[53] As in the *Roman de la rose* and its Middle English translation, Shame is here depicted as the enemy of love, but in this *Troy Book* episode the putative lover in question is a woman, not a man. It is thus particularly remarkable that Lydgate should draw on the discourse of manly force (or, in Shame's case, the lack thereof) in his description of Medea's emotional turmoil. On the one hand, we might read it as a comment on the quality of her womanly shamefastness, the very quality she hoped fellow banqueters would see in her silence in Jason's presence; but far from the formidable opponent depicted in texts like the *Roman de la rose* or *Psychomachia*, this figure of Shame is cowardly, barely able to obstruct Love unless he is aided by his conspiring brother, Dread. Read alongside Lydgate's earlier commentary on Medea's 'chere', this allegory-in-miniature would seem to suggest that her shamefastness is feeble or unstable, rather than the sure foundation of honourable female chastity. On the other hand, we might equally read this as a comment on the violence of Medea's sudden love for Jason, a passion that, as *Ami* argues in the *Roman*, would – or ought to – inspire more manly, forceful behaviour on the part of a would-be male lover, but which is, in the female person of Medea, temporarily unmanned by Shame and Dread:

> For Drede and Schame, whan þei ben allied,
> Of on assent haue pitously denyed
> Vn-to Loue, herte and hardines,
> Þat he ne durst out a worde expres;
> For whan þat Loue of manhod wolde speke,
> Þe wode fire out of his brest to vnreke,
> Vp-on þe point whan he schulde assey,
> Cometh Schame anoon, & outterly seith nay,
> And causeth Loue hornys for to schrynke,
> To [a]baische his chere & pitously to wynke,
> Cowardly his cause to appeire.
>
> (I. 2191–201)

But *should* Medea – or any other woman – be ruled by Love? Although Lydgate here describes Dread and Shame in bold and hardy terms, he also describes the experience of Love as a 'wode fire', something out of control and potentially destructive, a violent form of disorder rather than an admirable impulse.[54] This image of love is reinforced by subsequent reflections in which Lydgate expands on Guido's text by considering what the world would be like if shame did not exist in the first place:

> For dowt[e]les ȝif Schame nouȝt ne were—
> As it is kouþe, boþe niȝ and ferre—
> Love in his lawes often schulde erre,
> And wynden out of honeste[e]s cheyne,
> Of his boundis bridel breke a reyne,
> Ryȝt as an hors out of þe traise at large;
> For lite or nouȝt louers wolde charge
> To folwe her wille, and her lust to sewe[.]
>
> (I. 2204–11)

In this addition to his source material, Lydgate likens Shame to a horse's bridle or propriety's 'cheyne', a guiding force that keeps Love from error.[55] The image of a horse charging out of control – an image of uninhibited physical motion – suggests that, while Shame may be considered Love's enemy, it is also a necessary restraint. Although this discussion of shame might refer to its effects on *any* potential lover, male or female, its situation within an extended discussion of Medea's feelings suggests that Lydgate is

Shame under suspicion, shame under siege

referring to its effect as a restraint on women in love (or in lust). As Lydgate personifies it, shamefastness may be a cowardly impulse, but when it is genuinely felt it reins in a desire that would otherwise run amok. By contrast, Medea's feigned shamefastness – her careful control over her outward 'chere' – ultimately enables her to give full rein to her desire for Jason. It is this specifically female desire that so urgently needs to be reined in, as Lydgate explains:

> Recorde of wommen, for þei þe sothe knowe.
> For ne were Schame, as clerkys han compiled,
> Out of her hertis daunger were exiled,
> Al straungenes and feyned fals disdeyne.
> For ne were Schame pleinly þe wardeyne
> Of þis wommen, by writyng of þis olde,
> With-out assaut þe castel were y-ȝolde;
> It were no nede a sege for to leyn:
> For in swyche case longe trete were in veyne;
> For of nature þei loue no processe.
>
> (I. 2214–23)

This passage strongly recalls both the discourse and imagery of the *Roman de la rose*, most specifically its Ovidian suggestion that women are eager objects of masculine desire who are always already conquered, and its image of Shame as the 'wardeyne' of a castle under siege by male desire. In his depiction of Medea, Lydgate maintains that women are by nature so inclined to wantonness that shamefastness is the only thing that keeps them from running wild. No one would even need to lay 'sege' to shameless women, since they would capitulate immediately to their would-be lovers, and quickly – Lydgate notes that, 'of nature þei loue no processe'. In the line immediately following this passage, Lydgate makes his first and only use of the word *shamefastness* in the entire poem, declaring that only 'Drede & Schamefastnesse' (I.2224) prevent a woman from yielding to her desires.

Lydgate's allegory-in-miniature paints a vivid picture of Medea's internal battle between Love and Shame. Over the space of 200 lines, Lydgate depicts Medea as a woman trapped between her desires and her unstable shamefastness, and at their conclusion he repeatedly stresses how she experiences them: she is betwixt and between these two competing emotions, 'amyddes of þis ilke tweyne, / Of Loue and Schame' (I. 2230–1), 'in ful gret disioynt' (I. 2232), '[b]y-twyxe bothe' (I. 2235), '[v]n-euenly hanged in balaunce' (I. 2242), 'atwixe two' (I. 2249), until Fortune creates an opportunity for her to speak alone with Jason and warn him of the danger that awaits him. But the eventual capitulation of Medea's shamefastness seems to have been as inevitable as that of *Honte* in the *Roman de la rose*.

***

A single episode such as this cannot be taken as evidence of Lydgate's general attitude toward women, but its indebtedness to anti-feminist tropes demands our close attention for the way it enables Lydgate to discredit female shamefastness. Lydgate's expansion of Guido's story of Medea and Jason constitutes a particularly arresting example of how medieval writers might present the female practice of shamefastness as a practice worthy of suspicion. Lydgate depicts Medea's control over her *cher* as a calculated performance, a cunning exploitation of the conventional gestures of shamefastness that in turn points to the unreliability of such gestures as signifiers of a woman's virtue: the behavioural signs that should reveal Medea's hidden chastity instead conceal her desire for Jason. When Medea *does* give way to what appears to be shamefastness in the privacy of her room, that shamefastness is cowardly and feeble in Lydgate's allegorization of her emotional turmoil – there is no doubt that it will soon be overcome (and indeed, her restraint seems to evaporate the moment she is alone with Jason).

In the *Troy Book*, Medea bears out Lydgate's contention that there is 'no nede a sege for to leyn' against a woman who only appears to be shamefast, while the anti-feminist tropes he employs go further, suggesting that perhaps *no* woman's shamefast behaviour should be taken at face value. But what of women who *are* truly, even perfectly, shamefast? While Lydgate's ironic commentary on women's 'perfection' implies his doubt that such a woman could exist, his remarks concerning Shame's status as 'þe wardeyne / Of þis wommen' insinuate that it is female shamefastness that creates the 'nede' for the 'assaut' and 'sege' of chaste women. In the very act of rendering shamefastness suspect, Lydgate points to an even darker possibility, which I explore in the next chapter: that authentic female shamefastness must inevitably invite an aggressive male response.

Notes

This chapter includes some material that was previously published in Flannery, 'The Shame of the Rose'. I am grateful to the editors of that volume, and to Peter Lang, for permission to use this material here.

1 *Romaunt of the Rose*, in *The Riverside Chaucer*, C 6192 (all citations from this text are taken from this edition, and cited by fragment and line number). For other examples of the Middle English proverbial saying that 'the habit does not make the monk', see Whiting, *Proverbs, Sentences, and Proverbial Phrases*, H2. On the medieval Latin proverb, see Breen, *Imagining an English Reading Public*, p. 51.
2 *MED*, s. v. *daunger*, *straungenes(se*. All citations from the *Troy Book* are taken from John Lydgate, *Lydgate's Troy Book*, ed. Henry Bergen, EETS ES, 97, 103, 106, and 126 (London: Kegan Paul, Trench, Trübner & Co., 1906; repr. 1996 of EETS ES, 97, 103, and 106 as one volume) and cited above by line number.
3 For a wide-ranging and indicative compilation of such satire, see *Woman Defamed and Woman Defended*, ed. Blamires with Pratt and Marx. On the role of Ovid's *Ars Amatoria* in shaping medieval endorsements of masculine aggression within the context of erotic desire, see Marilynn Desmond, *Ovid's Art and the Wife of Bath: The Ethics of Erotic Violence* (Ithaca, NY: Cornell University Press, 2006).
4 See Flannery, 'Personification and Embodied Emotional Practice'.
5 See Chapter 2, pp. 81–2.
6 On the history of personification, see James J. Paxson, *The Poetics of Personification* (Cambridge: Cambridge University Press, 1994), pp. 8–34. See also Rita Copeland and Peter T. Struck, 'Introduction', in Rita Copeland and Peter T. Struck (eds), *The Cambridge Companion to Allegory* (Cambridge: Cambridge University Press, 2010), pp. 1–11 (especially pp. 6–8).
7 Some scholars have suggested that violence is an inherent component of allegory, see, for example, Gordon Teskey, *Allegory and Violence* (Ithaca, NY: Cornell University Press, 1996), and Noah Guynn, *Allegory and Sexual Ethics in the High Middle Ages* (New York, NY: Palgrave Macmillan, 2007), who maintains that that allegory turns 'all bodies into ideological battlefields' both for warfare within the human soul and psyche and for warfare within the body politic (p. 50).
8 One could argue, as Copeland and Struck have, that *Psychomachia*'s premise inverts allegorical interpretation: 'Here we encounter a transcendent truth directly through a set of abstractions which have been given concrete form at the narrative level, but which operate as universal, not particular values. What the characters represent is clear from their names, but the usefulness of the moral lesson depends on translating it out of its universal terms and back into a human, temporal perspective' ('Introduction', pp. 6–7).
9 '[Q]uid iuvat indomitos bello sedasse Furores / et sanctum Vitiis pereuntibus omne receptum, / si Virtus sub pace cadit?' ('What boots it by war to have reduced the ungovernable Passions and brought the good back without loss, while the Vices perished, if a Virtue falls in

time of peace?'); Prudentius, *Psychomachia*, in *Prudentius I*, trans. H. J. Thomson, The Loeb Classical Library (Cambridge, MA: Harvard University Press, 1949), pp. 274–323 (Latin on pp. 326, 328; English translation on pp. 327, 329). '[C]onpositis igitur rerum morumque secundis / in commune bonis, postquam intra tuta morari / contigit ac statione frui valloque foveri / pacificos Sensus' ('[A] fair and happy state of circumstance and life has been established over all, now that the peaceable Sentiments can dwell in security under the protection of guard-post and rampart'); Latin on p. 330; English translation on p. 331.

10 *Mens Humilis* is first mentioned in line 199 (p. 292), where she appears in battle against *Superbia* ('Pride'). *Superbia* also mocks *Pudicitia* (translated here as 'Chastity' by Thomson) at line 238, distinguishing her from *Pudor* (which Thomson translates as 'Purity') at line 245, and referring to her blush: 'sanguine vix tenui Pudor interfusus' ('Purity with scarce a tinge of blood to colour her cheeks'; Prudentius, *Psychomachia*, Latin on p. 296; English translation on p. 297). The concept of shamefastness as a weapon against pride is one that recurs in medieval devotional treatises; see the Introduction to this book, p. 16.

11 Both *pudicitia* and *pudor* describe a capacity for shame, but *pudicitia*'s frame of reference is more specific; see Rebecca Langlands, *Sexual Morality in Ancient Rome* (Cambridge: Cambridge University Press, 2006), p. 18. Both concepts anticipate the semantic range of the later English concept of shamefastness, which encompasses both *pudor*'s more general 'sense of shame' and *pudicitia*'s emphasis on sexual continence. For more on classical *pudor*, see Robert A. Kaster, *Emotion, Restraint, and Community in Ancient Rome* (Oxford: Oxford University Press, 2005); see also Kaster, 'The Shame of the Romans', *Transactions of the American Philological Association* 127 (1997), 1–19. As Langlands has shown in her study, *pudicitia* was also a concept that forged strong links between expectations of sexual continence and broader social concerns in Roman culture. As well as featuring in texts such as *Psychomachia*, *pudicitia* also appears in Roman society as 'a personified abstract virtue, a goddess described as playing an active role in the lives of ancient Romans, with her own shrines, cult statues and cult' (p. 37; see also pp. 39–61 for further discussion).

12 Prudentius, *Psychomachia*, Latin on p. 282, line 42; English translation on p. 283.

13 *Ibid.*, Latin on p. 282, line 41; English translation on p. 283.

14 *Ibid.*, Latin on p. 282, lines 42–52; English translation on p. 283.

15 Carruthers, *The Craft of Thought*, p. 148.

16 The meaning of *libido* ranges from 'inclination' to 'desire' to 'lust' (see William Smith and John Lockwood, *Chambers Murray Latin-English Dictionary* (Edinburgh: Chambers, 1933; repr. 2001), s. v. *libido*). Here, *Libido* is personified as the moral and emotional opposite of the sexual

continence *Pudicitia* represents: as the terms *lupa* and *meretrix* (both words for 'whore') indicate, *Libido* embodies unrestrained sexual appetite.
17 This may be in part a product of the Roman understanding of *pudicitia* as 'an ardent, heroic virtue, related to courage and patriotic sense of duty to the community, which, like all virtues in Roman culture, needs to be displayed in public acts which are often violent or startling' (Langlands, *Sexual Morality*, p. 31).
18 '[S]upremus / hic tibi finis erit, semper prostrata iacebis, / nec iam mortiferas audebis spargere flammas / in famulos famulasve Dei' ('This shall be thy last end; for ever shalt thou lie prostrate; no longer shalt thou dare to cast thy deadly flames against God's man-servants or his maid-servants'), Prudentius, *Psychomachia*, Latin on p. 282, lines 53–6; English translation on p. 283.
19 *Ibid.*, Latin on p. 284, lines 71–88; English translation on p. 285.
20 There are a variety of possible interpretations of the rose, but the later description of *Chasteez* as 'the lady of roses and buds' suggests that it most probably represents female chastity. Although I read the rose as a symbol of female chastity in general, it is also possible to read it as symbolizing the chastity of a particular lady, or as symbolizing a lady who thus far is chaste. Kathryn Gravdal, for example, reads the rose as a 'courtly lady' whose 'bud' is desired by the lover (*Ravishing Maidens: Writing Rape in Medieval French Literature and Law* (Philadelphia, PA: University of Pennsylvania Press, 1991), p. 68).
21 Other related terms, which seem eventually to have been superseded by *honte*, include *vergogne* and *pudeur*. The Anglo-Norman term *vergoigne* may be translated as both 'shame' and 'modesty, bashfulness', suggesting that, like the modern English word *shame*, it can refer both to actual disgrace and also to a sense of shame (*The Anglo-Norman Dictionary* online, s. v. *vergoigne*. See also Damien Boquet, 'Introduction: La vergogne historique: éthique d'une émotion sociale', *Rives Méditerranéennes* 31, special issue on *Histoire de la vergogne* (2008), http://rives.revues.org/2763 [accessed 22 April 2014]. *Pudeur* seems most closely related to a fear of disgrace, describing a disposition to fear shame or to fear behaving badly (*Dictionnaire du Moyen Français* online, s. v. *pudeur*. Guillemette Bolens distinguishes between *pudeur* and *vergoigne* by drawing on Kaster's work on Roman *pudor* (*Emotion, Restraint, and Community*); see Bolens, *The Style of Gestures*, pp. 100–22.
22 See *The Anglo-Norman Dictionary* online, s. v. *hunte*; *Dictionnaire du Moyen Français* online, s. v. *honte*.
23 Citations from the original French text of the *Roman de la rose* are taken from Guillaume de Lorris and Jean de Meun, *Le Roman de la Rose*, ed. by Felix Lecoy, Les Classiques Français du Moyen Âge 92, 95, and 98, 3 vols (Paris: Librairie Honoré Champion, 1965, 1966, 1970), and are cited above by line number. Citations from the English

translation are taken from *The Romance of the Rose*, trans. by Charles Dahlberg, 3rd edn (Princeton, NJ: Princeton University Press, 1995), and are cited above by page number.

24 *Jalousie*, who is one of the allegorical guardians of the rose, is not to be confused with *Le Jaloux*, the example of an abusive husband whom *Ami* uses to dissuade the lover from jealousy (see *Roman de la Rose*, lines 8425–9412; *Romance of the Rose*, pp. 156–70). Alarmed by the progress that the lover has made in his quest for the rose, *Jalousie* rebukes *Bel Acueil* for his friendly behaviour towards the lover, and remarks that *Honte* has been too far removed from the rose to be of any use (see *Roman de la Rose*, lines 3527–34; *Romance of the Rose*, p. 81).

25 See in particular *Ars Amatoria*, I. 485–6, 663–78. These are arguments I also make in 'A Bloody Shame' (see esp. p. 345). This kind of suggestion was one of the many reasons for Christine de Pizan's vigorous criticism of the *Roman de la rose*. See Marilynn Desmond, 'The *Querelle de la Rose* and the Ethics of Reading', in Barbara K. Altmann and Deborah L. McGrady (eds), *Christine de Pizan: A Casebook* (New York, NY: Routledge, 2003), pp. 167–80.

26 I explore the problematic implications of this paradox in Chapter 4.

27 The documents connected with the *Querelle* are edited in Christine de Pizan, Jean Gerson, Jean de Montreuil, Gontier and Pierre Col, *Le Débat sur le Roman de la Rose*, ed. Eric Hicks (Paris: Editions Honoré Champion, 1977). Translations of many of these materials may be found in *'La Querelle de la Rose': Letters and Documents*, ed. Joseph L. Baird and John R. Kane (Chapel Hill, NC: North Carolina Studies in the Romance Languages and Literatures, 1978).

28 Christine de Pizan, Jean Gerson, Jean de Montreuil, Gontier and Pierre Col, *Le Débat*, pp. 138–9; *La Querelle de la Rose*, number XIV, 135–6.

29 Desmond, 'The *Querelle de la Rose*', p. 171.

30 Gravdal highlights such euphemistic phrases as '*fame esforcer* (to force a woman), *faire sa volonté* (to do as one will), *faire son plaisir* (to take one's pleasure), or *faire son buen* (to do as one sees fit)', noting that they overlap with contemporary chivalric language related to strength and bravery (*Ravishing Maidens*, pp. 2–4).

31 *Ibid.*, pp. 68–70. Although critics differ in their interpretations of the significance of this 'rape' scene, Gravdal observes that they all appear to agree that the scene constitutes, 'if not a mordant commentary on, at least the logical extension of, the repressed violence in the romance of courtly love' (p. 71).

32 *Roman de la Rose*, lines 10689–702; *Romance of the Rose*, pp. 189–90.

33 This transition is also reflected in the way that *Honte* is said to be attired; as I have noted elsewhere, Guillaume describes *Honte* as attired like a nun, whereas Jean describes *Honte* as dressed for combat, wielding a sword and shield (Flannery, 'The Shame of the *Rose*', pp. 59, 63–8).

34 The following discussion of the *Romaunt of the Rose* builds on my brief reference to the poem in Flannery, 'The Concept of Shame', 171.
35 While the first two fragments (5810 lines) of the *Romaunt* cover Guillaume's text and the beginning of Jean's continuation, the third fragment (C) of the Middle English poem jumps ahead by several thousand lines to a later section of the French text (lines 10679–12360). The faithfulness of the Middle English translation is particularly clear when considered directly alongside the *Roman*, as presented in *The Romaunt of the Rose and Le Roman de la Rose: A Parallel-Text Edition*, ed. Ronald Sutherland (Berkeley, CA: University of California Press, 1967).
36 *The workes of Geffray Chaucer newly printed, with dyuers workes whiche were neuer in print before*, ed. William Thynne (London: Thomas Godfray, 1532), STC 5068, fols 128ra–68vb. The surviving fragments of the *Romaunt of the Rose* are found together in a single manuscript written in one early-fifteenth-century hand: Glasgow University Library MS Hunter 409 (V.3.7). A little over a decade ago, a single manuscript leaf containing text from the second fragment of the *Romaunt* (Fragment B) was discovered in the National Library of Scotland in Edinburgh: Sutherland Estates Papers, Acc. 10225, Box I, File 4 (see Simon Horobin, 'A New Fragment of the *Romaunt of the Rose*', *Studies in the Age of Chaucer* 28 (2006), 205–15).
37 Alfred David, '*The Romaunt of the Rose*', explanatory notes in *The Riverside Chaucer*, pp. 1103–16 (p. 1103, original emphasis). Fragment B was most quickly ruled the work of another author besides Chaucer, primarily on account of its many unusually Northern linguistic features. For a summary of the debate concerning the authorship of the *Romaunt*, see Aage Brusendorff, *The Chaucer Tradition*, 2nd edn (Oxford: Clarendon Press, 1967), pp. 383–7.
38 Cupid angrily tells the dreamer in the Prologue (who seems to be an avatar for Chaucer himself), 'Thou hast translated the Romaunce of the Rose, / That is an heresye ayeins my lawe, / And makest wise folk fro me withdrawe'; Geoffrey Chaucer, *The Legend of Good Women*, in *The Riverside Chaucer*, F 329–31.
39 *MED*, s. v. *ado*: 'Dealings, intercourse, traffic'.
40 *Roman de la Rose*, line 2829; *Romance of the Rose*, p. 70.
41 For discussion of the relationship between Lydgate's *Troy Book* and Guido's *Historia destructionis Troiae*, see John Finlayson, 'Guido de Columpnis' *Historia destructionis Troiae*, The "Gest Hystorial" of the Destruction of Troy, and Lydgate's *Troy Book*: Translation and the Design of History', *Anglia* 113 (1995), 141–62; Nicholas Watson, 'Outdoing Chaucer: Lydgate's *Troy Book* and Henryson's *Testament of Cresseid* as Competitive Imitations of *Troilus and Criseyde*', in Karen Pratt (ed.), *Shifts and Transpositions in Medieval Narrative: A Festschrift for Elspeth Kennedy* (Cambridge: D. S. Brewer, 1994), pp. 89–108

(esp. pp. 91–101); Anna Torti, 'From "History" to "Tragedy": The Story of Troilus and Criseyde in Lydgate's *Troy Book* and Henryson's *Testament of Cresseid*', in Piero Boitani (ed.), *The European Tragedy of Troilus* (Oxford: Clarendon Press, 1989), pp. 171–98; Lois A. Ebin, *John Lydgate* (Boston, MA: Twayne Publishers, 1985), pp. 39–52; and C. David Benson, *The History of Troy in Middle English Literature: Guido delle Colonne's "Historia destructionis Troiae" in Medieval England* (Cambridge: D. S. Brewer, 1980), pp. 97–129.

42 *MED*, s. v. *mocioun*. Guido remarks that women's souls are always in motion ('[c]uius animus semper consistit in motu'); Guido delle Colonne, *Historia destructionis Troiae*, ed. Nathaniel Edward Griffin (Cambridge, MA: The Mediaeval Academy of America, 1936), p. 17. On the relationship between affect and motion in the writings of Thomas Aquinas, see the Introduction to this book, p. 7. Although much work remains to be done on the language of emotion in Lydgate's works (and, indeed, in the medieval English literary canon), Lydgate is particularly fond of using the word 'mocioun' to describe human impulses, particularly unwise or reckless impulses. See, for example, his address to King Priam in Book II of the *Troy Book*, when he accuses the Trojan king of being 'travailed with wilful mocions, / Ouermaystred with þi passiouns, / For lak of resoun and of hiȝe prudence' (II.1809–11). On the theme of prudence as a control over such impulses in Lydgate's works, see Colin Fewer, 'John Lydgate's *Troy Book* and the Ideology of Prudence', *The Chaucer Review* 38 (2004), 229–45; Robert R. Edwards, 'Lydgate's *Troy Book* and the Confusion of Prudence', in Thomas R. Liszka and Lorna E. M. Walker (eds), *The North Sea World in the Middle Ages: Studies in the Cultural History of North-Western Europe* (Dublin: Four Courts, 2001), pp. 52–69; and C. David Benson, 'Prudence, Othea, and Lydgate's Death of Hector', *American Benedictine Review* 26 (1975), 115–23.

43 See Chapter 2.

44 Compare Guido delle Colonne, *Historia destructionis Troiae* (ed. Griffin), p. 18; English translation from Guido delle Colonne, *Historia destructionis Troiae*, trans. Mary Elizabeth Meek (Bloomington, IN: Indiana University Press, 1974), p. 16.

45 *MED*, s. v. *casten*.

46 Guido delle Colonne, *Historia destructionis Troiae* (ed. Griffin), p. 18; *Historia destructionis Troiae* (trans. Meek), pp. 16–17.

47 *MED*, s. v. *chere*.

48 See *How the Good Wife Taught Her Daughter*, in *Codex Ashmole 61*, lines 45–56; see also Chapter 2, pp. 67–9.

49 Ruth Morse makes frequent reference to the various classical and medieval depictions of Medea's intelligence and cunning in *The Medieval Medea* (Cambridge: D. S. Brewer, 1996).

50 Guido delle Colonne, *Historia destructionis Troiae* (ed. Griffin), p. 18; *Historia destructionis Troiae* (trans. Meek), p. 17.

51 In his notes accompanying these lines, Henry Bergen remarks that, 'It would seem, in view of the evident pleasure with which Lydgate amplified Guido's remarks, that his apology is not to be taken very seriously' (*Lydgate's Troy Book*, IV, p. 105). Lydgate would later go on to present a much less flattering portrait of Medea in his *Fall of Princes*, I. 2171–408.

52 For Guido's brief account, see *Historia destructionis Troiae* (ed. Griffin), pp. 18–19; *Historia destructionis Troiae* (trans. Meek), p. 17. In her survey of classical and medieval 'Medeas', Morse points out that some classical authors had depicted Medea as torn between *Amor* and *Pudor* after meeting Jason, noting in particular that, in his *Metamorphoses*, 'Ovid gives Medea an internal monologue, adapted from [Virgil's] Dido, and with Dido's debate between *amor* and *pudor*' (*The Medieval Medea*, p. 118). The extent to which Lydgate might have been drawing on such models is unclear, although his own treatment of Medea's internal conflict differs in its treatment of this conflict from an external, third-person perspective, rather than as an internal monologue.

53 Lydgate both amplifies and puts a more courtly spin on Guido's account, which notes that '[i]nstat amor vt audeat sed propter ignominiam pudor vetat' ('Love urged that she be bold, but shame forbade it because of the dishonor'); *Historia destructionis Troiae* (ed. Griffin), p. 18; *Historia destructionis Troiae* (trans. Meek), p. 17.

54 The Middle English term *wode* can describe someone as 'emotionally distressed or agitated', but is more commonly used to describe someone as deranged, frenzied, or unreasoning (*MED*, s. v. *wode*).

55 The word *honeste* can refer to one's good name or reputation, or to propriety in general (*MED*, s. v. *honeste*).

4
Death or dishonour: the problem of exemplary shame

Ther been two weyes, outher deeth or shame, / That thou most suffer[.]
(*The Physician's Tale* 214–15)[1]

When Virginius tells his daughter Virginia that she must endure either 'deeth' or 'shame' in *The Physician's Tale*, he is not offering her a choice. As he explains to her, the 'sentence' (224) upon which he has already decided is death, a decision he seems to have reached even before he arrives (Chaucer tells us that he comes '[w]ith fadres pitee stikynge thurgh his herte, / Al wolde he from his purpos nat converte' (211–12)). From Virginius's perspective, Virginia, the epitome of shamefast chastity, must either die or suffer violation at the hands of a lustful judge; but Chaucer nowhere suggests that the latter is really an option for Virginius. After a prolonged exchange, Virginia submits to her father's logic, and Virginius cuts off the maiden's head to preserve her maidenhead.

Medieval readers and writers were alternately fascinated and horrified by the stories of Virginia and her fellow Roman heroine Lucretia, classical examples of women faced with the prospect of either death or dishonour. Their martyrdoms – Virginia's at the hand of her father, and Lucretia's by her own hand – variously provoked lamentation, adulation, and criticism from different quarters. While Lucretia had received praise in earlier accounts, Augustine famously labelled her suicide the act of 'a Roman lady, too greedy of praise' who 'feared that if she remained alive, she would have been thought to have enjoyed suffering the violence that she had suffered while alive' ('Romana mulier, laudis avida nimium, verita est ne putaretur, quod violenter est passa cum viveret, libenter passa si viveret').[2] Lydgate, who related the stories of both Lucretia and Virginia in his *Fall of Princes* (written between 1431 and 1438–9), placed them side by side as examples of 'tragedie' (II. 1429), but also particularly praised the 'manli' Virginius (II. 1382) for keeping his daughter's maidenhead 'ondefoulid' (II. 1388).[3] And yet, writing nearly a millennium apart and from very different perspectives, both Augustine's critique and Lydgate's 'tragedie' draw our attention to the same questions raised by both narratives: what might have been, what *if*.

This urge to indulge in counterfactual fantasy – to imagine what *might* have happened – lies at the heart of these narratives' longstanding fascination, as well as their varied reception.[4] For at the same time that they invite readers to create counterfactual versions of these classical histories (witness Augustine's *si viveret*, 'if she were alive'), the stories of Virginia and Lucretia foreclose the possibility of doing so. This foreclosure stems from the problematic binary underlying these narratives, a binary neatly articulated by the epigraph from Chaucer's story of Virginia at the head of this chapter: Virginius assures his daughter that there are only 'two weyes' open to her, either death or shame. Chaucer's retellings of the stories of Virginia and Lucretia bring this troubling binary to the surface and force readers to linger uncomfortably in their recognition of it.[5] The discomfort we are urged to feel in turn constitutes an opportunity to reconsider the tensions that inhere in the logic behind female shamefastness as it is fetishized in medieval English literature.

As we have seen in the case of medieval conduct literature for women, the suggestion of what *might* happen was used to teach women the importance of practising shamefastness, and to cultivate in them a hypervigilance concerning the possibility of disgrace.[6] Here, however, the implicit invitation to ponder what might have happened to Virginia and Lucretia, had they lived, also raises the question of why death and dishonour are the only options for honourable women faced with the possibility of sexual shame in these texts. I will argue that the key to the issue lies in how medieval literature depicts the relationship between 'hardy' masculinity (reflected in the language of force employed in the medieval discourse of both erotic love and rape) and honourable female shamefastness. In the Ovid-inflected medieval discourse of erotic desire found in the *Roman de la rose* and other medieval texts, shamefastness emerges as a troubling point of opposition between masculine desire and an honourable female habit of shamefastness. This chapter takes up this problematic relationship between female shamefastness and the model of hardy masculinity and considers its disturbing implications for female exemplarity founded on shamefastness. As Chaucer's adaptations of the narratives of Virginia and Lucretia demonstrate, women's shamefast chastity is not only under threat from masculine hardiness, but can even *provoke* that threat, either by stimulating masculine desire or by inviting men to prove their manhood. I begin by exploring how Chaucer represents the irreconcilability of shamefast femininity and forceful masculinity elsewhere in his work. As I show, *Troilus and Criseyde* offers a particularly pointed critique of the logic that suggests manliness is proven through triumph over female shamefastness. I then continue on to the stories of Virginia and Lucretia, and show that Chaucer and his contemporary, John Gower (c. 1330–1408), approach the theme of 'manly force' from very different angles. In the case of Gower's *Confessio Amantis*, the stories of Virginia and Lucretia echo the concerns of their classical forebears by presenting the binary of death or dishonour as the result of corrupt rule and the violation (or threatened violation) of chaste women by rulers incapable of controlling their lust. Chaucer, on the other hand, deliberately shifts attention away from issues of correct rule and towards the practice of shamefastness that distinguishes these women's exemplarity. Whereas Gower invites readers to consider what might have happened in a Rome that was justly governed by chaste rulers, Chaucer engages readers in a deeply uncomfortable experiment in counterfactual thinking about female honour, an experiment that threatens to reopen the question of whether the binary of death or dishonour need exist in the first place.

Maidenly shamefastness and hardy masculinity

Chaucer's Physician remarks of Virginia that '[s]hamefast she was in maydens shamefastnesse' (*The Physician's Tale* 55), a peculiarly tautological observation that defines Virginia in terms of her emotional practice: her sense of shame is so finely tuned that it directs her virtuous behaviour and renders her secure ('fast') against the threat of dishonour. But Chaucer's poetry repeatedly suggests that honourable female shamefastness conflicts with the expectations of hardy masculinity, leaving honourable women no choice other than that of dying to be chaste.

As various recent critics of Middle English literature have pointed out, 'masculine' and 'feminine' are not fixed or 'universal characteristics that each person throughout history possesses to a greater or lesser degree'.[7] Rather, they are constructed, performed, and imagined differently in different places and times, and for different groups and subgroups. While multiple and competing concepts of both femininity and masculinity existed alongside one another in the Middle Ages, some aspects of each (such as the ideal of female chastity) appear to have remained more constant than others. For example, in her investigation of how men 'learned to be men' in late-medieval Europe, Ruth Mazo Karras contends that 'one core feature of medieval masculinity ... is the need to prove oneself in competition with other men and to dominate others'.[8] A man's ability to demonstrate his manliness 'depended particularly upon [his] forcefulness, his "hardynesse" or "manhode".'[9] This reading of medieval masculinity has informed the distinctions scholars have made between honourable masculine behaviour and honourable feminine behaviour among medieval 'gentils' (that is to say, knights and ladies). In his work on honour in Chaucer, for example, Derek Brewer observed that '[t]he honour of knights rests on the dominant biological characteristic of most young men, their aggressiveness'.[10] Siegfried Christoph, writing on the relationship between honour, shame, and gender in Arthurian romance, has noted that a knight or nobleman whose honour has been compromised 'is expected to redeem his honor, if necessary by force of arms. The opponent's defeat re-establishes not only the court's order, but also the hero's claim to honor.'[11] In these contexts, masculine honour was sharply distinguished from the honour of women, which was determined almost exclusively by their sexual behaviour.[12] What most studies of medieval gender have overlooked, however, is that shamefastness plays a key role in distinguishing female honour from masculine honour.[13] Female honour was defined and preserved almost entirely by the careful practice of shamefastness, whose kinesic markers – blushing, hesitation, modest behaviour – were in turn deemed so definitively or conventionally feminine that anything resembling it in a man might be interpreted as inconsistent with models of hardy, aggressive masculinity.[14] Although there were contexts in which it was appropriate for a well-bred man to display some degree of modesty or humility, 'manly' behaviour tended in the opposite direction, towards overcoming one's shame and winning public recognition through boldness, aggression, and violence.

The Physician's praise of Virginia is one of several passages in *The Canterbury Tales* that link shamefastness with the physical determinant of a woman's honour. In his description of the temple of Diana (Roman goddess of chastity) in *The Knight's Tale*, for example, the Knight says that, 'Depeynted been the walles up and doun / Of huntyng and of shamefast chastitee' (*The Knight's Tale* 2054–5), phrasing that evokes how chastity is kept safe – 'fast' – by the practice of shamefastness. In the prologue to her tale, the Wife of Bath makes two references to womanly shamefastness. The first, discussed in the Introduction to this book, is a quotation from the first epistle of St Paul to Timothy (1 Timothy 2: 9) declaring that women should apparel themselves '[i]n habit maad with chastitee and shame' (*The Wife of Bath's Prologue* 342–3).[15] The second reports her most recent husband Jankyn's declaration that '[a] womman cast hir shame away, / Whan she cast of hir smok' (*The Wife of Bath's Prologue* 782–3), which derives from St Jerome's citation from Herodotus.[16] In both instances, shame refers to shamefastness, sensibility and susceptibility to disgrace, which is depicted as a virtue appropriate to the female sex.[17] Elsewhere, the Host's addresses to the Clerk explicitly link shamefastness to ideals of female behaviour and explicitly dissociate it from ideals of male behaviour. During the drawing of lots in *The General Prologue*, the Host urges the Clerk to 'lat be youre shamefastnesse' (*The General Prologue* 840), the unmanly timidity that the Host lightly mocks in the prologue to *The Clerk's Tale*: '"Sire Clerk of Oxenford," oure Hooste sayde, / "Ye ryde as coy and stille as dooth a mayde / Were newe spoused, sittynge at the bord"' (*The Clerk's Prologue* 1–3). Here, *shamefastnesse* seems to refer to general hesitation or reluctance, which the Host identifies as behaviour more appropriate to a 'mayde' than to a man.[18] Although the Host's jibe invokes a common medieval image of 'shamefast' clerkly masculinity, the image of a new bride sitting at her husband's table for the first time infuses the Host's remarks with all the associations of womanly shamefastness.[19] The Host's comments suggest that the Clerk is inhibited by an overly strong sense of shame from speaking in the way that a man *ought* to speak. While Harry Bailly's comments are not necessarily being endorsed as correct opinion, his remarks indicate the extent to which shamefastness constitutes an important dividing line between medieval concepts of masculinity and femininity. Men might be expected to seek out public opportunities to prove their excellence to their peers and to themselves; by contrast, 'an honourable woman, born with the proper sentiment of shame, strives to avoid the human contacts which might expose her to dishonour'.[20] Shamefast women shun the public arena; only shameless women inhabit it without a second thought.[21]

These kinds of distinctions take on particular significance in Chaucer's *Troilus and Criseyde*, whose titular characters have provided much fodder for scholarly debates regarding Chaucer's treatment of gender. Troilus has been the subject of several studies on 'manliness', which have explored Chaucer's handling of masculinity within the poem.[22] For her part, Criseyde has sparked apparently irresolvable disagreement concerning whether Chaucer intended to depict her sympathetically (as a helpless victim) or critically (as the woman who wrongly abandoned Troilus). During the extended courtship of these two characters, the theme of shamefastness plays an important role, particularly in those passages where Pandarus (Troilus's friend and Criseyde's uncle) offers advice to the lovers. Although Pandarus encourages both Troilus and Criseyde to set aside 'nyce shame' in Book II (Criseyde at II. 1286, and Troilus at II. 1500), the phrase has very different implications for each. In both cases, Pandarus is suggesting that each lover *should not worry about* shame; to do so would be 'nyce' (foolish, cowardly, scrupulous).[23] However, in the case of Criseyde, her uncle's 'lat be youre nyce shame' inappropriately urges her towards precisely the kind of shameless behaviour that honourable women were expected to avoid; when directed at Troilus, the reference to 'nyce shame' functions as a boisterous urging away from the shamefastness more appropriate to women. Sensibility to shame is thus a crucial point of tension between Troilus's masculinity and Criseyde's feminine honour. Pandarus's point is that, as a man seeking to win Criseyde for himself, Troilus ought not to allow bashfulness, modesty, or fear of shame to stand in his way. If Criseyde were to do as Pandarus suggests, however, her status as an honourable woman would be compromised.

Pandarus's advice suggests the extent to which the model of hardy masculinity is fundamentally at odds with the ideals of female shamefastness. A woman's honourable behaviour is determined by her possession of a sense of shame, whereas the expectations of hardy masculinity – for example, in the context of erotic desire – can present a woman's shamefastness as something to be overcome, if necessary, through manly aggression.[24] This tension is exacerbated by the link between female honour and what Rachel Warburton has termed 'rapability'. As she remarks in her discussion of the theme of rape in Chaucer's works, '[n]otions of femininity, particularly the evaluative "good women," are intimately linked to conceptions of rapability[,] [… which] is deemed essential to our understanding of women and their moral agency'.[25] In other words, a woman's honour is inextricably tied to the potential for its violation. The honourable woman is the woman who can be raped, who can be shamed, who can be violated. Conversely, the *dis*honourable woman is, by definition, the woman who cannot be shamed or violated, in part because she is perceived to have no sense of shame.

The link between female honour and the potential for rape existed in medieval law as well as in literature. As Barbara Hanawalt has observed in her study of crime in early fourteenth-century England, a woman's social condition could affect the probability of her attacker's indictment for rape: 'If the woman involved was a young girl, a virgin, or a noble or very high status woman, indictment was likely. But if she was of low status or some slur could be put upon her, the jury would not indict or the case would end in acquittal.'[26] (A similar link may still be seen in modern rape trials in the United States, in which the prosecution and the defence push equally hard for the accuser's sexual history to be withheld or admitted, respectively.)

Once we start to read shamefast female 'rapability' alongside medieval discourses of rape, disturbing implications arise. As Kathryn Gravdal has pointed out in her study of rape in medieval French literature and law, the euphemistic language used to speak of rape and ravishment (phrases such as *fame esforcer*, 'to force a woman', or *faire sa volonté*, 'to do as one will') was closely tied to the 'chivalric rubric of admirable strength and heroic efforts [and to] the word *esforcement*, denoting effort, power, military force, bravura, and rape'.[27] The language of rape is thus interwoven with the language of aggressive masculinity. This is well illustrated by the Ovidian passage in the *Roman de la rose* examined in the previous chapter, in which *Ami* gives the lover advice regarding how he should deal with the allegorical figures of *Dangiers* ('Resistance'), *Honte* ('Shame'), and *Peor* ('Fear'): 'cuillez la rose tout a force / et moutrez que vos estes hon' ('cut the rose by force and show that you are a man').[28] We hear echoes of *Ami*'s advice in Book IV of *Troilus and Criseyde*, when Pandarus encourages Troilus to take matters into his own hands in order to avoid losing Criseyde to the Greeks:

> Frend, syn thow hast swych distresse,
> And syn the list myn argumentz to blame,
> Why nylt thiselven helpen don redresse
> And *with thy manhod* letten al this grame?
> Go ravysshe here! Ne kanstow nat, for shame?
> And other lat here out of towne fare,
> Or hold here stille, and leve thi nyce fare.
>
> Artow in Troie, and hast non hardyment
> To take a womman which that loveth the

> And wolde hireselven ben of thyn assent?
> Now is nat this a nyce vanitee?
> *Ris up anon, and lat this wepyng be,*
> *And kith thow art a man*; for in this houre
> I wol ben ded, or she shal bleven oure.
>
> (IV. 526–39, my emphases)

Chaucer's use of the word 'ravysshe' in the passages above allows its multiple meanings (both 'carry off' and 'rape') to filter in; although Pandarus is ostensibly suggesting that Troilus take Criseyde out of Troy, he is also using the uneasy medieval vocabulary of rape.[29] Calling Troilus's 'hardyment' into question, Pandarus's recommendation to abandon impotent grief and seek 'redresse ... with thy manhod' suggests that ravishment (whether through kidnapping or illegal coitus) is the appropriate action for a manly man to take. Pandarus's advice is of course not necessarily meant to seem like *good* advice, particularly at this stage of a war that began with the ravishment of a foreign beauty; but like Harry Bailly's mockery of the Clerk, Pandarus's words reflect a presumed link between masculinity and forcefulness. His assurance that Criseyde 'wolde hireselven ben of thyn assent' recalls the assumption expressed by *Ami* in the *Roman de la rose*: that women are always ready and willing to be ravished by masculine force. In effect, Pandarus is trying to shame Troilus into acting boldly, or as if he were without shame, in order to solve his problem and prove his manliness. Ironically enough, Pandarus is counting on Troilus's ability to *feel ashamed about having such a strong sense of shame* in order to persuade him to set that very sense of shame aside. Pandarus's words point to the assumption that, at the same time that a woman's honour is compromised by the act of ravishment, a man's masculinity is confirmed. And in that moment, the honourable woman – the woman defined by her shamefast habit – ceases to exist.

Crucially, almost immediately after Pandarus suggests the plan to 'ravysshe' Criseyde, Troilus rejects it. Although he acknowledges that 'Al this have I myself yet thought ful ofte, / And more thyng than thow devysest here' (IV. 542–3), he explains that he is loath to compound the disastrous rape of Helen with another act of ravishment (particularly when Criseyde is being exchanged with the Greeks 'for the townes goode' (IV. 553)). He is also certain that any direct pleas to his father will be rejected; but most of all, he does not want to treat Criseyde with any kind of violence, or to damage her good name:

> Yet drede I moost hire herte to perturbe
> With violence, if I do swich a game;
> For if I wolde it openly desturbe,
> It mooste be disclaundre to hire name.
> And me were levere ded than hire diffame –
> As nolde God but if I sholde have
> Hire honour levere than my lif to save!
>
> Thus am I lost, for aught that I kan see.
> For certeyn is, syn that I am hire knyght,
> I moste hire honour levere han than me
> In every cas, as lovere ought of right.
> Thus am I with desir and reson twight:
> Desir for to destourben hire me redeth,
> And reson nyl nat; so myn herte dredeth.
>
> (IV. 561–74)

Despite harbouring the 'desir' to claim Criseyde by force, Troilus recognizes that such an act would result in her 'diffame'. He rejects both Pandarus's rhetoric of masculine aggression and his own desires in favour of his beliefs concerning what a lover and a knight 'ought of right' to do. Eschewing one concept of manliness, he embraces another, one that incorporates sensibility to shame not only on his own behalf, but on behalf of Criseyde. One could argue that Troilus's choice does not get him the best results; after all, he is eventually abandoned and Criseyde's name becomes synonymous with female infidelity. But this exchange between Pandarus and Troilus constitutes an example, a critique, and, ultimately, a rejection of the logic that subjects honourable female shamefastness to the force held up as proof of manliness.

The very fact that Troilus twice declares his willingness to defend Criseyde from defamation with his life is testament to how high the stakes can be for a woman of good repute, but it also suggests that masculine violence poses both the ultimate threat to and the ultimate defence of female honour. This continues to leave shamefast women at the mercy of male force, which, if misdirected or uncontrolled, can obliterate the quality by which female honour is preserved. As I will show in the following discussion of the *Confessio Amantis*, Gower reproduces this problematic reasoning in his narratives of Virginia and Lucretia, which act as foils for Chaucer's versions by putting the chastity of male rulers forward as the solution to the clash between masculine force and female shamefastness.

Rapacious rule in Gower's *Confessio Amantis*

It is unclear whether Gower or Chaucer was first to compose his version of the stories of Virginia and Lucretia.[30] Both Chaucer's *Physician's Tale* and *The Legend of Lucrece* are commonly dated to before his *Canterbury Tales* period or very early on in it, to sometime between 1386 and 1390, dates that roughly coincide with Gower's work on the *Confessio Amantis* between approximately 1385 and 1393.[31] Evidence in Gower's works and in those of Chaucer indicates that the two poets knew each other and were familiar with each other's work.[32] Despite working on the same narratives during the same period, however, the two authors produced very different accounts of these exemplary Roman women. As I will show, Gower employs the death-or-dishonour binary faced by Virginia and Lucretia to connect the theme of uncontrolled kingly lust to corrupt rule: in Gower's versions of their stories, the violence that demonstrates or preserves female honour is of secondary importance in relation to the male violence that subsequently ejects tyrants from Rome.

A highly political poem written during a turbulent period of English history, the *Confessio Amantis* remains the best known of Gower's works. Its 33,000 lines recount the confessions of the narrator – initially called 'Amans' but later named as Gower himself – to Genius, the 'priest' of Venus, and use this extended series of confessions to meditate on virtues and vices. Among the poem's eight books, the seventh (in which Virginia's and Lucretia's stories appear) stands out as an example of the 'mirror for princes' genre so popular in medieval literature.[33] In this book, Gower primarily concerns himself with good rule and its relationship to a king's self-governance.[34]

The stories of Virginia and Lucretia appear in Book VII among a series of admonitions concerning kingly chastity. This section is introduced with four lines of Latin verse:

> Corporis et mentis regem decet omnis honestas,
> Nominis ut famam nulla libido ruat.
> Omne quod est hominis effeminat illa voluptas,
> Sit nisi magnanimi cordis, ut obstet ei.
>
> (VII. xi.104)

> Every sort of honorableness of body and mind is proper for a king, so that no lust destroys his name's repute. Sensuous indulgence effeminizes everything there is in a man, unless he be a great-hearted man who can oppose it.[35]

Gower's Latin verses gender lustfulness and sexual incontinence as effeminate and effeminizing behaviour that can jeopardize good rule.[36] While these remarks echo popular misogynist arguments, by describing lustfulness in explicitly feminizing terms they also link the practice of good kingship with the correct performance of gender. The examples contained in Book VII of the *Confessio Amantis* are therefore intended to support Aristotle's fictional advice to Alexander the Great in the *Secretum secretorum*: 'that he schal mesure / His bodi, so that no mesure / Of fleisshly lust he scholde excede' (VII. 4235–7). Gower warns that, if a king is unable 'his wille / Fro lustes of his fleissh restreigne' he is creating a dangerous trap for himself, 'Into the which if that he slyde, / Him were betre go beside' (VII. 4454–8).

Gower was far from the first author to frame the narratives of Virginia and Lucretia within larger social and political concerns. As Rebecca Langlands observes, in his history of Rome Livy groups both narratives together as stories focusing on '*stuprum*, the transgressive sexual act that damages its victim, as the threat to and testing point of *pudicitia* [shamefast sexual continence], and on the implications of an individual's sexual experience for the wider community, for liberty, for political structures and even for national security'.[37] In Livy's account, the main issue in both stories is not the emotional experience of the female victims in relation to shame (although this is made more prominent in the narrative of Lucretia), but how those around them react to the potential for their violation. Livy includes both narratives within a larger history of the Roman state: the stories of Lucretia and Virginia are relevant to this history because of how their *pudicitia* is tied to the fate of Rome. Lucretia's story, which occurs in Book I of Livy's history, depicts its heroine as possessing *obstinatam pudicitiam* (translated in one edition as 'resolute modesty'): it is only when Tarquin threatens to kill Lucretia and lay a dead slave's body alongside her that 'her resolute modesty was overcome, as if with force, by his victorious lust' ('vicisset obstinatam pudicitiam velut vi victrix libido').[38] When she relates the rape to her husband, her father, and their trusted friends, she declares that they must pledge that 'the adulterer shall not go unpunished' ('inpune adultero fore').

The problem of exemplary shame

Once Lucretia has killed herself, Brutus snatches up the knife from her body and leads the revolution that will expel the Tarquinii from Rome.[39] Likewise, Livy introduces Virginia's narrative by describing it as an event that was 'inspired by lust and was no less shocking in its consequences than that which had led, through the rape and the death of Lucretia, to the expulsion of the Tarquinii from the City and from their throne', explaining that the corrupt decemvirs of Virginia's time met the same fate.[40] Similarly, Ovid, who relates only Lucretia's story in his *Fasti*, connects her fate to the political fate of Rome when he concludes with the declaration that '[t]hat day was the last of kingly rule' in Rome ('dies regnis illa suprema fuit').[41]

By including these Roman tales in a book on good and bad rule, Gower follows his classical predecessors – particularly Livy – in linking these stories of actual or threatened rape to the theme of rapacious rule.[42] In the story of Lucretia, Gower characterizes the rapist Aruns, one of Tarquin's many sons – as a 'tyrannysshe knyht' (VII. 4889) and as possessing 'melled love and tirannie' (VII. 4899), references that play upon the flexibility of the Middle English word *tiraunt*, which can not only describe a wicked or unjust ruler, but also a ruler who seizes power by force.[43] As a representative of an unjust regime and a man who aims to conquer chastity by force, Aruns is indeed a tyrant in both senses of the Middle English word. But, as Gower's Latin heading indicates, Aruns also exemplifies a kind of warped masculinity, at once effeminate in his inability to control his lust and violent in his efforts to satiate it. This effect is magnified by the tale's framing of the rape as the result of masculine competition: Aruns and his companions debate whose wife is most virtuous, 'and ther began a strif, / For Arrons seith he hath the beste' (VII. 4772–3). This 'strif' is only resolved when Collatin, a knight and cousin to Aruns, suggests that they ride home to see how things stand:

> 'It is,' quod he, 'of non emprise
> To speke a word, bot of the dede,
> Therof it is to taken hiede.
> Anon forthi this same tyde
> Lep on thi hors and let ous ryde:
> So mai we knowe bothe tuo
> Unwarli what oure wyves do,
> That that schal be a trewe assay.'
>
> (VII. 4778–85)

In this passage, Gower deviates ever so slightly from Livy's account, in which *all* of the men proceed home in order to catch their wives unawares. Here, what began as a debate among a group of men evolves into individualized competition between 'tuo' men, in which victory depends on proof of a wife's superior honour.[44]

The language and imagery leading up to the rape continue to develop Gower's depiction of Aruns as a man whose masculine hardiness is misdirected. Having decided upon his course of action, Aruns reflects that 'Fortune unto the bolde / Is favorable forto helpe' (VII. 4902–3), employing a proverbial phrase that presents his pending actions as both justification and, in his own eyes, proof of his manly boldness.[45] The rape itself, which is briefly described, is stripped down to its bare elements in such a way as to stress that it is an uneven clash between unchecked male force and female shamefastness: Gower gives no account of the extended pleas, threats, or declarations of love that Livy describes Tarquin making, but instead simply notes that Aruns declares that 'if sche made noise or cry ... his swerd lay faste by / To slen hire and hire folk aboute' (VII. 4979–81).[46] Lucretia's response to this abrupt threat to her chastity is instantaneous: she loses her voice 'thurgh tendresce of wommanhiede' (VII. 4975) as soon as Aruns awakens her with his embrace, and Gower likens her emotions to those of 'a Lomb whanne it is sesed / In wolves mouth' (VII. 4983–4). Overwhelmed, she swoons, an adjustment to the original narrative that enables Gower to present the rape of Lucretia as absolutely, unequivocally, rape; the unjust act of a tyrant carried out on the helpless body of an honourable woman. Swooning seems to be the only possible response of womanly shamefastness in the face of such violent masculine lust.

The language of violated femininity also pervades Gower's account of Lucretia's devastation after her rape:

> And sche, which thoghte hirself unmete
> And the lest worth of wommen alle,
> Hire wofull chiere let doun falle
> For schame and couthe unnethes loke.
> ... And sche, which hath hire sorwes grene,
> Hire wo to telle thanne assaieth,
> Bot tendre schame hire word delaieth,
> That sondri times as sche minte
> To speke, upon the point sche stinte.
> ... Hire tale between schame and drede
> Sche tolde, noght withoute peine.
>
> (VII. 5030–49)

Gower's description of Lucretia as feeling 'unmete' ('undeserving of some honour', 'displeasing') and 'the lest worth of wommen alle' stresses not just Lucretia's shame, but her shame *as a woman*, her sense that her womanly worth has been compromised.[47] Such devastation can only be felt by a woman like Lucretia, a woman closely identified with her shamefast chastity. One could argue that, in this moment, Lucretia is besieged by shame on all sides: Gower's first reference to her shame (5033) seems to be both retrospective and ongoing – what Aruns has done to her has deprived her of her once-perfect chastity, and she feels this most intensely in the presence of her family and friends. At the same time, it is anticipative shame that repeatedly prevents her from explaining her state to those around her. Gower's use of the phrase 'tendre schame' recalls his earlier reference to Lucretia's 'tendresce of wommanhiede', which rendered her speechless when Aruns awakened her. Shamefastness is above all a *womanly* quality; it is what made Lucretia so honourable, chaste, and 'rapable' in the first place. But although Gower stresses Lucretia's emotional state before her suicide in these lines, his objective is to show how her violation and her emotional response to it work upon the men around her and inspire them to defend the state from any further tyranny. In this instance, the death-or-dishonour binary is invoked by Lucretia herself, who slays herself so that '[n]evere afterward the world ne schal / Reproven hire' (VII. 5063–4), but any opportunity to ponder what might have transpired had she let herself live is swallowed up in the action that follows. Brutus leaps into action and stirs up bystanders into an uprising, and the story ends with a description of the end of the 'tirannie' of the Tarquins: 'Awey, awey the tirannie / Of lecherie and covoitise!' (VII. 5118–19). This is the outcome that matters; the rallying cry of the Romans as they drive the Tarquins from Rome reinforces the association between a ruler's sexual incontinence and tyrannous rule, and Genius concludes the narrative by warning readers that righteous rule and lechery are mutually exclusive: 'That rihtwisnesse and lecherie / Acorden noght in compaignie / With him that hath the lawe on honed, / That mai a man wel understonde' (VII. 5125–8).

These remarks create a bridge between Lucretia's story and the story of Virginia that immediately follows. In Gower's version of this story, Appius is no longer a corrupt judge who asks one of his minions to bring a trumped-up case against Virginia, but is instead a king who conspires with his brother, Marcus Claudius, a knight and 'a man of such riote / Riht as the king himselve was' (VII. 5168–9). These hierarchical adjustments not only translate the classical narrative into fourteenth-century social terms, but also fit it into the didactic framework of Book VII of the *Confessio Amantis*. As in the case of Lucretia's narrative, the story is more about bad rulers than it is about the female subjects they violate; Virginia is never named, but is simply referred to as the 'Maide' and as Virginius's daughter. The only shame anyone seems to be concerned about is Virginius's: when Appius's motives become clear to Virginia's friends, they warn Appius that Virginius

> for the comun riht
> In thilke time, as was befalle,
> Lai for the profit of hem alle
> Upon the wylde feldes armed,
> That he ne scholde noght ben harmed
> Ne schamed, whil that he were oute;
> And thus thei preiden al aboute.
>
> (VII. 5190–7)

Gower's references to the 'comun riht' and 'the profit of hem alle' play upon highly charged political terms in late fourteenth-century England, when common profit was believed to be the chief aim of good rule.[48] Virginius's friends place the potential rape of Virginia in an explicitly political context by contrasting Appius's violation of due process with Virginius's defence of Rome's welfare, which is depicted as under threat from within and without (a parallel with the situation of Gower's England).

When Virginius returns and finds he has no means of protecting his daughter, he kills her in public and justifies his actions by describing them as the necessary consequences of Appius's corrupt rule:

> Lo, take hire ther, thou wrongfull king,
> For me is levere upon this thing
> To be the fader of a Maide,
> Thogh sche be ded, than if men saide
> That in hir lif sche were schamed
> And I therof were evele named.
>
> (VII. 5247–52)

As in Gower's narrative of Lucretia, here the death-or-dishonour binary lurks just beneath the surface of Virginia's story; Virginia could have *either* lived with shame *or* died with honour, but the former is deemed by Virginius to be too horrifying a prospect. Gower here contrasts Virginius's determination to protect his daughter's honour at all costs with the actions of the 'wrongfull king' Appius,

The problem of exemplary shame   137

who is determined to violate that honour at all costs: Virginius is a better protector of Rome's common good than the man charged with that role. Virginius's concern for Rome after his daughter's death makes this clear; after being forced to flee, Virginius goes to 'ther as the pouer was / of Rome' (VII. 5265–6) and warns them that his own predicament proves that

> thus stant every mannes lif
> In jeupartie for his wif
> Or for his dowhter, if thei be
> Passende an other of beaute.
>
> (VII. 5273–6)

Gower's rendition of Virginia's story – or, rather, of Virginius's story – focuses on the ramifications of rapacious rule for a corrupt king and his subjects, rather than on the consequences for Virginia herself. What matters here is what Appius's actions mean for Virginius and his fellow Romans, not the death of a virgin. At the same time, however, Virginia's shamefastness is what makes the whole story work: just as death is the only thing that can preserve her from sexual defilement, the very threat of that defilement and the consequences that proceed from it derive from her shamefast chastity.

Gower's stories of Virginia and Lucretia ultimately focus on the consequences of embattled female shamefastness for men and male rule. The exemplarity of the women themselves is tangential to the narratives' concern with the link between male lust and corrupt rule; instead of being encouraged to contemplate the shamefast example set by these women, the princely readers to whom Gower directs these stories are shown counterexamples of male conduct as warnings concerning what kind of sexual behaviour to avoid while in power. If readers are encouraged to indulge in counterfactual thinking here, it is in relation to the fate of Rome and its rulers, not in relation to the fates of Virginia and Lucretia, a dynamic that is almost entirely reversed by Chaucer's versions of these classical narratives.

No other remedy: *The Physician's Tale*

Perhaps the most fundamental change that Chaucer makes to his sources for *The Physician's Tale* is to shift focus towards the character of Virginia. Both Livy's history of Rome (to which Chaucer refers, but which most scholars agree he probably did not consult directly) and the *Roman de la rose* (Chaucer's primary source) present their readers with almost no Virginia to speak of: she is merely a silent, faceless casualty, the person who is ultimately killed, or, in the words of Anne Middleton, 'a non-person'.[49] All of this changes with *The Physician's Tale*, which provides a lengthy description of Virginia's many wonderful qualities, gives examples of her active practice of virtue, and endows her with a voice. Nevertheless, it is difficult to know what to do with Virginia, whose virtues and apparent passive acquiescence in her own destruction have prompted many to read her either as 'a mere helpless victim' or as an allegorical figure of virtue and virginity.[50] Virginia's shamefastness is so perfect that it verges on allegory:

> As wel in goost as body chast was she,
> For which she floured in virginitee
> With alle humylitee and abstinence,
> With alle attemperaunce and pacience,
> With mesure eek of beryng and array.[51]
>
> (*The Physician's Tale* 43–7)

The fact that Virginia is as completely chaste 'in goost' as she is 'body' is significant. Not only does it point back to the expectation that women be chaste in body and mind, but it also conveys the extent to which Virginia maintains a disciplined habit of shamefastness. Her outwardly virtuous behaviour is a reflection of (and support for) her equally virtuous nature. Through his references to her 'abstinence', 'attemperaunce', and 'mesure' in these lines, Chaucer stresses not just Virginia's chastity, but also her exemplary shamefast behaviour.[52] She is neither outspoken nor boastful, nor does she carry or array herself in a manner calculated to attract attention. Quite the contrary: she seems eager to avoid it. In an addition to Chaucer's source for the tale, the Physician elaborates on his description of Virginia's shamefast ways by noting that

> And of hir owene vertu, unconstreyned,
> She hath ful ofte tyme syk hire feyned,
> For that she wolde fleen the compaignye
> Where likly was to treten of folye,
> As is at feestes, revels, and at daunces,
> That been occasions of daliaunces.
>
> (*The Physician's Tale* 61–6)

Chaucer's use of the word 'unconstreyned' (under no compulsion, free) testifies to Virginia's ability to behave virtuously without external guidance or coercion, but it also characterizes her shamefast practice as a closed circuit. Her shamefastness is so genuine, so deeply felt, that it *automatically* prompts her to shy away from events that offer opportunities not only for 'daliaunces', but for other potential threats of exposure to masculine eyes and ears.[53] Her withdrawal from these social spaces manifests and secures her perfect chastity. The only 'feigning' she does is in aid of that chastity, rather than to falsely convince others of virtues she does not have. In any other context, feigning headaches or illness for the sake of preserving one's honour might seem ludicrous or extreme, but in the context of the Physician's comments on Virginia's shamefastness, it reinforces her chastity and confirms her status as a chaste and honourable maiden. Unlike earlier versions of Virginia's narrative, it places her exemplary shamefastness at centre-stage.

Holly Crocker has drawn attention to the way that Chaucer foregrounds Virginia's agency in the performance of her own virtue. Crocker suggests that the fact that Virginia's feminine passivity is under her own direction (rather than under that of any masculine authority figure) is a source of 'patriarchal panic' for Virginius, who must 'suppress the visible influence that feminine passivity exerts over his character, attempting instead to assert his masculinity through a violent exercise of manifest agency'.[54] While I agree that Chaucer deliberately draws attention to the visibility of Virginia's 'unconstreyned' virtuous behaviour, I would suggest that he does so in order to highlight the threat that Virginia's shamefast exemplarity poses to her chastity, and ultimately to her life. This is suggested when, following on from the Physician's account of Virginia's habitual withdrawal from revelry, the tale considers how she first enters into the public arena: through public fame. Ironically, her entry into the public sphere comes about precisely because of the disciplined shamefastness that urges her to withdraw from it. Chaucer's introduction of the subject of fame into the tale marks a shift in the course and tone of the narrative:

> This mayde, of which I wol this tale expresse,
> So kepte hirself hir neded no maistresse,
> For in hir lyvyng maydens myghten rede,
> As in a book, every good word or dede
> That longeth to a mayden vertuous,
> She was so prudent and so bountevous.
> For which the fame out sprong on every syde,
> Bothe of hir beautee and hir bountee wyde,
> That thurgh that land they preised hire echone

> That loved vertu, save Envye allone,
> That sory is of oother mennes wele
> And glad is of his sorwe and his unheele.
>
> *(The Physician's Tale* 105–16)

The Physician's reflections on Virginia's superlative exemplarity are accompanied here by the suggestion of danger. This brief description of Virginia's renown concludes with foreboding, and gestures towards one of the major potential pitfalls of fame: there are always those who are happy to hear (and speak) ill of others. The scope of Virginia's exemplarity expands with alarming speed over the course of a dozen lines, from an example accessible 'as in a book' to the eyes of other maidens, to an unbounded fame that 'sprong on every syde'. Even more firmly establishing public fame as especially dangerous for shamefast women is the fact that this reference to Virginia's renown is immediately followed by an account of the event that seals her doom: the moment when the judge Appius sees Virginia and declares, 'This mayde shal be myn, for any man!' (*The Physician's Tale* 129).[55] Virginia's entrance into the public sphere proves to be her undoing; she becomes the target of a man's lustful plotting.

That a chaste and honourable woman might be endangered by her presence in the public sphere or (implicitly) by her good reputation is also implied elsewhere in Chaucer's works. In *The Man of Law's Tale*, for example, the heroine Custance's trials are set in motion when the sultan of Syria is told of her 'excellent renoun' (*The Man of Law's Tale* 150), which inflames his desire to be married to her and sets her on course for years of wandering and hardship.[56] And, as I will discuss in more detail below, Lucrece's rape in the *Legend of Good Women* results directly from her husband's boasts about her virtue. These examples, as well as that of Virginia herself, point to a correlation between an honourable woman's accessibility to others, whether through sight or speech, and the possibility of her violation.

The idea that Virginia's entrance into the public arena invites her violation and, indeed, destruction, complements the work of R. Howard Bloch, who has linked the 'fatality' underlying *The Physician's Tale* with 'medieval definitions of virginity' and with 'the specifically literary effects of a poetics of praise'.[57] According to Bloch, the medieval 'logic of virginity' 'implies not only that Virginia is not a virgin from the moment she is seen, but that her death is inferred the moment she steps into the street'.[58] Examining patristic definitions of perfect chastity, Bloch observes that a true virgin is a woman who has not only never slept with a man, but who has also never desired to do so, who has never been desired by a man, and, in fact, 'who has never been *seen* by a man'.[59] This argument is pursued to its fullest extent, as Bloch posits that virginity is so constantly under threat from the gazes, words, and thoughts of others that 'a certain inescapable logic of virginity' leads to the conclusion that 'the only true virgin – is a dead virgin'.[60] But to insist, as Bloch does, on reading Virginia allegorically, as 'the figure of virginity', is to miss the other cultural contexts with which Chaucer's depiction of Virginia is engaging.[61] By reading Virginia's exemplary virginity solely in relation to the writings of the Early Church Fathers, Bloch overlooks the new contexts in which women are being urged to undertake the labour of chastity in later medieval England. In the late fourteenth century, patristic doctrine was not the only discourse available for thinking about or praising female chastity and virginity, nor would it necessarily have been foremost in the minds of lay, vernacular readers. While strict patristic doctrine would view total withdrawal from the world as the only sure guardian of female chastity, conduct literature for women was also concerned with how chastity might be practised and perfected *in* the world. In conduct texts, female honour depends in part upon women's ability to perform their chastity before others; it is through these performances that a woman can 'show the full potential of her nature'.[62]

Whereas Bloch argues that, according to patristic lines of thinking, Chaucer's praise of Virginia makes him complicit in the abstract deflowering of Virginia, I would argue that Chaucer's depiction of Virginia's exemplary shamefastness alerts his readers to the extremely problematic way that masculine and feminine gender roles conflict, leaving women with the choice of only 'two weyes, outher deeth or shame'.[63] The rest of *The Physician's Tale* makes it clear that the inevitability surrounding Virginia's death stems not simply from her virginity, but from the dynamic of shamefastness and gender within the tale. Chaucer's adjustments to the narrative highlight the innate tension between the model of aggressive masculinity and the ideals of feminine behaviour, which underlies the violence that *must* ultimately be committed against Virginia, one way or another. Although Virginia and her shamefastness are at the centre of the tale, they are framed by the language, tools, and requirements of hardy masculinity, which are present from the very start of the narrative. The story in fact begins with Virginius's reputation, rather than with Virginia's virtue:

> Ther was, as telleth Titus Livius,
> A knyght that called was Virginius,
> Fulfild of honour and of worthynesse,
> And strong of freendes, and of greet richesse.
> *(The Physician's Tale* 1–4)

While most of the details concerning Virginius's renown are taken directly from Chaucer's main source, the *Roman de la rose*, there they appear somewhere in the middle of the story, whereas here they are the first facts we learn about any of the protagonists. The story begins, therefore, with the issue of masculine worth, rather than with female chastity, and once that chastity is threatened, although Virginia is seen as the prize, man is seen as the adversary: inflamed with desire for Virginia, Appius declares, 'This mayde shal be myn, for any man!' (*The Physician's Tale* 129). This is not to say that Appius's main goal is to antagonize Virginius (or any other man); nothing in the text suggests that his goal is anything less singleminded than to 'hasten his delit al that he may' (*The Physician's Tale* 159). But the language he uses to express his determination to achieve that goal identifies men as his opponents. This is the language of aggressive masculinity.

Chaucer also later invokes masculine aggression by means of another small detail. Once Appius's accomplice has concluded his demand that Virginia be turned over to him,

> Virginius gan upon the cherl biholde,
> ... And wolde have preeved it as sholde a knyght,
> And eek by witnessyng of many a wight,
> That al was fals that seyde his adversarie[.]
> *(The Physician's Tale* 191–5)

Whereas the churl had offered to prove the truth of his case '[b]y witnesse, lord, so that it nat yow greeve' (*The Physician's Tale* 186), Virginius is eager to prove his case not just by the testimony of his own witnesses, but also 'as sholde a knight' – in other words, through trial by combat. But the option of defence through (lawful) violence against another man is not one that Virginius is allowed to have; he is stripped of every means of defending his daughter that the public arena might have permitted him.

The problem of exemplary shame 143

As the story moves towards its conclusion, it becomes more and more bound by absolutes. Chaucer's addition of the exchange between Virginius and his daughter before her death makes this abundantly clear, as Virginius bleakly sets out his daughter's options in what forms the epigraph to this chapter: 'Ther been two weyes, outher deeth or shame, / That thou most suffre' (*The Physician's Tale* 214–15). This statement has troubled many readers as either illogical or unfeeling; indeed, Virginius's apparent intractability has often been cited as evidence that Chaucer blamed him for Virginia's death.[64] But I would argue that such responses are precisely the reactions we are intended to have to the death-or-dishonour binary that Virginius describes. Even Virginia cannot help but call her father's reasoning into question:

'O mercy, deere fader!' quod this mayde,
And with that word she bothe hir armes layde
Aboute his nekke, as she was wont to do.
The teeris bruste out of hir eyen two,
And seyde, 'Goode fader, shal I dye?
Is ther no grace, is ther no remedye?'
(*The Physician's Tale* 231–6)

In light of the tale's underlying concern with shame and gender, this exchange provides a poignant commentary on the expectations of hardy masculinity and shamefast femininity, which seem to offer shamefast women no escape from violence. As the moments leading up to Virginia's death are drawn out by Chaucer's descriptions of her pleas and swooning, readers are moved to consider and echo Virginia's request for 'grace' or some other 'remedye'.

Whereas Chaucer's sources had unequivocally blamed Appius for Virginia's death, *The Physician's Tale* places responsibility not only with the judge, but also with 'a curious array of vaguely motivated sources of trouble: Nature, governesses, fathers, mothers, "the feend," Virginius and Virginia themselves, and finally, in perhaps the most startling *non sequitur* of all, those who having failed to forsake sin are forsaken by it'.[65] I would suggest that what we see in the tortuous moralization that concludes the tale is a repeated attempt to fit the story into an interpretive framework, to make it have meaning. In the eyes of its narrator and his audience of pilgrims, it is a story that *should* have lessons to bestow, but precisely what those lessons might be remains unclear. The fact that, as so many critics have noted, the climax of the story seems to be such a pointless destruction of an innocent life (a moment whose pathos is deliberately heightened by Chaucer) invites the reader, like Virginia, to ask for some other kind of meaning, something beyond the framework of death-or-dishonour that shapes the tale: is there no grace, or any other remedy?

The repeated attempts to draw a moral from the story contribute to its sense of inflexibility and inevitability, and highlight the apparently insoluble tension between masculine aggression and female shamefastness that drives its plot. Chaucer's tale of Virginia suggests that being held in high public esteem for one's virtue or beauty was not always an asset for a woman, and could in fact be a liability. Might the safest option for an honourable shamefast woman be not to have a good reputation, but to have no public reputation whatsoever?

The trouble with Chaucer's Lucrece

If Chaucer uses the inflexibility of *The Physician's Tale* to underscore the tension between female shamefastness and hardy masculinity, his *Legend of Lucrece* provides an even sharper critique of the masculine aggression that endangers female chastity. Like Gower, Chaucer adjusts his source to lay greater emphasis on the violence of Tarquin's lust and to highlight the theme of male competition. But whereas Gower presents these new elements as evidence of the Tarquins' corrupt rule, Chaucer focuses on their consequences for Lucrece in order to question the inevitability of her fate.

After expressing his intention to 'seyn the exilynge of kynges / Of Rome' (F 1680–1), he declares, 'But for that cause telle I nat this storye, / But for to preyse and drawe to memorye / The verray wif, the verray trewe Lucresse' (F 1684–6). Not all scholars have interpreted this stated objective of praising Lucrece to be genuine, or to be reflected in the remainder of the text.[66] But, as in the case of Virginia, Chaucer dissociates Lucrece's narrative from issues of governance and makes her more central to his version of the story. He achieves this, firstly, by omitting any mention of other, less honourable Roman wives. In the version included in Ovid's *Fasti* (Chaucer's main source for the *Legend of Lucrece*), for example, the Roman soldiers first visit their own wives, who are engaged in raucous carousing, before visiting the house of Tarquinius Collatinus, where they find Lucretia virtuously spinning wool with her handmaids.[67] Even Gower, who restricts the competition to Aruns and Collatin, begins by describing the initial debate taking place between Aruns and his entire 'compaignie'. But Chaucer omits any mention of other soldiers participating in the debate or visiting Lucrece's house. These omissions focus attention entirely on the conversation and actions of Tarquin and Collatine as two Roman men engaged in (perhaps initially friendly) competition with one another, which later has disastrous consequences for the woman at the centre of that competition. The legend might usefully be viewed as focusing on ill-considered masculine speech and its consequences for Lucrece's chastity and honour. Tarquin (described by Chaucer as 'lyght of tonge' (F 1699)) idly encourages his men to 'speke of wyves, that is best; / Preyse every man his owene as hym lest' (F 1702–3), and this prompts Lucrece's husband to respond,

> 'Nay, sire, it is no nede
> To trowen on the word, but on the dede.
> I have a wif,' quod he, 'that, as I trowe,
> Is holden good of alle that evere hire knowe.
> Go we to-nyght to Rome, and we shal se.'
>
> (F 1706–10)[68]

Although Tarquin's words seem to be addressed to a group of his fellow soldiers, the 'we' that Collatine suggests should return to Rome does not include anyone apart from himself and Tarquin. Tarquin's response, 'That liketh me' (F 1711), is also individualized, and Chaucer's description of their journey to Rome mentions only 'Tarquinius and ek this Colatyn' (F 1714). Consequently, and even more thoroughly than in Gower's version of the story, competition between two men forms the backdrop for Collatine's boast, which in turn illustrates the dangers of speaking about things (such as a wife's honour) that are best kept private; he shifts from the pleasures derived from 'the word' to actually *seeing* with one's own eyes, but also lays open the possibility of believing through 'the dede'.

Just as Virginia's chastity was threatened by Appius's sight of her ('Allas, that evere Apius the say!' (VI. 227)), Lucrece's status as a chaste wife is endangered the moment that Collatine's boastfulness enables Tarquin to catch sight of her at home. Tarquin's thoughts following the initial encounter with Lucrece illustrate how female chastity was believed to be threatened by the male gaze in medieval culture.[69] The next day, his thoughts are full of her, and it is then that he decides to rape her:

> A-morwe, whan the brid began to synge,
> Unto the sege he cometh ful privily,

> And by hymself he walketh soberly,
> Th'ymage of hire recordynge alwey newe:
> 'Thus lay hire her, and thus fresh was hyre hewe;
> Thus sat, thus spak, thus span; this was hire chere;
> Thus fayr she was, and this was hire manere.'
> Al this conseit hys herte hath newe ytake.
> (...)
> Ryght so, thogh that hire forme were absent,
> The plesaunce of hire forme was present;
> But natheles, nat plesaunce but delit,
> Or an unrightful talent, with dispit –
> 'For, maugre hyre, she shal my leman be!
> Hap helpeth hardy man alday[.]'
>
> (F 1757–73)

Whereas in the *Confessio Amantis* Aruns had simply noted that 'Fortune unto the bolde / Is favorable forto helpe' (VII. 4902–3, closely echoing Ovid), Tarquin's declaration that *'maugre hyre*, she shal my leman be' carries the same threat of force as Appius's vow that 'This mayde shal be myn, for any man!' (VI. 129), but this time it is Lucrece's shamefastness and chastity which are the objects of masculine aggression. Tarquin believes that his boldness or 'hardynesse' will help him to overcome Lucrece's shamefastness: 'Hap helpeth hardy man alday'. This passage strikingly recalls *Ami*'s advice to the narrator in the *Roman de la rose*, when female shame and resistance are recast as opponents who must be defeated by the manly force of the lover. By altering Ovid's 'viderit!' ('let her look to it!') to 'maugre hyre', Chaucer makes clear that honourable feminine shame is being regarded by Tarquin as something that must be overcome through masculine force. This is further reinforced by Chaucer's description of the moments leading up to Lucrece's rape, which adapts Ovid's remarks regarding the imbalance of the situation:

> No word she spak, she hath no myght therto.
> What shal she seyn? Hire wit is al ago.
> Ryght as a wolf that fynt a lomb alone,
> To whom shal she compleyne or make mone?
> What, shal she fyghte with an hardy knyght?
> Wel wot men that a woman hath no myght.
> What, shal she crye, or how shal she asterte
> That hath hire by the throte with swerd at herte?
> She axeth grace, and seyth al that she can.
>
> (F 1796–804)[70]

This passage provides a clear critique of Tarquin's earlier declaration, which, like the kind of advice offered by *Ami* and Pandarus, extols masculine forcefulness and implicitly assumes that women are in effect waiting to be overcome by it. Tarquin's perspective is sharply undercut by Chaucer's series of rhetorical questions, which highlights the tension between the model of hardy masculinity and the shamefast ideals of feminine behaviour. The narrator points to the impossibility of her situation when he asks, 'What, shal she fyghte with an hardy knyght?' The rhetorical nature of the question helps to paint this as an image of misdirected masculine aggression, a tableau in which the force that should be used to defend female shamefastness is instead used to violate it. In the context of his rape of Lucrece, this reference to Tarquin's 'hardynesse' is as double-edged as it was in Pandarus's speech to Troilus: on the one hand, it refers to the boldness or audacity appropriate to a man; but on the other, it is associated with the ability and willingness to commit rape. The passage emphasizes the painful contrast between the tools of masculinity ('myght', 'swerd') and the sensorimotor inhibitions of shamefast femininity. Confronted by an armed man threatening dishonour, a medieval man would be expected to respond in kind in order to avoid shame, but the assumption at work here is that a woman would not be equipped to respond effectively with physical force. While Lucrece does not respond physically, she makes an effort to persuade Tarquin with words: 'she axeth grace, and seyth al that she can'. But as the bestial imagery of the wolf and the lamb suggests, Tarquin is incapable of being persuaded by her words as – Chaucer implies – he *should* be. Whereas Troilus's reasoning led him to reject Pandarus's suggestion of rape, Tarquin's rapacity drives his behaviour. His subsequent rape of Lucrece is both heinous and a kind of failure, and thrusts the essential problem to the fore: female resistance to masculine aggression must inevitably fail.[71] Chaucer's rhetorical questions both invite the reader to consider an alternate ending and simultaneously foreclose the possibility of any such thing. Like Virginia, Lucrece is compelled to ask for grace, which is not an option. Given the choice between two kinds of dishonour (rape on the one hand, and posthumous defamation on the other), Lucrece swoons 'for fer of sclaunder and drede of deth' (F 1814). Like Gower's depiction of a silently swooning Lucretia, this Chaucerian addition both absolves Lucrece of having made any choice between violation and slander, and renders her mercifully unconscious at the moment of her violation.

Once the deed has been done, Chaucer digresses into criticism of Tarquin's behaviour, which is beneath him as a knight and a king's son:

> Tarquinius, that art a kynges eyr,
> And sholdest, as by lynage and by ryght,
> Don as a lord and as a verray knyght,
> Whi hastow don dispit to chivalrye?
> Whi hastow don this lady vilanye?
> Allas, of the this was a vileyns dede!
>
> (F 1819–24)

This digression is notably different from Ovid's commentary, which focuses on the consequences for Tarquin's rulership:

> quid, victor, gaudes? haec te victoria perdet.
> heu quanto regnis nox stetit una tuis!
>
> Why, victor, dost thou joy? This victory will ruin thee. Alack, how dear a single night did cost thy kingdom![72]

In comparison with Ovid and Gower, Chaucer is less concerned with dynasties or common profit and more concerned with how Tarquin has behaved as a lord, a knight, and a man. Lucrece's rape is here reconstituted as a violation not just of *her* honour, but also of *his*. His deed has 'don dispit to chivalrye', and should have been beneath him. Chaucer treats the rape of Lucrece as a moment in which masculine aggression runs amok, overrunning the shamefast foundations of female honour.[73]

After her rape, Lucrece's shamefastness continues to be evident in her understandable reluctance to speak of her violation, even 'in halle' before her intimate circle of family and friends: 'A word, for shame, forth ne myght she brynge, / Ne upon hem she durste nat beholde' (F 1835–6). But once she has explained what has happened, her immediate concern appears to be not for herself and her own reputation, but for that of her husband:

> She sayde that, for hir gylt ne for hir blame,
> Hir husbonde shulde nat have the foule name,
> That wolde she nat suffre by no wey.
>
> (F 1844–6)

Lucrece's anxiety returns the reader's attention to the issue of male rivalry evoked by the competition between Tarquin and Collatine. Because masculine aggression has been driven more by masculine competition than by an urge to protect female shamefastness, in the end both womanly chastity and the woman herself must be erased. Despite the fact that her family and friends forgive her because 'It was no gilt, it lay not in hir myght' (F 1849), Lucrece defiantly refuses to 'have noo forgyft for nothing' (F 1853) and takes her own life. Lucrece's final effort to cover her feet even 'as she fel adoun' (F 1856) bespeaks a shamefast habit rivalling that of the chaste Virginia; her shamefastness is so automatic that, even in the act of dying, Lucrece is shamefast to the end.[74] And while, like Ovid, Chaucer notes that her death ended the Tarquins' reign ('never was ther kyng in Rome toun / Syn thilke day' (F 1870)), he concludes her story by reflecting on her exemplarity, her saintliness, and her 'stable herte' (F 1876), which stands in stark contrast to the 'brotel' hearts of men (F 1885).

The suddenness and the conviction of Lucrece's suicide call to mind the infuriating inflexibility of *The Physician's Tale*. Like Virginia's death, Lucrece's suicide seems to have been inevitable, and returns us to the problematic binary of death-or-dishonour underlying both tales. It suggests that Lucrece grasps the impossibility not just of her own situation, but of the situations of all women whose honour is framed by the same violence that perpetually threatens to negate it: women's honour is always already subject to masculine violence because that violence must always either protect or threaten it. In his references to honourable female shamefastness, Chaucer redeploys the language of aggressive masculinity in order to problematize it in their narratives. In Chaucer's works, 'hardynesse', 'myght', and 'force' shed their congratulatory overtones and are made more clearly recognizable as the enemies of female honour. The handling of shamefastness in Chaucer's works and the sense of fatality plaguing the stories of Virginia and Lucrece raise deeply troubling questions regarding gendered definitions of honour. Can honourable female shamefastness exist without the male aggression that helps to define it? Can female honour exist securely in the same context as masculine honour, which is so often won and preserved through aggression? Both Virginia and Lucrece are left asking after grace, searching for something outside the choices offered to them, and finding nothing.

Like Gower, Chaucer suggests that both the problem and its solution lie in the choices that men make, but his focus is on the impact of these choices on women. The moment a man decides to exercise his hardiness by violating female shamefastness, he places not only her chastity, but her very life, in jeopardy. In Gower's

Confessio Amantis, this predicament is for the most part symbolic and symptomatic of bad governance: the ruler who cannot govern his own lusts is an unjust ruler, and – if Gower's historical exempla are to be believed – will not rule for long. A king's energies must be directed towards preserving the common good of his nation, not towards exploiting his power and violating their trust. By shifting the focus away from the theme of governance in *The Physician's Tale* and *The Legend of Lucrece*, Chaucer explores the same dynamic between individual men and women, and pinpoints the masculine failure to respond appropriately to the spectacle or desirability of female shamefastness as the chief cause of the dilemma faced by superlatively honourable women. But this leaves shamefast women with little room to manoeuvre. Lucretia, Virginia, and other honourable women remain dependent on the choices made by the men around them, and on masculine attitudes towards female shamefastness. Ultimately, these narratives suggest that all honourable women can do is watch, wait, and, if necessary, die well when there is no other remedy.

***

As *The Physician's Tale* and the *Legend of Lucrece* make clear, both Virginia and Lucrece are exemplary figures of female shamefastness and chastity. Their exterior gestures of concealment and withdrawal are not presented as problematically 'practised', but rather as the embodied result and manifestation of a shamefastness that has been thoroughly *interiorized* – in this respect, they can both be said to be chaste '[a]s wel in goost as body'. Yet, in both cases, their exemplarity seems to leave them with no options beyond death or dishonour when their chastity is threatened by uncontrolled or misdirected male aggression. The discomfort Chaucer urges us to feel upon reading these stories heightens their emotional impact, but it also opens up a space in which the tensions that inhere in the female practice of shamefastness become more discernible. Just how absolute must a woman's devotion to honour be? Can anything ever be acceptable as definitive proof of that honour? And how are women meant to strive for shamefastness that is both perfectly interiorized and legible in their exterior behaviour when the very exemplarity of such virtue might inspire male lust or violence? By raising such questions, Chaucer's stories of Virginia and Lucrece invite us to consider not only what might have happened differently in those stories, but also whether the emotional practices upon which those narratives depend might themselves be reimagined.

Even if Chaucer's narratives point to the fundamental ways in which the models of shamefast femininity and hardy masculinity are at odds with one another, they adhere to the notion that the correct practice of shamefastness is one that combines inner virtue with virtuous outer conduct. The unfeigned artlessness of their shamefastness is what demonstrates Virginia's and Lucrece's perfect chastity. But while their shamefastness may be exemplary, it is also conventional in the sense that it comprises gestures and behaviour that are visibly recognizable as proper shamefast comportment, the very same comportment outlined in medieval conduct literature for women and mendaciously replicated by Medea in Lydgate's *Troy Book*. As I will show in my final chapter, while the conventionality of shamefast conduct was precisely what made it imitable even by shameless women, it could also be exploited by male authors to disarm their readers.

Notes

This chapter includes material that was previously published in Flannery, 'A Bloody Shame'. I am grateful to the editors of *The Review of English Studies* for permission to use this material here.

1 All citations of Chaucer's works in this chapter are drawn from editions in *The Riverside Chaucer* and cited above by line number.
2 Augustine, *The City of God Against the Pagans, Vol. I: Books I–III*, trans. McCracken, pp. 88–9. Augustine's comment occurs in the middle of an extended discussion of Lucretia which forms part of his argument for survival rather than suicide in the aftermath of rape. Suzanne M. Edwards investigates this and other 'early discourses of survival' in *The Afterlives of Rape in Medieval English Literature* (New York, NY: Palgrave Macmillan, 2016).
3 Lydgate, *Lydgate's Fall of Princes*, cited above by book and line number. Lydgate tells the story of Lucretia twice in the *Fall of Princes*: once in book II (II. 1002–344), and once in book III (III. 932–1148). The book II version is taken from Coluccio Salutati's *Declamatio Lucretiae* (see E. P. Hammond, 'Lydgate and Coluccio Salutati', *Modern Philology* 25 (1927), 49–57). On the *Declamatio Lucretiae* (and for a transcription of the text), see Stephanie H. Jed, *Chaste Thinking: The Rape of Lucretia and the Birth of Humanism* (Indianapolis, IN: Indiana University Press, 1989).

4 On counterfactual thinking, see Neal J. Reese and Mike Morrison, 'The Psychology of Counterfactual Thinking', *Historical Social Research* 34 (2009), 16–26.
5 Glenn Burger has made a similar argument concerning the depiction of love in Chaucer's *Legend of Good Women*, which he suggests compels readers to linger in 'ugly feelings' generated by 'the profound unease created when Chaucer's good women are forced to inhabit the gap between love felt as overwhelming passion and love recognized as that which will never be the kind of ennobling and *trotheful* experience you were taught it should be' ('"Pite renneth soone in gentil herte": Ugly Feelings and Gendered Conduct in Chaucer's *Legend of Good Women*', *The Chaucer Review* 52 (2017), 66–84 (p. 68)). Burger here draws on the concepts outlined in Sianne Ngai, *Ugly Feelings* (Cambridge, MA: Harvard University Press, 2005).
6 On the ways that medieval texts sought to teach shamefastness, see Chapter 2.
7 See, for example, Ruth Mazo Karras, *From Boys to Men: Formations of Masculinity in Late Medieval Europe* (Philadelphia, PA: University of Pennsylvania Press, 2003), p. 3 (quoted here); Derek G. Neal, *The Masculine Self in Late Medieval England* (Chicago, IL: The University of Chicago Press, 2008); Carolyn P. Collette, *Performing Polity: Women and Agency in the Anglo-French Tradition, 1385–1620* (Turnhout: Brepols, 2007); or Tara Williams, *Inventing Womanhood: Gender and Language in Later Middle English Writing* (Columbus, OH: The Ohio State University Press, 2011), which argues that later Middle English writers use words like *womanhood*, *femininity*, and *motherhood* 'to signal moments where the writers are particularly interested or invested in exploring new ideas about femininity' (p. 3). Much work has been undertaken on the subject of gender in Chaucer's writings; recent major studies include Tison Pugh and Marcia Smith Marzec (eds), *Men and Masculinities in Chaucer's Troilus and Criseyde* (Cambridge: D. S. Brewer, 2008); Holly A. Crocker, *Chaucer's Visions of Manhood* (New York, NY: Palgrave Macmillan, 2007); Alcuin Blamires, *Chaucer, Ethics, and Gender* (Oxford: Oxford University Press, 2006); and Peter G. Beidler (ed.), *Masculinities in Chaucer: Approaches to Maleness in the Canterbury Tales and Troilus and Criseyde* (Cambridge: D. S. Brewer, 1998).
8 Karras, *From Boys to Men*, p. 10.
9 Alcuin Blamires, 'Chaucer's Revaluation of Chivalric Honor', *Mediaevalia* 5 (1979), 245–69 (p. 246).
10 Derek Brewer, 'Honour in Chaucer', in *Tradition and Innovation in Chaucer* (London: Macmillan Press, 1982; repr. 1983), pp. 89–109 (p. 96).
11 Siegfried Christoph, 'Honor, Shame and Gender', in Friedrich Wolfzettel (ed.), *Arthurian Romance and Gender/Masculin/Féminin dans le roman arthurien medieval/Geschlechterrollen im mittelalterlichen Artusroman:*

Selected Proceedings of the XVIIth International Arthurian Congress, Internationale Forschungen zur Allgemeinen und Vergleichenden Literaturwissenschaft 10 (Amsterdam: Rodopi, 1995), pp. 26–33 (p. 28). A number of studies have expanded our understanding of medieval masculinity in recent years; see in particular Neal, *The Masculine Self*, which considers how qualities like 'trueness', husbandry, and clothing and physical appearance informed medieval ideas concerning masculinity and manhood.

12 Karras, *From Boys to Men*, p. 60.
13 In general, a strong sensibility to shame was thought to be more appropriate for women and young people than it was for men: as I point out in my Introduction, in book 4 of his *Il Convivio*, for example, Dante glosses Aristotle's *Ethics* when he declares that shame ('vergogna') is 'good and praiseworthy' ('buona e laudabile') 'in women and in young people' ('nelle donne e nelli giovani'; English from *Il Convivio (The Banquet)*, p. 205; Italian from *Dante Alighieri Convivio*, vol. 3 (second volume of the text), 383). Dante is here discussing Aristotle's remarks in *Nicomachean Ethics* IV. 9.
14 This rule is not without exceptions; as I discuss in the next chapter, a certain 'maidenly shamefastness' was believed to be appropriate to clerks (see Chapter 5).
15 1 Timothy 2: 9 is also cited by St Jerome in *Adversus Jovinianum* 1. 27: 'Similiter et mulieres in habitu ornato, cum verecundia [translatable as shame, respect, modesty] et castitate, ornantes se, non in tortis crinibus, aut auro, vel margaritis, sive veste pretiosa' (St Jerome, *Adversus Jovinianum, in Patrologiae cursus completus, series latina, vol. 23*, ed. J.-P. Migne (Paris, 1844–64), columns 211–338 (column 248).
16 This is taken from Jerome, *Adversus Jovinianum*, 1. 48 ('Scribit Herodotus, quod mulier cum veste deponat et verecundiam' (column 279)), and is originally from Herodotus, *Histories* 1. 8.
17 As I have already noted, shamefastness is one of several possible meanings of the Middle English word *shame*; see 'Introduction', pp. 24–5, n. 9; and *MED*, s. v. *shame*.
18 See *MED*, s. v. *shamefast*, which may be defined as '[r]eluctant, unwilling, hesitant'. There are a number of Middle English proverbs regarding the appropriately quiet, modest behaviour of maidens; see, for example, Whiting, *Proverbs, Sentences and Proverbial Phrases*, entries M4, M5, M6, M7, M8, M9, M11, M13, M14, M15, and M18.
19 In Huling E. Ussery, 'How Old Is Chaucer's Clerk?', *Tulane Studies in English* (*TSE*) 15 (1967), 1–15, Ussery points out that several medieval sources describe such timidity as appropriate behaviour for clerks. Jill Mann, *Chaucer and Medieval Estates Satire* (Cambridge: Cambridge University Press, 1973), who cites Ussery's study, notes that, while 'Chaucer makes the image more concrete and in so doing gives it a comic touch', the original metaphor was 'neither his nor comic' (p. 243, n. 112; see also p. 76).

20 J. G. Peristiany (ed.), *Honour and Shame: The Values of Mediterranean Society* (Chicago, IL: The University of Chicago Press, 1966), p. 46.
21 On advice regarding appropriate womanly behaviour in medieval conduct literature, see Chapter 2.
22 See, for example, Beidler (ed.), *Masculinities in Chaucer*, and Pugh and Marzec (eds), *Men and Masculinities*.
23 *MED*, s. v. *nice*.
24 See Chapter 3.
25 Rachel Warburton, 'Reading Rape in Chaucer: or Are Cecily, Lucretia, and Philomela *Good Women*?', in Mihoko Suzuki and Roseanna Lewis Dufault (eds), *Diversifying the Discourse: The Florence Howe Award for Outstanding Feminist Scholarship, 1990–2004* (New York, NY: Modern Language Association of America, 2006), pp. 270–87 (p. 270).
26 Barbara Hanawalt, *Crime and Conflict in English Communities 1300–1348* (Cambridge, MA: Harvard University Press, 1979), p. 105. For a survey of the evolution of rape law and vocabulary in medieval England, see Corinne Saunders, *Rape and Ravishment in the Literature of Medieval England* (Cambridge: D. S. Brewer, 2001), pp. 33–119.
27 Gravdal, *Ravishing Maidens*, pp. 2–4 (also discussed in Chapter 3).
28 Guillaume de Lorris and Jean de Meun, *Le Roman de la Rose*, lines 7660–1; *The Romance of the Rose*, pp. 144–5. For Ovid's similar advice, see in particular *Ars Amatoria*, I. 485–6, 663–78.
29 See *MED*, s. v. *ravishen*.
30 For a comparison of Chaucer's and Gower's treatments of the narratives of Virginia and Lucretia, see Carol Weiher, 'Chaucer's and Gower's Stories of Virginia and Lucretia', *English Language Notes* (*ELN*) 14 (1976), 7–9. Studies that have considered Gower's likely influence on Chaucer's *Legend* include John M. Bowers, 'Rival Poets: Gower's *Confessio* and Chaucer's *Legend of Good Women*', in Elisabeth Dutton with John Hines and R. F. Yeager (eds), *John Gower, Trilingual Poet: Language, Translation, and Tradition* (Cambridge: D. S. Brewer, 2010), pp. 276–87; Nicola McDonald, 'Games Medieval Women Play', in Carolyn Collette (ed.), *The Legend of Good Women: Context and Reception* (Cambridge: D. S. Brewer, 2006), pp. 176–97; and Nicola F. McDonald, 'Chaucer's *Legend of Good Women*, Ladies at Court, and the Female Reader', *The Chaucer Review* 35 (2000), 22–42. Studies arguing for Chaucer's influence on Gower include Richard Axton, 'Gower – Chaucer's Heir?', in Ruth Morse and Barry Windeatt (eds), *Chaucer Traditions: Studies in Honour of Derek Brewer* (Cambridge: Cambridge University Press, 2009), pp. 21–38; and Norman Callan, '"Thyn Owne Book": A Note on Chaucer, Gower, and Ovid', *Review of English Studies* new series (n. s.) 22 (1946), 269–81. Andrew Cole has recently put forward the suggestion that the influence runs both ways; see Andrew Cole, 'John Gower Copies Geoffrey Chaucer', *The Chaucer Review* 52 (2017), 46–65.

31 On the dating of *The Physician's Tale* and *The Legend of Lucrece*, see *The Riverside Chaucer*, pp. 901–2 and 1059.
32 In addition to having given Gower power of attorney before travelling to Italy in 1378, Chaucer claims to dedicate *Troilus and Criseyde* to 'moral Gower' (V. 1856), although in the introduction to *The Man of Law's Tale* he refers to the 'wikke' stories of incest related by Gower in the *Confessio Amantis* (*Introduction to the Man of Law's Tale* 77–89). Interpretations of the latter reference vary: while Patricia J. Eberle remarks in her explanatory notes to *The Man of Law's Tale* that 'this passage has been viewed as a slighting reference to Gower' (*The Riverside Chaucer*, p. 856), Diane Watt is inclined to view them as playful ('John Gower', in Larry Scanlon (ed.), *The Cambridge Companion to Medieval English Literature 1100–1500* (Cambridge: Cambridge University Press, 2009), pp. 153–64 (p. 154; see also p. 153, on Gower's power of attorney)). Gower in turn describes Chaucer as 'mi disciple and mi poete' in his *Confessio Amantis* (VIII. 2942*). All references to the *Confessio Amantis* are taken from *The English Works of John Gower*, ed. G. C. Macaulay, EETS ES 81, 82 (Oxford: Oxford University Press, 1900; repr. 1969), and are cited above by book and line number, with an asterisk indicating where line numbers are cited from the unrevised version of Gower's text (following Macaulay).
33 On the 'mirror for princes' or *Fürstenspiegel* genre, see Judith Ferster, *Fictions of Advice: The Literature and Politics of Counsel in Late Medieval England* (Philadelphia, PA: University of Pennsylvania Press, 1996), p. 2; and Larry Scanlon, *Narrative, Authority, and Power: The Medieval Exemplum and the Chaucerian Tradition* (Cambridge: Cambridge University Press, 1994).
34 These themes also prevail in its three major sources: the *Secretum secretorum*, Brunetto Latini's *Trésor*, and Giles of Rome's *De regimine principum*. See *The English Works of John Gower*, II, p. 522, and Elizabeth Porter, 'Gower's Ethical Microcosm and Political Macrocosm', in A. J. Minnis (ed.), *Gower's 'Confessio Amantis': Responses and Reassessments* (Cambridge: D. S. Brewer, 1983), pp. 135–62.
35 English translation by Andrew Galloway, in John Gower, *John Gower: Confessio Amantis, Book 7*, ed. Russell Peck, TEAMS (Kalamazoo, MI: Medieval Institute Publications, 2004), http://d.lib.rochester.edu/teams/text/peck-gower-confessio-amantis-book-7 [accessed 10 April 2018].
36 Thus, Gower warns his (male) reader not to 'change for the wommanhede / The worthinesse of his manhede' (VII. 4255–6), and argues that 'To sen a man fro his astat / Thurgh his sotie effeminat, / And leve that a man schal do, / It is as Hose above the Scho, / To man which oghte noght ben used' (VII. 4303–7). Richard II himself (to whom Gower first dedicated the *Confessio*, before rededicating the revised version to Henry Bolingbroke) was the subject of rumours regarding

his court's alleged debauchery. In his 1422 English adaptation of the *Secretum secretorum*, the Dublin notary James Yonge claimed that after Richard's second marriage, 'Than regnyde avoutry and lechurie in hym and his howse-maynage, that al the roialme thanne rumourt and lothit for that rousty Synne' (James Yonge, *The Gouernaunce of Prynces*, in *Three Prose Versions of the Secreta Secretorum*, ed. Robert Steele, EETS ES, 74 (London: Kegan Paul, Trench, Trübner & Co., 1898; repr. 1996), 121–248 (pp. 136–7)).

37 Langlands, *Sexual Morality*, p. 84.
38 Livy, *History of Rome, Vol. 1, Books 1–2*, trans. B. O. Foster, The Loeb Classical Library (Cambridge, MA: William Heinemann, Ltd, 1967), pp. 200–1 (I. LVIII.5).
39 *Ibid.*, pp. 202–3 (I. LVIII.7).
40 Livy, *History of Rome, Vol. 2, Books 3–4*, trans. B. O. Foster, The Loeb Classical Library (Cambridge, MA: William Heinemann, Ltd, 1967), pp. 142–3 (III. XLIV.1–2): 'Sequitur aliud in urbe nefas ab libidine ortum, haud minus foedo eventu quam quod per stuprum caedemque Lucretiae urbe regnoque Tarquinios expulerat, ut non finis solum idem decemviris qui regibus sed causa etiam eadem imperii amittendi esset.'
41 Ovid, *Fasti*, trans. J. G. Frazer, rev. G. P. Goold, The Loeb Classical Library, 6 vols (Cambridge, MA: Harvard University Press, 1989), vol. 5, 118–19 (II. 852).
42 As Weiher has noted, Gower's version of these stories follows Livy more closely than Ovid, whereas Chaucer's follow Ovid more closely than Livy ('Chaucer's and Gower's Stories').
43 *MED*, s. v. *tiraunt*. The word can also describe a generally wicked person, or a cruel lover.
44 This point corresponds with arguments made by such scholars as Bolens, who remarks that '[b]oasting is the starting point of the legend of Lucrece' (*The Style of Gestures*, p. 105).
45 Chaucer derives the phrase from Ovid's account: 'audentes forsque deusque iuvat' ('God and fortune help the daring'; *Fasti*, 112–13 (II. 782)).
46 For Livy's account of this scene, see *History of Rome, Vol. 1*, pp. 200–1 (LVIII. 5).
47 *MED*, s. v. *unmete*.
48 On the subject of common profit or the common good in late medieval England, see M. S. Kempshall, *The Common Good in Late Medieval Political Thought: Moral Goodness and Political Benefit* (Oxford: Clarendon Press, 1999). On Gower's treatment of common profit, see Russell A. Peck, *Kingship and Common Profit in Gower's Confession Amantis* (Carbondale, IL: Southern Illinois University Press, 1978).
49 Anne Middleton, 'The *Physician's Tale* and Love's Martyrs: "Ensaumples mo than ten" as a Method in the *Canterbury Tales*', *The Chaucer Review* 8 (1973), 9–32 (p. 13).

50 Quote from Lee Patterson, *Chaucer and the Subject of History* (Madison, WI: University of Wisconsin Press, 1991), p. 369. For allegorical readings of *The Physician's Tale*, see Frederick Tupper, 'Chaucer and the Seven Deadly Sins', *PMLA* 29 (1914), 93–128; Beryl Rowland, 'The Physician's "Historial Thyng Notable" and the Man of Law', *English Literary History (ELH)* 40 (1973), 165–78; Brian S. Lee, 'The Position and Purpose of the *Physician's Tale*', *The Chaucer Review* 22 (1987), 141–60; Bloch, 'Chaucer's Maiden's Head'; and Marta Powell Harley, 'Last Things First in Chaucer's Physician's Tale: Final Judgment and the Worm of Conscience', *Journal of English and Germanic Philology* 91 (1992), 1–16.
51 These characteristics closely match those listed in the discussion of womanly chastity in *The Parson's Tale*, 946.
52 The *MED* cites 'modesty' (which is also one possible meaning of *shamefastness*) as one definition of *mesure* (s. v. *mesure*). For a discussion of Virginia as the embodiment of temperance, see Denise Baker, 'Chaucer and Moral Philosophy: The Virtuous Women of *The Canterbury Tales*', *Medium Aevum* 60 (1991), 241–56 (pp. 246–9).
53 *MED*, s. v. *unconstreined*.
54 Crocker, *Chaucer's Visions of Manhood*, p. 53. In Crocker's view, Virginius kills his daughter in order to 'usurp control over the agency that makes her a pattern of feminine submission'. On 'the fictionality of gender distinctions based on displays of agency or passivity', see Holly A. Crocker, 'Performative Passivity and Fantasies of Masculinity in the Merchant's Tale', *The Chaucer Review* 38 (2003), 178–98 (p. 179).
55 Gower's version of Virginia's story in the *Confessio Amantis* makes the link between public fame and the potential for a woman's violation even more explicit, since Apius does not lust after Virginius's daughter until he hears of her fame: 'Men seiden that so fair a lif / As sche was noght in al the toun. / This fame, which goth up and doun, / To Claudius cam in his Ere, / Wherof his thoght anon was there, / Which al his herte hath set afyre, / That he began the flour desire / Which longeth unto maydenhede, / And sende, if that he myhte spede / The blinde lustes of his wille' (*Confessio Amantis*, VII. 5138–47).
56 Despite the fact that her subsequent travels and ordeals result in her converting many of those she encounters to Christianity, Custance nevertheless suffers almost unending persecution, the threat of rape, and the possibility of starvation with her infant child.
57 Bloch, 'Chaucer's Maiden's Head', p. 115.
58 *Ibid*., 121.
59 *Ibid*., 117 (original emphasis).
60 *Ibid*., 120. By contrast, in her discussion of medieval discourses of survival after rape, Edwards posits that 'a rape survivor might be a real virgin, a true virgin, even if God alone can know her as such' (*Afterlives of Rape*, p. 22).

61 Bloch, 'Chaucer's Maiden's Head', p. 115.
62 Burger, *Conduct Becoming*, p. 7.
63 Bloch, 'Chaucer's Maiden's Head', p. 124.
64 For critical approaches to Virginius, see, for example, Crocker, *Chaucer's Visions of Manhood*, pp. 51–76; John Hirsch, 'Modern Times: The Discourse of the *Physician's Tale*', *The Chaucer Review* 27 (1993), 387–95; John A. Pitcher, 'Chaucer's Wolf: Exemplary Violence in *The Physician's Tale*', *Genre* 36 (2003), 1–27; Richard L. Hoffman, 'Jephthah's Daughter and Chaucer's Virginia', *The Chaucer Review* 2 (1967), 20–31; Robin L. Bott, '"O, keep me from their worse than killing lust": Ideologies of Rape and Mutilation in Chaucer's *Physician's Tale* and Shakespeare's *Titus Andronicus*', in Elizabeth Robertson and Christine M. Rose (eds), *Representing Rape in Medieval and Early Modern Literature* (New York, NY: Palgrave Macmillan, 2001), pp. 189–211; and Enrico Giaccherini, 'Tradition as Collaboration: The Public and the Private in *The Physician's Tale*', in Silvia Bigliazzi and Sharon Wood (eds), *Collaboration in the Arts from the Middle Ages to the Present*, Studies in European Cultural Transition, 35 (Aldershot: Ashgate, 2006), pp. 7–15. For a more sympathetic reading of Virginius as a father figure, see Jill Mann, 'Parents and Children in the "Canterbury Tales"', in Piero Boitani and Anna Torti (eds), *Literature in Fourteenth-Century England: The J. A. W. Bennett Memorial Lectures, Perugia, 1981–1982* (Cambridge: D. S. Brewer, 1983), pp. 165–83.
65 Emerson Brown, Jr., 'What is Chaucer Doing with the Physician and His Tale?', *Philological Quarterly* 60 (1981), 129–49 (p. 133).
66 Warburton, for example, has argued that 'Lucretia seems incidental' to Chaucer's actual narrative, citing the dominance of masculine perspective in the legend (Warburton, 'Reading Rape', p. 276).
67 Ovid, *Fasti*, vol. 5, 110–13 (II. 741–58).
68 Gower's use of the verb *janglen* ('to talk idly', 'to gossip') similarly characterizes the debate as idle speech (VII.4774); see *MED*, s. v. *janglen*.
69 See Bloch, 'Chaucer's Maiden's Head'.
70 Ovid describes Lucretia's situation in similar terms: 'She answered never a word. Voice and power of speech and thought itself fled from her breast. But she trembled, as trembles a little lamb that, caught straying from the fold, lies low under a ravening wolf. What could she do? Should she struggle? In a struggle a woman will always be worsted. Should she cry out? But in his clutch was a sword to silence her.' ('illa nihil: neque enim vocem viresque loquendi / aut aliquid toto pectore mentis habet, / sed tremit, ut quondam stabulis deprensa relictis / parva sub infesto cum iacet agna lupo. / quid faciat? pugnet? vincetur femina pugnans. / clamet? at in dextra, qui vetet, ensis erat.'), Ovid, *Fasti*, vol. 5, 114–15 (II. 797–802).
71 One Chaucerian exception to this rule would be Custance, who memorably fights off a would-be rapist who comes on board her ship

in the *Man of Law's Tale*. Indeed, she fights him off so successfully that 'with hir struglyng wel and myghtily / The theef fil over bord al sodeynly, / And in the see he dreynte for vengeance' (921–3). However, her ability to fight him off is ascribed to 'blisful Marie' (920) and to Jesus, and therefore appears to be more their victory than hers: 'And thus hath Crist unwemmed kept Custance' (924). For the importance of signs of force as proof of rape (rather than consensual sex), see the discussion of developments in medieval rape law in Saunders, *Rape and Ravishment*, pp. 33–119.
72 Ovid, *Fasti*, vol. 5, 114–15 (II. 811–12).
73 For Chaucer's criticism of chivalric honour, see Blamires, 'Chaucer's Revaluation of Chivalric Honor'.
74 Crocker, in 'Medieval Affects Now', ascribes Lucrece's gesture to her love of 'clennesse and eke trouthe' (F 1860), and, citing its oft-remarked similarity to Caesar's gesture at the moment of his death in the *Monk's Tale*, suggests that, 'The resemblance between these scenes, notably, rewrites the gendered script for both. Because both suggest a love for honesty is a defining feature of a heroic death, these moments are paired, stuck together, in ways that reimagine how certain feelings might invest women *and* men with excellence' (p. 93). But while Chaucer does indeed frame the deaths of both characters in terms of their shared 'love of honesty', in the case of Lucrece this framing emerges out of a long historical and literary tradition in which her name is virtually synonymous with a specifically feminine form of shamefast chastity.

5
Shamefast Hoccleve and shameless craving

Towards the end of his appeal to Lord Thomas Fourneval in *La Male Regle*, a petitionary poem he composed in 1405–06, Thomas Hoccleve explains that his circumstances compel him to make a direct request for payment. Having prefaced his request with some 400 lines of verse recounting his misspent youth (which has contributed to his current impecunious state), Hoccleve can beat about the bush no longer, but must instead get down to the business of asking Fourneval to 'paie me þat due is for this yeer / Of my yeerly x li. in th'eschequeer, / Nat but for Michel terme þat was last' (420–2) (although Hoccleve protests that 'I dar nat speke a word of ferne yeer, / So is my spir[i]t symple and sore agast' (423–4)).[1] Lest this request seem too abrupt, Hoccleve explains that he is 'looth' to ask for payment (426), but that he is forced to imitate 'the shamelees crauour', whose boldness and persistence pay off where the timidity of the 'poore shamefast man' goes unrewarded (429–31). In order to beg effectively, Hoccleve implies, he must now learn how to be shameless.

At first glance, Hoccleve here seems to be invoking a broader understanding of shamefastness than we have encountered thus far. The shamefastness to which he refers does not seem to be embodied hypervigilance against the possibility of being or seeming unchaste, but rather a more general kind of bashfulness or hesitation; as he explains, Hoccleve does not wish to seem 'importune' (425) – that is, overeager or insistent.[2] He contrasts this bashfulness with the shamelessness of beggars, who, he suggests, are sufficiently bold (or perhaps lacking in decency) to ask for what they need unblushingly.[3] *La Male Regle* presents us with an author who claims to view his own shamefastness as more of a hindrance than a virtue. Yet the poem's concluding petition is preceded by a depiction of Hoccleve's self-described shamefastness that draws upon the conventional language and imagery associated with the practice of female shamefastness outlined in the first four chapters of this study. As I have shown, while medieval women were encouraged to practise shamefast behaviour, the success of this practice was partly dependent on its not appearing too 'practised'. A woman's shamefast conduct should never appear calculated purely to achieve a certain effect on the viewer, but should rather appear to be conduct arising from genuine inner chastity. This ideal engaged women in a series of complicated gestures involving concealing and revealing, applying effort in order to appear effortlessly, authentically chaste. Complex as these gestures were for women, their relationship to masculine ideals of behaviour is more complicated still. For if hardy masculinity tended towards boldness and aggression, clerkly masculinity was believed to be distinguished by a certain 'maidenly shamefastness' (to which the Host's mocking treatment of the Clerk in *The Canterbury Tales* makes reference). As will become clear, however, while Hoccleve's self-presentation in *La Male Regle* may be drawing on this clerkly ideal, it also explicitly draws on the familiar conventions of feminine shamefastness in an effort to disarm the target of Hoccleve's petition.

This final chapter examines Hoccleve's engagement with both female shamefastness and masculinity in two of his early works, the *Letter of Cupid* (his translation of Christine de Pizan's anti-misogynist *Epistre au dieu d'Amours*) and *La Male Regle*, through the lens of what has been characterized as Hoccleve's distinctive pattern of self-effacement. 'Embarrassment' has come to be thought of as a defining characteristic of Hoccleve's poetics, one which emerges primarily out of Hoccleve's efforts to honour and imitate the recently deceased Chaucer.[4] While Hoccleve's work is undoubtedly self-effacing, if we adopt the postmedieval language of 'embarrassment' in our discussions of the phenomenon we overlook the Middle English discourse and imagery of shamefastness that Hoccleve uses, as well as its gendered associations.[5] As I will show, in presenting himself as a 'poore shamefast man' Hoccleve plays on two of the key beliefs underpinning the medieval practice of honourable female shamefastness: the belief that such emotional practices can be learned, and the belief that they can also be counterfeited.

I begin by taking a closer look at the Middle English language of 'manhood' and 'manliness' in relation to shamefastness. Returning to Chaucer's depiction of the interactions between the Host and the Clerk, I suggest that it not only illustrates a familiar binary that contrasts masculine boldness with feminine bashfulness and hesitation, but also that it may have inspired some of Hoccleve's own self-representation. I then turn to Hoccleve's treatment of misleading appearances in his *Letter of Cupid*, in which Hoccleve claims to have proto-feminist intentions but ultimately suggests that the behaviour of neither men nor women can be taken at face value. Finally, I return to *La Male Regle* in order to show how Hoccleve exploits the idea of shamefastness as a replicable practice, transforming what medieval women were encouraged to make an apparently artless performance of virtue into a performance of conspicuous artifice. By reappropriating shamefastness in order to amuse and to beg, Hoccleve demonstrates how the literary trope of feminine shamefastness might be co-opted by male authors.

Feeling like a man?

Ethan Knapp has argued that 'the element of embarrassment is something distinct, and crucial, to Hoccleve's poetics'.[6] In making this observation, Knapp draws on the modern English understanding of *embarrassment* as an '[i]ntense emotional or social discomfort', in Hoccleve's case stemming from 'an awareness that one's own … words or actions are inappropriate or compromising, or that they reveal inadequacy of foolishness'.[7] This trait has typically been identified as a characteristic of Hoccleve's paeans to Chaucer and his allusions to himself or his own life, moments in Hoccleve's work where he articulates his supposed sense of personal and professional inadequacy most clearly.[8] Yet it is important to note that on these occasions Hoccleve himself employs the Middle English vocabulary and kinesic imagery of shame and shamefastness, concepts that carry a rich variety of gendered associations that have largely been overlooked in Hoccleve scholarship.[9] In order to bring these associations to light, I will begin by considering how Hoccleve might also be engaging with the mode of masculinity against which feminine shamefastness is defined – that is, a view of manliness that is linked to the boldness, aggression, and even violence used to lay siege to female chastity.

Although the word *manli* was certainly in use in Middle English literature, it could be associated with a range of characteristics, including resolution and steadfastness, generosity, and courteousness.[10] Hoccleve himself, in a section of the *Regiment of Princes* on kingly magnanimity ('De regis magnanimitate'), uses the word *manhode* as a Middle English synonym for *magnanimitas*.[11] As Holly Crocker notes in her study of Chaucerian masculinity, the Middle English term *manhed* (also *manhode*) has multiple meanings, and can refer to 'the human condition', virtues deemed to be 'manly', or 'the race of man'.[12] Among *manli* qualities or virtues, boldness and bravery are cited with the greatest regularity. J. A. Burrow has shown how this trend is reflected in the works of poets such as Chaucer, Langland, and Hoccleve, in which the most 'prominent' idea linked to manliness was 'the idea of male courage and prowess in battle'.[13] Although Burrow acknowledges that these writers do not always reference the concept of manliness without irony or criticism, he also remarks that in other contexts words like *man*, *manly*, and *manhode* denote male virtues 'that Chaucer, Langland, and Hoccleve all, in their different ways, look for in knights and lords, hosts and householders, as representing common ideals of what a real Man should be like'.[14] That courage and prowess in battle are ranked so highly among these ideals suggests a widespread investment in masculine boldness and aggression, traits that, as we have seen, are often represented as masculine counterparts of (and potential threats to) female shamefastness.

Shamefastness, modesty, and humility were by no means off limits to men in medieval English literature. Middle English devotional writings encouraged men as well as women to cultivate a carefully gauged sense of shame in order to forestall the sin of pride.[15] Modesty was likewise considered appropriate to the practice of chivalry (which is very likely one reason for the emphasis on Sir Gawain's humility in the early fitts of *Sir Gawain and the Green Knight*).[16] In *The General Prologue* to *The Canterbury Tales*, for example, Chaucer describes the Knight as 'of his port as meeke as is a mayde. / He nevere yet no vileynye ne sayde / In al his lyf unto no maner wight. / He was a verray, parfit gentil knyght' (69–72). Following hard upon a long list of the many battles he has fought, the reference to the Knight's meekness and its likeness to that of a maiden stresses his ability to balance martial prowess with the courtesy expected of a knight.[17] But outside of such contexts, boldness is a quality that medieval texts also explicitly state distinguishes men from women, and manliness from womanly behaviour. This distinction comes to the fore in the words of the Host to the Clerk in the prologue to Chaucer's *Clerk's Tale*:

> 'Sire Clerk of Oxenford,' oure Hooste sayde,
> 'Ye ryde as coy and stille as dooth a mayde
> Were newe spoused, sittynge at the bord;
> This day ne herde I of youre tonge a word.
> ... For Goddes sake, as beth of bettre cheere!
> It is no tyme for to studien heere.

Telle us som myrie tale, by youre fey!
For what man that is entred in a pley,
He nedes moot unto the pley assente.'
(*The Clerk's Prologue* 1–11)

As I noted in the preceding chapter, the image conjured up by the Host's jibe is a familiar one of feminine shamefastness: a blushing bride, sitting silent at her husband's breakfast table for the first time, publicly visible for the first time after losing her virginity on her wedding night.[18] Here, the bride functions as a byword for the shamefastness that the Clerk is seen to be performing; he is acting 'as' or like a maid, rather than like a man. It is not the first time in *The Canterbury Tales* that the Host accuses the Clerk of shamefastness (in *The General Prologue* he instructs the Clerk to 'lat be youre shamefastnesse' (840)), but the choice of simile makes the feminization of the emotional disposition particularly pointed here. In and of itself, the Clerk's silence or timidity is not necessarily a sign of unmanliness; indeed, it was considered appropriate behaviour for a medieval clerk.[19] But what the Host recognizes as the Clerk's shamefast model of masculinity is not the kind of bold, outspoken masculinity the Host subscribes to. Instead, in the Host's eyes, the performance the Clerk offers the world is closer to the model of honourable shamefast femininity expected of new brides.

The Host's remarks are rendered even more cutting by the way that the Host himself is (like another pilgrim, the Monk) presented as a manly man:[20]

A semely man Oure Hooste was withalle
For to been a marchal in an halle.
A large man he was with eyen stepe—
A fairer burgeys was ther noon in Chepe—
Boold of his speche, and wys, and wel ytaught,
And of manhod hym lakkede right naught.
(*The General Prologue* 751–6)

Not only is the Host presented as a self-appointed arbiter of manliness in *The General Prologue*, but he is also presented as a kind of archetypal Man, one who 'lakkede right naught' of manly qualities.[21] 'Boold of his speche' and 'large', he displays none of the sensorimotor inhibitions of a timid, shamefast individual; in other words, as the Host's teasing of the Clerk reflects, he is the opposite of a coy young maiden. My intention is not to claim that Chaucer is presenting the Host as the ideal man, nor the Host's remarks to the Clerk as a more 'correct' construction of masculinity vs femininity, but I wish to stress the ways in which this episode is illustrative of a familiar binary that links masculinity with boldness and aggression, and femininity with shamefastness. This binary represents a widespread cultural and social practice, which is also an intrinsically emotional one.

This episode from *The Canterbury Tales* is also one with which Hoccleve may very well have been familiar. Scholars have already pointed out that Hoccleve seems to have modelled his own eulogies to Chaucer on Chaucer's praise of Petrarch in *The Clerk's Prologue* (31–56).[22] If Hoccleve found inspiration in the Clerk's references to Petrarch, it is possible that he also found the Clerk himself to be a useful model for the modesty that he wished to perform in relation to his fourteenth-century predecessor, and that the potentially gendered nature of that modesty was not lost on him.

Hoccleve's attitude towards and self-positioning in relation to concepts of manliness have proven difficult to pin down. Ruth Nissé has maintained that, particularly in the *Regiment of Princes* and the 'Address to Oldcastle', Hoccleve exhibits a powerful sense of nostalgia for a more masculine, martial England, and calls for a 'remasculinization' of England and English knighthood.[23] By contrast, Andrew Lynch has argued that Hoccleve's verse sets up 'a clerkly counter-discourse to the norms of chivalric masculinity' based on a 'sustained personal antipathy to violence' and war.[24] Knapp suggests that Hoccleve uses the *Letter of Cupid* to 'carve out a space from which to speak that would be identical to neither of the dominant types of masculine literary authority, the competing models of *chevalerie* and *clergie*'. He submits that, '[i]n his evasion of these models, Hoccleve is indebted both to the general example of Christine's feminized authorial voice and also to specific tactics she uses in her *Epistre*'.[25] In the discussion that follows, I will argue that what might at first seem confusing or inconsistent in Hoccleve's stance towards manliness may be ascribed to his investment in creating authorial personas for himself, personas that he is fully aware need bear no relation to his own beliefs or character. As I will show, in the *Letter of Cupid* Hoccleve articulates a particularly cynical perspective regarding the unreliability of appearances, one with profound implications for our interpretation of his own shamefast performances.

Hoccleve and gender: the *Letter of Cupid*

Much of the dispute concerning whatever feminist credentials Hoccleve might have has centred on the *Letter of Cupid*, his translation of Christine de Pizan's anti-misogynist *Epistre au dieu d'Amours*. Whereas Christine's poem is clearly a proto-feminist (or at least 'profeminine', to use the term preferred by Alcuin Blamires) condemnation of the various ways that male behaviour puts women and their reputations at risk, Hoccleve's Middle English translation-adaptation of the *Epistre* is more difficult to place.[26] Although Hoccleve retains (and even intermittently reinforces) some of Christine's arguments, his occasional slippages into satire result in a text that claims to advocate honourable women but which ultimately suggests that the behaviour of neither sex can necessarily be taken at face value.

Christine wrote the *Epistre au dieu d'Amours* in 1399. The text has sometimes been identified as the opening salvo in the *Querelle de la Rose*, the written debate between Christine and several French intellectuals concerning the perceived merit of the *Roman de la rose*, or its lack thereof (although Thelma Fenster notes that the debate did not begin for another two years after Christine composed the *Epistre*).[27] The poem certainly bears the hallmarks of Christine's objections to the *Roman de la rose*: in addition to scornfully referencing Jean de Meun and his text, the *Epistre* is deeply concerned with women's honour, with the various means by which men scheme to overcome female chastity or tarnish female reputations, and with defending women against spoken and written attacks.[28] Over more than 800 lines of verse, Christine's Cupid expresses his intention to redress the complaints he has received 'de toutes femmes generaument' ('[f]rom all of womankind'; 13):

> Des grans extors, des blames, des diffames,
> Des traÿsons, des oultrages tres griefs,
> Des faulcetez et de mains autres griefs
> Que chacun jour des desloyaulx reçoivent,
> Qui les blament, diffament, et deçoivent.
>
> (Of damage done, of blame and blemished name,
> And of betrayals, very grievous wrongs,
> Of falsehoods uttered, many other griefs,
> Endured each day from those disloyal men
> Who blame and shame, defame and deceive them.)
> (*Epistre au dieu d'Amours* 18–22)

As the women's complaint suggests, it is not simply their broken hearts that are at stake, but also, and even more urgently, their honour. Cupid intimates that women have singled out France as the chief home of men who deceive women with flattery, brag about their sexual exploits (whether or not they actually happened), and constantly defame women as wicked, lustful, and inconstant. He responds by chastising deceitful and gossiping men (whom he distinguishes from his own loyal followers), mocking and rebuking those men who defame women simply because they have had no success with them, and reminding his readers of women's many redeeming qualities, not the least of which is the fact that it was a woman who was chosen to bear the son of God. The *Epistre* repeatedly calls on men to cherish, honour, and defend women, and concludes by declaring that all those who do not will be punished at Cupid's command.

Written only three years after Christine's poem, Hoccleve's *Letter of Cupid* is probably best characterized as an abbreviated adaptation-translation of the *Epistre*.[29] Mary Carpenter Erler has gone so far as to declare that, 'for much of its length', the *Letter* is 'quite independent of Christine's work'.[30] Hoccleve's poem rearranges many of Christine's arguments, and inserts reflections on or expansions of those arguments.[31] In addition to these changes, Hoccleve introduces fluctuations in tone throughout his poem that destabilize the proto-feminist thrust of his source, and which have caused considerable scholarly debate as to his view of women. The poem has been used as evidence both by those who would describe the poet as a proto-feminist and by those who see him as inherently anti-feminist. Jerome Mitchell has contended that Hoccleve's *Letter of Cupid* 'is at least as feminist in outlook as its French source'.[32] Conversely, Jonathan Stavsky has suggested that, despite Hoccleve's quickness to translate the *Epistre au dieu d'Amours* (a poem written in defence of women), he attempts 'to ingratiate himself into a distinctly masculine literary coterie that was forming around Chaucer's legacy by imbuing the *Letter* with irony and ambivalence towards womankind'.[33] Diane Bornstein has offered one of the sharpest critiques of Hoccleve's *Letter*:

> The exaggerated defense that Cupid offers in support of women, the proverbial language used to comment on their behavior, the omission of actual and literary examples of the good deeds of women, and the omission or softening of Christine's criticism of disrespectful men and anti-feminist clerks all combine to undermine Christine's

argument and make the work more of a parody of feminism rather than a judicious, courtly defense of women.[34]

The question of precisely what attitude towards women is represented by Hoccleve's *Letter* seems to have been no less complicated for Hoccleve's contemporary readers, if Hoccleve's *Series* (1419–21) is anything to go by. In *Dialogue with a Friend*, one of the poems within the *Series*, Hoccleve's friend warns him that his translation of the *Epistre* has written 'so largeliche' of women (broadly; also, improperly and without restraint) 'That they been swart wrooth and ful euele apaid' (755–6).[35] Although Hoccleve acknowledges that 'doutelees sumwhat ther is therin / Þat sowneth but right smal to hir [women's] honour', he first defends himself by describing himself not as the 'auctour' but only as 'a reportour' of what others had already said (757–63). And even so, he complains,

> What world is this? How vndirstande am I?
> Looke in the same book. What stikith by?
> Whoso lookith aright therin may see
> Þat they me oghten haue in greet cheertee,
>
> And elles woot I neuere what is what.
> The book concludith for hem, is no nay[.]
> (*Dialogue with a Friend* 774–9)

Despite Hoccleve's protestations that the *Letter* 'concludith' in women's favour, he ends his *Dialogue* by resolving to write something that will make amends for his earlier poem.

Although the *Letter of Cupid* has been identified as both misogynist and proto-feminist since the century in which it was composed, its slipperiness prevents it from fitting neatly into either camp. Moreover, the way that Hoccleve destabilizes material that had, in Christine's hands, been earnestly wielded in the defence of women drives a wedge between the appearances of both men *and* women and the reality of their natures. This is in keeping with a theme expressed in the *Letter*'s opening stanzas, which muse upon the difficulty of seeing past appearances and manners to a man's character, the very same dilemma upon which later Middle English treatments of habit turn. In these lines, which appear to be original to Hoccleve, the poem warns that

> Ful hard is it to knowe a mannes herte,
> For outward may no man the truthe deeme,
> Whan word out of his mowth may ther noon sterte,

> But it sholde any wight by reson queeme.
> So is it seid of herte, it wolde seeme.
> O faithful womman, ful of innocence,
> Thou art betrayed by fals apparence.
>
> (*The Letter of Cupid*, 36–42)[36]

Appearances can be deceiving: this is one of the fundamental problems that underlie Middle English discussions of virtuous habits like female shamefastness, and consequently one of the reasons that women must practise and perfect that shamefastness so consistently. And as Hoccleve suggests here, it is impossible to know a man's heart merely by observing his speech or appearance. Notably, in this passage Hoccleve is concerned not with women's ability to deceive men, but with the ability of men to mislead women, 'ful of innocence', by means of 'fals apparence'. Indeed, even when men speak, their words can deceive women, who, 'meeued of pitee, / Weenyng al thyng wer as þat tho men seye, / Granten hem grace of hir benignitee' (43–5). Hoccleve notes that, after having won these women, such men abandon them as soon as they can find other willing women in town (50–5).

Whether or not one reads the reference to female innocence ironically, the problem of outward appearance versus the truth in one's heart is made explicit by the poem's emphasis on the unreliability of men's words, which can so easily lead women astray. Pitying women, '[w]eenyng al thyng wer as þat tho men seye' (44), grant men their affection only to discover that men do not keep their word ('[a] man, for al his ooth, is hard to leeue' (56)). Even worse, such men are eager to recount their exploits to their friends:

> And for þat euery fals man hath a make,
> As vnto euery wight is light to knowe,
> Whan this traitour the womman hath forsake
> He faste him speedith vnto his felowe.
> Til he be ther his herte is on a lowe.
> His fals deceit ne may him nat souffyse,
> But of his treson tellith al the wyse.
>
> (*The Letter of Cupid*, lines 57–63)

Hoccleve here captures the malicious pleasure such men take in bragging of their 'fals deceit' to one another.[37] The picture painted here recalls the warnings in the *Book of the Knight* concerning how men speak about women behind their backs, particularly when those women have granted men their favour too quickly.[38] Hoccleve points out that such talk brings honour neither to the speaker nor to the woman he boasts of having duped:

> Is this a fair auant, is this honour,
> A man himself to accuse and diffame?
> Now is it good confesse him a traitour,
> And brynge a wommoman to a sclaundrous name,
> And telle how he hir body hath doon shame?
> No worsship may he thus to him conquere,
> But ful greet repreef vnto him and here.
>
> To her, nay, yit was it no repreef,
> For al for pitee was it þat shee wroghte,
> But he þat breewid hath al this mescheef,
> Þat spak so fair and falsly inward thoghte,
> His be the shame, as it by reson oghte,
> And vnto her thank perpetuel,
> Þat in a neede helpe can so wel.
>
> (*The Letter of Cupid*, lines 64–77)

Here, Hoccleve, turns what in Christine's text is an exasperated outburst against male gossip ('Dieux, quieulx parleurs!'; 'Good God, what gossips!'; *Epistre au dieu d'Amours* 163) into a half-serious, half-satirical meditation on what women deserve from the men upon whom they take pity.[39] To not only deceive women in the first place, but then to go on to boast about having done so, brings a man only shame. The second stanza here makes a rather feeble attempt to recuperate the honour of the woman who takes pity on such a man, claiming that '[t]o her, nay, yit was it no repreef', but rather to him to 'spak so fair and falsly inward thoghte' (and who owes her 'thank perpetuel' for having taken pity on him). Yet even as these lines point to the disjunction between outward appearance and inner reality as the reason why men are to blame in such situations, the very same disjunction threatens to undermine the praise of apparently 'pitying' women, who may, after all, merely *seem* virtuous and innocent. Indeed, the suggestion that these deceptive men should be thanking the women they've deceived seems to invite such eyebrow-raising by taking the defence of women a stretch too far. Shouldn't truly honourable, shamefast women be capable of withstanding even these demands for 'pity'?

The final line of the above stanzas executes one of several satirical turns in Hoccleve's adaptation of Christine's material. Christine's *Epistre* likewise warns men that slandering women is dishonourable behaviour, and that they should honour the women who are always ready '[a] corps d'omme souëvement nourrir' ('[g]ently to serve the creature needs of man'), both '[a] son naistrë, au vivre, et au mourir' ('[a]t birth, in life, and at his time of death'; *Epistre au dieu d'Amours* 175–6). Drawing on familiar models of virtuous female pity, Christine paints a picture of woman as mother, sustainer, and nurse throughout a man's life, constantly '[a] son besoing piteuse et secourable' ('piteous and helpful to him in his need'; *Epistre au dieu d'Amours* 172 (my translation)) and therefore as worthy to be honoured by man.[40] While Hoccleve echoes much of Christine's argument, he narrows the field from all of womankind to only those women who have been duped and slandered by the men in question. Hoccleve's proposal that duplicitous men should *thank* their female victims who 'in a neede helpe can so wel' seems to play upon the association of the Middle English word *nede* with the sexual 'needs' and desires of the human body, an association that in turn transforms Christine's elevation of womankind into the suggestion that a true gentleman always says 'thanks for last night' to the women he's seduced.[41]

The slipperiness of Hoccleve's tone extends to his condemnation of the ways that men slander women when their attempts at deceit are not met with success:

To his felawe anothir wrecche seith,
'Thow fisshist fair. Shee þat hath thee fyrid,
Is fals and inconstant and hath no feith.
Shee for the rode of folk is so desyrid,
And as an hors fro day to day is hyrid,
That whan thow twynnest from hir conpaignie
Anothir comth, and blerid is thyn ye.

'Now prike on faste and ryde thy iourneye.
Whyl thow art ther, shee, behynde thy bak,
So liberal is shee can no wight withseye,
But qwikly of anothir take a snak,
For so the wommen faren, al the pak.
Whoso hem trustith, hangid moot he be!
Ay they desiren chaunge and noueltee.'

Wherof procedith this but of enuye?
For he himself here ne wynne may,
Repreef of here he spekth, and villenye,
As mannes labbyng tonge is wont alway.
Thus sundry men ful often make assay

> For to destourbe folk in sundry wyse,
> For they may nat accheuen hir empryse.
>
> (*The Letter of Cupid*, lines 99–119)

These stanzas draw heavily on Christine's *Epistre*, which also remarks on how men will slander women both by claiming to have bedded them (even if they haven't) and by teasing other men about the likely infidelity of their alleged lovers.[42] However, Hoccleve expands upon his source: here, instead of confining themselves to the specific cases of their female victims, men exchange commonplace misogynist warnings that *all* women are inconstant and insatiable, likely to take up with another man as soon as the first's back is turned ('so the wommen faren, al the pak'). Hoccleve also introduces the image of such a woman as a 'hors' (surely also punning on the Middle English word *hor*) who 'fro day to day is hyrid', a comparison that is particularly degrading in its implication that anyone with enough cash may 'ride' her.[43] Such a woman is reduced not merely to the level of a prostitute, but to that of an animal for hire. What the *Letter* had previously cast as an example of virtuous female pity is here a form of gross sexual liberality: this imaginary woman is so generous with her favours (and perhaps so excessive in her desires) that 'shee can no wight withseye'. Shamefastness has no hold on her; indeed, she is so voracious that she takes a 'snak' ('bite') from another as soon as a man's back is turned.[44] Like the *Epistre*, Hoccleve's poem quickly declares such vicious attacks to be nothing more than the words of sore losers, men who 'may nat accheuen hir empryse', but Hoccleve's expansions on its source material make it difficult to take him at his word.

Hoccleve's slippery treatment of Christine's arguments transforms her case for women into a text that (mis)leads in multiple directions. In this respect, it lives up to Hoccleve's warning that it is hard 'to knowe a mannes herte': it is certainly difficult to know Hoccleve's. He treats Christine's poem like a costume to be altered and worn while parading around in half-serious, half-mocking fashion; he restates her arguments and then riffs on them, occasionally leading to suggestions that most women would likely find far from flattering. That he is aware of what is at stake for women who are seduced and deceived is abundantly clear; that he takes these stakes seriously is not clear at all. The result is a reappropriation of a proto-feminist text for his own literary gain.[45] In the final section of this chapter,

Shamefast Hoccleve and shameless craving 173

I will show how, in *La Male Regle*, Hoccleve aims to create a misleading appearance for himself when he reappropriates female shamefastness for his financial gain. By mimicking the language and postures that would have been closely identified with the shamefastness women were encouraged to practise, Hoccleve turns a pathetic and entertaining account of his youthful misrule into a petition for payment.

Practising shamelessness

Hoccleve professes his inadequacy with great regularity, whether in relation to the achievements of his predecessor Chaucer, when addressing current or potential patrons, or when speaking of his own personal failings and setbacks. In the final section of this chapter, I will consider a poem that has often been cited as a striking example of Hoccleve's characteristic (if self-interested) self-effacement: *La Male Regle*. While this poem might at first seem to exemplify what Knapp has referred to as Hoccleve's poetics of embarrassment, the language of shamefastness/-lessness to which Hoccleve resorts enables him to call up the gendered associations of these concepts, and to redeploy them to suit his needs. Hoccleve masquerades behind the shamefast manners women were encouraged to learn in order to present himself as someone who must now learn to be shameless in order to get paid.

The title *La Male Regle* is open to multiple interpretations, including 'The Misrule' (*mal regle*); the misruled purse or 'bagge' (*male*); and the regulated male (*mâle reglé*). All of these meanings converge in the content of Hoccleve's poem, which comprises both his account of how, in his youth, he painted the town red with nights of overeating, copious drinking with tavern wenches, and lavish spending, as well as Hoccleve's concluding request for financial support. Although the poem's opening stanza addresses itself to the '[e]rthely god ... helthe' (8), Hoccleve's actual target seems to have been England's Treasurer, Lord Thomas Fourneval, whose name is mentioned in the poem's concluding petition to 'Health', whom Hoccleve asks to remind 'my lord the Fourneval' (417) to pay the annuity due him.

The form of *La Male Regle* fuses penitential lyric with bureaucratic petition – appropriately enough, since, with the exception of an apparent breakdown in the second decade of the fifteenth century, Hoccleve was for his entire working life a clerk of the Privy Seal.[46]

La Male Regle opens with a lament for Hoccleve's current 'sickness' (poverty), and then describes his youthful 'riot' or misrule, using Hoccleve's own susceptibility to flattery as a bridge to discussing flattery and misrule at court before veering back to Hoccleve's own situation. It closes with an expression of the poet's resolution to live moderately, and with a roundabout petition to Fourneval. The main business of *La Male Regle* is therefore twofold: (1) to 'confess' the youthful waywardness of the author, and (2) to appeal for 'coyn' to purchase the 'medecyne' (446) that will relieve the sickness resulting from his youthful misbehaviour.[47]

The question of how Hoccleve's poetic petitions should be interpreted (and whether he was ever really *that* strapped for cash) has long been debated.[48] Whatever Hoccleve's actual circumstances, his repeated, earnest professions of shamefastness in *La Male Regle* contribute significantly to the comedy of his chagrined references to his misbehaviour and his penury. After spending the first quarter of the poem complaining of his daily suffering (25) and lamenting the 'folie and inprudence' (62) of his youth, Hoccleve gives details of his misbehaviour, which he prefaces with *occupatio*, claiming that he can barely speak of them. Thus begins perhaps the most famous passage of the poem:

> I dar nat telle how þat the fressh repeir
> Of Venus femel lusty children deer
> Þat so goodly, so shaply wer, and feir,
> And so plesant of port and of maneere,
> And feede cowden al a world with cheere,
> And of atyr passyngly wel byseye,
> At Poules Heed me maden ofte appeere,
> To talke of mirthe and to disporte and pleye.
> (*La Male Regle* 137–44)[49]

Of course, part of the entertainment here is the fact that, although Hoccleve claims that he 'dar nat telle', he *does* tell – at least a little bit. He then goes on to recount how frequently he bought 'sweet wyn' and 'wafres thikke' for his 'likerous' company at the tavern, in the hope that he might 'wynne loue and thank' (145–52). One can easily envisage Hoccleve as the eager outsider plying female companions with food and drink in order to win their favour, a picture that is by turns amusing, pathetic, and sympathetic. One might also read this as Hoccleve's effort to be seen as *manli*, insofar as he is able: magnanimous and generous, if not bold. The theme of manliness resurfaces in the following stanza, in which we learn just how far Hoccleve was able to take matters with his female companions (the answer seems to be: not very far at all):

> Of loues aart yit touchid I no deel.
> I cowde nat, and eek it was no neede.
> Had I a kus, I was content ful weel,
> Bettre than I wolde han be with the deede.
> Theron can I but smal, it is no dreede.
> Whan þat men speke of it in my presence
> For shame I wexe as reed as is the gleede.
> Now wole I torne ageyn to my sentence.
> (*La Male Regle* 153–60)

For any reader hoping for a juicy account of Hoccleve's escapades, this stanza is, to say the least, a bitter disappointment. Hoccleve claims he did not participate at all in what he euphemistically terms 'loues aart'. This is apparently because he 'cowde nat' or didn't know how to, but also because he was more content with just a kiss than he would have been 'with the deede'. Knapp observes that we might see 'a suggestion of physical impotence' in these lines, but the emphasis in this stanza is just as much on Hoccleve's purported innocence ('[t]heron can I but smal') as it is on his inability to perform.[50] Perhaps the most comical image Hoccleve presents us with is that of him blushing 'as reed as is the gleede' (glowing coal) when men so much as speak of 'the deede' in his presence. His sense of shame is apparently so intense that he cannot even listen to other men recounting their own sexual exploits (which they apparently do, as Christine would have expected), let alone perpetrate any himself. Like the Host's joking comparison of the Clerk to a newly wedded maiden, Hoccleve's description of his own blush activates the feminine associations of that shamefast brand of clerkly masculinity. While men blush for any number of reasons in medieval English literature, the fact that Hoccleve describes himself as blushing at his companions' sexual boasts aligns that blush with maidenly shamefastness.[51]

As *La Male Regle* makes clear, it is not only in relation to 'loues aart' that Hoccleve does not 'dare' – he presents himself as paralysed by shamefastness, an 'enfeebled persona' (to use Sarah Tolmie's phrase).[52] This becomes increasingly apparent as Hoccleve's confession continues. Immediately after describing his uneventful visits to the taverns, Hoccleve criticizes those who 'hauntith tauerne of custume', drink too much, and 'speke of folk amis', for, as he ruefully notes, heavy drinkers seldom speak well of their fellow man (161–6).[53] In this case, Hoccleve's shamefastness has one advantage:

> But oon auantage in this cas I haue:
> I was so ferd with any man to fighte,
> Cloos kepte I me. No man durste I depraue
> But rownyngly I spak, nothyng on highte.
> And yit my wil was good, if þat I mighte,
> For lettynge of my manly cowardyse,
> Þat ay of strokes impressid the wighte,
> So þat I durste medlyn in no wyse.
>
> (*La Male Regle* 169–76)

Just as he claims to be too overcome with shame even to speak about or listen to stories of sexual encounters, he claims to be so afraid at the prospect of physical confrontation that he can barely speak at all, and then only 'rownyngly' (in whispers). The phrase 'manly cowardyse' is particularly suggestive; given Hoccleve's professed inability to perform (or speak of) 'loues aart', the phrase seems to function both as an oxymoronic comment on his lack of manhood and as another example of his shamefastness. The phrase has also been interpreted in other ways; Lynch, for instance, has argued that 'the rhetoric of "fear"' is one element of an overall anti-war stance that may be observed in Hoccleve's works.[54] I would argue that here Hoccleve intends his 'cowardyse' to stand as confirmation of his persona's overwhelming embodied timidity. Indeed, in the poem's subsequent stanzas, Hoccleve claims to be so timid that he cannot even stand up to *himself*:

> Whan I departe sholde and go my way
> Hoom to the Priuee Seel, so wowed me
> Hete and vnlust and superfluitee
> To walke vnto the brigge and take a boot
> þat nat durste I contrarie hem all three,
> But dide as þat they stired me, God woot.
>
> (*La Male Regle* 187–92)

Hoccleve's wording here is noteworthy: instead of describing himself as too tired or overwhelmed, he explains that he 'durste nat' 'contrarie' his own inclination to take a boat home. Particularly in the wake of his alleged blushing in response to other men's sexual bragging, this passage enhances Hoccleve's self-representation as a comically shamefast man – that is, as a man who is comically unmanly.

Unable even to defy his own 'hete', 'vnlust', and 'superfluitee', Hoccleve understandably can neither 'stele' to support himself 'ne begge also for shame' (367–8). Hoccleve transforms the embodied shamefastness that would be taken as a sign of virtue in a woman into a performance that he showcases as proof of his unmanly weakness, his excuse for not having begged more effectively. Hoccleve uses the first 350 lines of his 448-line poem to present proof that he is a 'shamefast man' persistently overcome by debilitating timidity.

This extended self-portrait is not an innocent prelude to Hoccleve's conclusion: it is what makes his concluding petition work. Conventionally enough, Hoccleve begins his petition by claiming to be 'contryt and of ful repentance' (403–5) for having displeased the 'god' Health with his misbehauiour. However, Hoccleve follows up his request for 'mercy' and 'grace' by reminding 'Health' somewhat pointedly that '[i]t sit a god been of his grace free' (407), a remarkably direct statement for someone so avowedly timid. But while he begs Health to urge 'my lord the Fourneval' (417–18) to pay him, he insists that, 'I dar nat speke a word of ferne yeer, / So is my spir[i]t symple and sore agast' (423–4). Once more, claiming that he 'dare not' speak allows Hoccleve to do precisely that: to lay claim to all that is owed him under the guise of a man too stricken by shamefastness to do so.

At this point, we arrive at the passage with which I opened this chapter, after which only two stanzas remain in *La Male Regle*. It is here that Hoccleve *finally* professes himself willing to learn from the example of the 'shameless crauour'. Indeed, the preceding narrative of his shamefastness is now cited as proof that sham*eless*ness is something that Hoccleve urgently needs to learn how to practise. Hoccleve has adopted a pose modelled on the behaviours associated with women's shamefast practice in order to inspire pity, amusement, and receptiveness to his upcoming petition. He then presents that petition as his first attempt to cast off his former shamefastness and emulate the boldness of beggars:

> The prouerbe is, the doumb man no lond getith.
> Whoso nat spekith and with neede is bete,
> And thurgh arghnesse his owne self forgetith,
> No wondir, thogh anothir him forgete.
> Neede hath no law, as þat the clerkes trete,
> And thus to craue artith me my neede,
> And right wole eek þat I me entremete,
> For þat I axe is due, as God me speede.
>
> (*La Male Regle* 433–40)

After his extended performance of unmanly shamefastness, Hoccleve concludes by playing the part of a man forced by his circumstances to speak up: 'to craue artith me my neede'.[55] Hoccleve justifies his newfound bold directness with a proverb ('the doumb man no lond getith'), a strategy he later revisits in his *Regiment of Princes*.[56] But in the wake of Hoccleve's extended recounting and performance of his shamefastness, this stanza seems to hold out a moment of relief for both author and reader: *finally*, Hoccleve can ask for what is due; *finally*, we come to the heart of the matter:

> And þat that due is, thy magnificence
> Shameth to werne, as þat I byleeue.
> As I seide, reewe on myn inpotence,
> Þat likly am to sterue yit or eeue,
> But if thow in this wyse me releeue.
> By coyn, I gete may swich medecyne
> As may myn hurtes all, þat me greeue,
> Exyle cleene, and voide me of pyne.
>
> (*La Male Regle* 433–48)

In this stanza, Hoccleve professes himself to be staging his *début* as a 'shamelees crauour'. Most remarkable of all, that *début* hinges on the shamefast performance he has just delivered: he presents his 'inpotence' as a spectacle that ought to move his addressee to pity. We might be inclined to read this as an example of what Tolmie has described as Hoccleve's tendency toward 'a poetics of extortion' in his petitionary writing.[57] But I would suggest that what we are seeing here is Hoccleve's appeal to Fourneval's status as a *manli* man, one who is justly generous to those who are dependent on him. Indeed, Hoccleve's reference to Fourneval's 'magnificence' (grandeur, splendour, or wealth, but also great-mindedness) deliberately invokes the very models of manliness Hoccleve claims he tried and failed to emulate during his misrule, and frames Hoccleve's petition as an opportunity for Fourneval to perform his own manhood: by taking pity on Hoccleve and offering him payment, Fourneval can prove himself to be a manly man.

***

Perhaps more than any other Middle English author, Hoccleve is a poet of personas. His poems are filled with reflections on how he must appear to others or how others are speaking of him, debates with interlocutors concerning how he should present himself to those around him, and accounts of his efforts to control how others see him. *La Male Regle* stands as one of many examples of the ways in which Hoccleve makes texts by 'staging his life', presenting himself as an *un*manly man who is neither in a position to spend money as lavishly (if foolishly) as he would like nor bold enough to demand payment.[58] This particular mode of self-representation relies to a great extent on the association of shamefastness with femininity, and on the idea of shamefastness as a practice: having been thus far handicapped by his maidenly timidity, Hoccleve claims he must now learn to practise shamelessness in order to survive. But whereas shamefastness might be viewed as a sign of virtuous fortitude ('fastness') in a woman, Hoccleve flaunts it as an accessory to his misrule, one that demonstrates his inadequacy and ineptitude as a 'manly' man. In this respect, Hoccleve makes comedy out of what is ordinarily a source of uncertainty and anxiety in relation to the female practice of shamefastness. As this book has shown, women's honour resides to a large extent in their ability to effectively practise and perform the behaviour associated with shamefastness, but their honour is also called into question when that behaviour is deemed to be too practised, too studied, performed merely to counterfeit virtue. The stakes are different for Hoccleve, whose staging of his own shamefastness would be viewed as deceitful in a woman, but can be viewed as simply disarming in a mendicant male poet. Whereas women must be careful to be artless in their shamefastness, Hoccleve is free to make his avowed shamefastness into art, a performance that in turn 'artith' him to practise the shamelessness that will enable him to beg effectively.

Notes

1 *La Male Regle de T. Hoccleue*, in Thomas Hoccleve, *'My Compleinte' and Other Poems*, ed. Roger Ellis (Exeter: University of Exeter Press, 2001), pp. 64–76. All citations from this text are taken from this edition and cited above by line number.
2 *MED*, s. v. *shamefast(e, importune*.
3 *MED*, s. v. *shameless*. The word can also mean 'blameless', which is perhaps another meaning Hoccleve is drawing on: just as he should not fear disgrace in making his request, neither should his addressee find his request disgraceful.
4 Knapp, 'Thomas Hoccleve', p. 196.
5 Although the word *embarrassment* has been in use in English since the mid seventeenth century (when it referred to a hindrance or some kind of trouble), its currently more familiar definition of 'emotional

or social discomfort' has only been traced back to the mid eighteenth century (see *OED*, s. v. *embarrassment*).
6 Knapp, 'Thomas Hoccleve', p. 196.
7 *OED*, s. v. *embarrassment*. As Stearns points out in his history of shame, although shame and embarrassment are 'neighbouring' emotions, embarrassment 'is simply less intense and noticeably less durable than shame, and is more quickly forgotten by the same token ... In contrast, shame often lasts longer – up to forty-eight hours – and its sensations can be revived through community pressure, again, in contrast to embarrassment' (although he also notes that this distinction does not explain why 'one person might be merely embarrassed by a miscue that would cause others even in the same culture and certainly between two cultures, to feel shame'); *Shame*, p. 3. Scheff, 'Shame and the Social Bond', suggests that embarrassment is essentially the contemporary equivalent of shame.
8 Hoccleve's professions of authorial inadequacy have most frequently been cited as examples of the conventional modesty topos so common to much of medieval literature. Reading Hoccleve's self-effacing declarations in this light, Amy N. Vines has described them as 'insincere performances', although she suggests that, in his *Series*, Hoccleve experiments with 'an alternate way of participating in the patronage system' ('The Rehabilitation of Patronage in Hoccleve's *Series*', *Digital Philology* 2 (2013), 201–21 (p. 203)). Robert J. Meyer-Lee connects Hoccleve's distinctive poetics of subjection to the poet's self-representation as a beggar (*Poets and Power from Chaucer to Wyatt* (Cambridge: Cambridge University Press, 2007; repr. 2009), pp. 88–123; see also his 'Laureates and Beggars in Fifteenth-Century English Poetry: The Case of George Ashby', *Speculum* 79 (2004), 688–726 (pp. 697–9)). Most famously, David Lawton identified Hoccleve's use of the modesty topos with the 'extravagant guise of dullness' adopted by authors of fifteenth-century English literature; 'Dullness and the Fifteenth Century', *ELH* 54 (1987), 761–99 (p. 764).
9 This is not to say that critics have ignored the ways in which Hoccleve might be presenting himself as effeminate; Andrew Lynch, for example, argues that Hoccleve adopts 'a feminized voice of personal experience' (as opposed to 'clerkly and manly authority') in his confessions in *La Male Regle*, in which he presents himself as cowardly and 'sexually timid' ('"Manly Cowardyse": Thomas Hoccleve's Peace Strategy', *Medium Ævum* 73 (2004), 306–23 (p. 307)), although Lynch does not connect this self-representation to the discourse of shamefastness/-lessness Hoccleve employs.
10 *MED*, s. v. *manli*. Among the many recent studies of medieval masculinity are Isabel Davis, *Writing Masculinity in the Later Middle Ages* (Cambridge: Cambridge University Press, 2007); Crocker, *Chaucer's Visions of Manhood*; Clare Lees, *Medieval Masculinities: Regarding Men in the Middle Ages* (Minneapolis, MN: University of

Minnesota Press, 2004); Neal, *The Masculine Self*; Jeffrey Jerome Cohen and Bonnie Wheeler (eds), *Becoming Male in the Middle Ages* (New York, NY: Garland, 1997); Pugh and Marzec (eds), *Men and Masculinities*; and Karras, *From Boys to Men*.
11 Thomas Hoccleve, *The Regiment of Princes*, ed. by Charles R. Blyth, TEAMS (Kalamazoo, MI: The Medieval Institute, 1999), http://d.lib. rochester.edu/teams/text/blyth-hoccleve-regiment-of-princes [accessed 13 April 2018], with the section in question taking up lines 3900–4004 (3906: 'Yee moot of kynde to manhode enclyne'). See also J. A. Burrow's discussion of these lines: 'Versions of "Manliness" in the Poetry of Chaucer, Langland, and Hoccleve', *The Chaucer Review* 47 (2013), 337–42 (p. 341).
12 Crocker, *Chaucer's Visions of Manhood*, pp. 9–11, 158 n. 31; see also *MED*, s. v. *manhed(e*.
13 Burrow, 'Versions of Manliness', p. 337. Burrow notes that terms such as *manhood*, *man*, and *manly* 'did not belong to the official moral discourse of medieval England, as displayed in the many sermons and treatises of the time. Rather, they represent judgments passed in common parlance, at a level of everyday usage for which the evidence is more scanty.'
14 Burrow, 'Versions of Manliness', p. 342.
15 See, for example, Walter Hilton's *The Scale of Perfection*, which urges readers who feel any 'stirynge of pride' to 'doo al the shame that thou mai therto' (*The Scale of Perfection*, 89, fol. 80v). Valerie Allen has argued that 'Christian morality valorizes shame ... because it seeks to compensate for and protect against the spiritual frailty that is our universal condition' ('Waxing Red', pp. 194–5).
16 *Sir Gawain and the Green Knight* is almost certainly the Middle English text that has been most thoroughly mined by studies of shame in medieval English literature. See, for example, Allen, 'Waxing Red', p. 192 (in which *Sir Gawain* is the first text to be cited, after the Wycliffite Bible); Stephanie Trigg, '"Shamed be...": Historicizing Shame in Medieval and Early Modern Courtly Ritual', *Exemplaria* 19 (2007), 67–89; Burrow, 'Honour and Shame'; Kindrick, 'Gawain's Ethics'; and Wasserman, 'Honor and Shame'.
17 See *MED*, s. v. *mek*, which may refer to someone who is 'gentle', 'humble', or 'submissive'.
18 See also *The Merchant's Tale*, which notes that after her wedding night, May '[h]eeld hire chambre unto the fourthe day, / As usage is of wyves for the beste' (1859–61), as well as Ussery, 'How Old Is Chaucer's Clerk?', which notes examples of this sort of bashful behaviour being attributed to clerks in medieval sources.
19 See Ussery, 'How Old Is Chaucer's Clerk?'; and Mann, *Chaucer and Medieval Estates Satire*, pp. 76, 243 n. 112.
20 Chaucer describes the Monk as a 'manly man' in *The General Prologue* to *The Canterbury Tales* (167). On the masculinity of Chaucer's monk,

see Michael D. Sharp, 'Reading Chaucer's "Manly man": The Trouble with Masculinity in the *Monk's Prologue* and *Tale*', in Beidler (ed.), *Masculinities in Chaucer*, pp. 173–85. On the Monk's and Host's competing notions of manliness, see Kurt Olsson, 'Grammar, Manhood, and Tears: The Curiosity of Chaucer's Monk', *Modern Philology* 76 (1978), 1–17.

21 This is not to say that the Host is necessarily invulnerable to mockery or criticism. John J. McGavin, for example, has suggested that the Host's 'sexual comparison' of the Clerk to a newly wedded maiden 'may reflect more on the speaker, Harry Bailley, showing his need to subordinate, and control by sexual comedy, the learning which he fears in the Clerk' (*Chaucer and Dissimilarity: Literary Comparisons in Chaucer and Other Late-Medieval Writing* (Madison, WI: Fairleigh Dickinson University Presses, 2000), p. 103). Mark Allen has suggested that the Host embodies a specifically bourgeois masculinity ('Mirth and Bourgeois Masculinity in Chaucer's Host', in Beidler (ed.), *Masculinities in Chaucer*, pp. 9–19).

22 See, for example, Scanlon, *Narrative, Authority, and Power*, p. 312; William Kuskin, 'The Erasure of Labor: Hoccleve, Caxton, and the Information Age', in Kellie Robertson and Michael Uebel (eds), *The Middle Ages at Work* (New York, NY: Palgrave, 2004), pp. 229–60 (pp. 234–35); Jerome Mitchell, *Thomas Hoccleve: A Study in Early Fifteenth-Century English Poetic* (Urbana, IL: University of Illinois Press, 1968), pp. 110–15.

23 Ruth Nissé, '"Oure Fadres Olde and Modres": Gender, Heresy, and Hoccleve's Literary Politics', *Studies in the Age of Chaucer* 21 (1999), 275–99 (pp. 298–9).

24 Lynch, '"Manly Cowardyse"', p. 307.

25 Ethan Knapp, *The Bureaucratic Muse: Thomas Hoccleve and the Literature of Late Medieval England* (University Park, PA: The Pennsylvania State University Press, 2001), p. 50.

26 For Blamires's discussion of the distinctions between terms such as 'profeminine', 'proto-feminist', 'profeminist', and 'feminist', see Alcuin Blamires, *The Case for Women in Medieval Culture* (Oxford: Clarendon Press, 1997), pp. 11–12.

27 See pp. 3–4 of Thelma S. Fenster's introduction to her edition and translation of Christine de Pizan's poems in *Poems of Cupid, God of Love: Christine de Pizan's Epistre au dieu d'Amours and Dit de la Rose, Thomas Hoccleve's The Letter of Cupid*, ed. Thelma S. Fenster and Mary Carpenter Erler (Leiden: Brill, 1990). As Fenster points out (p. 8), this identification of the *Epistre* with the *Querelle* may be seen in the first printed edition containing the *Epistre*, which retitled the poem '*Contre Roman de la Rose*'. The documents connected with the *Querelle* are edited in Christine de Pizan, Jean Gerson, Jean de Montreuil, Gontier and Pierre Col, *Le Débat sur le Roman de la Rose*; translations of

28 See Christine de Pizan, *Epistre au dieu d'Amours*, in *Poems of Cupid, God of Love*, pp. 34–75. All citations from this poem are taken from this edition, as are all English translations, except where noted; both are cited by line number above.

many these materials may be found in *'La Querelle de la Rose'*. I discuss some of Christine's objections to the *Roman de la rose* in Chapter 3, pp. 99–100.

29 Meyer-Lee suggests that, in choosing to translate Christine's *Epistre au dieu d'Amours*, Hoccleve 'chose to translate what was at that time likely Christine's best-known poem, hoping, we may suppose, to build a career as court poet on the model of Chaucer, whose reworking of contemporary French poetry marked the first phase of his career' (*Poets and Power*, p. 95).

30 See p. 159 of Mary Carpenter Erler's introduction to her edition of the *Letter of Cupid* in *Poems of Cupid, God of Love*.

31 *Ibid.*, p. 160.

32 Mitchell, *Thomas Hoccleve*, p. 53.

33 Jonathan Stavsky, 'Hoccleve's Take on Chaucer and Christine de Pizan: Gender, Authorship, and Intertextuality in the *Epistre au dieu d'Amours*, the *Letter of Cupid*, and the *Series*', *Philological Quarterly* 93 (2014), 435–60 (p. 436).

34 Diane Bornstein, 'Anti-feminism in Hoccleve's Translation of Christine de Pizan's *Epistre au dieu d'amours*', *ELN* 19 (1981), 7–14 (p. 14).

35 *MED*, s. v. *largeli(e*. Hoccleve, *A dialoge*, in *'My Compleinte' and Other Poems*, pp. 131–55.

36 *L'epistre de Cupide [The Letter of Cupid]*, in Thomas Hoccleve, *'My Compleinte' and Other Poems*, pp. 93–107. All citations from this text are taken from this edition and cited above by line number. On the contrast between outward appearance and inner truth as a theme in Hoccleve's verse, see Stephen Medcalf, *The Later Middle Ages* (London: Holmes & Meier, 1981), pp. 123–40.

37 Hoccleve here seems to be adapting Christine's account of how false male lovers enjoy bragging about their supposed conquests to their companions: 'Ne leur souffit ce qu'ainsi les traÿssent, / Ains ont compains de leur male aliance; / Si n'y remaint ne fait ne couvenance / Qui ne soit dit l'un a l'autre' ('Not satisfied with just betraying them [the ladies in question], / They've partners in their nasty liaison, / No deed performed or promise made can fail / To be retold around'; *Epistre au dieu d'Amours* 108–11).

38 See discussion in Chapter 2, pp. 78–9.

39 As I discuss in this book's afterword, at this point in her poem Christine argues that men are destroying women's honour when they should be defending it (*Epistre au dieu d'Amours*, 163–7).

40 Fenster translates this line as 'When he's in need, she understands and helps'.

41 *MED*, s. v. *ned(e* (n. (1)).
42 'La rigolent l'un l'autre, et par reprouches / S'entredient: "Je sçay bien de tes fais: / Tele t'aimë, et tu le jolis fais / Pour seue amour, mais plusieurs y ont part; / Tu es receu quant un autre s'en part!" / La diffament les envïeux la belle / Sans achoison ne nul mal savoir d'elle' ('They rib each other, and by means of taunts / Exchanged, they say: "I know what you're about: / Your sweetheart's such a one, you play the beau / To have her love; but many get their part, / For you are greeted as another parts!" / The lady's slandered by the envious, / Who have no cause, who know no ill of her'; *Epistre au dieu d'Amours*, 126–32).
43 *MED*, s. v. *hor(e* (n. 2): a whore.
44 *MED*, s. v. *snacche*.
45 Hoccleve's poem may not have had quite the impact on his career that he was likely hoping for. On the early reception of the *Letter of Cupid*, see Rory G. Critten, 'Imagining the Author in Late Medieval England and France: The Transmission and Reception of Christine de Pizan's *Epistre au dieu d'Amours* and Thomas Hoccleve's *Letter of Cupid*', *Studies in Philology* 112 (2015), 680–97.
46 For a biography of Hoccleve, see J. A. Burrow, *Thomas Hoccleve*, Authors of the Middle Ages, 4 (Aldershot: Variorum, 1994). Knapp traces the connections between Hoccleve's work as a clerk of the Privy Seal and his poetic writings in *The Bureaucratic Muse*; see also Ethan Knapp, 'Bureaucratic Identity and the Construction of the Self in Hoccleve's *Formulary* and *La Male Regle*', *Speculum* 74 (1999), 357–76; and Knapp's account of Hoccleve's career in Knapp, 'Thomas Hoccleve'). On Hoccleve's breakdown, see R. Lawes, 'Psychological Disorder and the Autobiographical Impulse in Julian of Norwich, Margery Kempe, and Thomas Hoccleve', in Denis Renevey and Christiania Whitehead (eds), *Writing Religious Women: Female Spiritual and Textual Practices in Late Medieval England* (Cardiff: University of Wales Press, 2000), pp. 217–43.
47 While the extent to which we should take Hoccleve's autobiographical references at face value remains debatable, it seems reasonable to assume that we are meant to read the 'I' as Hoccleve in *La Male Regle*. Not only does Hoccleve address himself at one point ('Bewaar, Hoccleue, I rede thee therfore, / And to a mene reule thow thee dresse' (351–2)), but in the autograph manuscript held in the Huntington Library (MS HM 111), Hoccleve prefaces the poem with a colophon reading, 'Cy ensuyt la male regle de T. Hoccleue' (Nicholas Perkins, 'Thomas Hoccleve, *La Male Regle*', in Peter Brown (ed.), *A Companion to Medieval English Literature and Culture, c. 1350–1500* (Chichester: John Wiley & Sons Ltd, 2009), pp. 585–603 (p. 597)).
48 As D. C. Greetham has pointed out, '[Hoccleve] does, admittedly, make so much of his own life in his poetry that critics are inevitably tempted to allow such ostensibly autobiographical statements more

value and credit than they might otherwise receive in a more reticent author' ('Self-Referential Artifacts: Hoccleve's Persona as a Literary Device', *Modern Philology* 86 (1989), 242–51 (p. 244)). For a sceptical treatment of Hoccleve's frequent references to his poverty, see, for example, A. Compton Reeves, 'Thomas Hoccleve, Bureaucrat', *Medievalia et Humanistica* n. s. 5 (1974), 201–14. In the case of *La Male Regle*, Perkins has argued that, 'Hoccleve's 'lack of "mesure", once taken at face value by critics, is a strategic waywardness intended to ambush his audience into pity for the speaker's naivety, and to accept his problematic claim that his diseased body and purse can be cured by the "medecyne" of money' ('Thomas Hoccleve', pp. 445–6)).

49 Some, like Tolmie, have suggested that we shouldn't take Hoccleve's denials here at face value (they could merely be an extension of the preceding *occupatio*; see Sarah Tolmie, 'The Professional: Thomas Hoccleve', *Studies in the Age of Chaucer* 29 (2007), 341–73 (pp. 368–70)). I would argue that, whether they are 'genuine' or not, recounting them as he does enables Hoccleve to take up a mantle of shamefastness.

50 Knapp, *The Bureaucratic Muse*, p. 40.

51 On blushing and gender in medieval literature and culture, see Allen, 'Waxing Red'.

52 Tolmie, 'The Professional', p. 347.

53 On the association of drinking with 'unlicensed speech' in the late fourteenth and early fifteenth centuries, see Nicholas Perkins, *Hoccleve's Regiment of Princes: Counsel and Constraint* (Cambridge: D. S. Brewer, 2001), pp. 8–9.

54 Lynch, '"Manly Cowardyse"', 317.

55 *MED*, s. v. *arten* (v.): to confine or compel.

56 The passage in question occurs at lines 248–59 of the *Regiment of Princes*: 'Thow seest al day the begger is releeved / That sit and beggith blynd, crookid, and lame, / And why? For he ne lettith for no shame / His harmes and his povert to bywreye / To folk as they goon by him in the weye. / For and he keepe him cloos and holde his pees, / And nat out shewe how seek he inward is, /He may al day so sitten helpelees; / And, sone myn, althogh he fare amis / That hydeth so, God woot, the wyt is his; / But this begger his hurtes wole nat stele; / He wole telle al and more – he can naght hele.' For variations on the proverb 'Seldom gets a dumb man land', see Whiting, *Proverbs, Sentences, and Proverbial Phrases*, M276. (Notably, at line 1807 of the *Regiment*, Hoccleve also claims that his overwhelming shame prevents him from begging: 'To begge, shame is myn impediment'.)

57 See Sarah Tolmie, 'The *priue scilence* of Thomas Hoccleve', *Studies in the Age of Chaucer* 22 (2000), 281–309 (p. 299).

58 Perkins, 'Thomas Hoccleve', p. 597.

Afterword

In the literature of medieval England, being an honourable woman is a matter of emotional practice and performance – it requires learning how to feel in a specific way. While certain emotions like pity or compassion might be closely associated with ideals of womanhood or womanliness, a very different, more specific emotional disposition was required to preserve female honour: hypervigilance against the possibility of shame. In their engagement with this concept, and with its possibilities and complications, medieval English texts reveal a keen interest in what Peter N. Stearns has described as 'the *anticipation* aspect that extends shaming's social utility' by making a virtue out of one's efforts to avoid shame.[1] This alertness to shame might also be seen as a kind of *proneness* to shame, a hypersensitivity and predisposition to the experience of shame. Thus, somewhat ironically, a woman like Chaucer's Virginia who might be described as '[s]hamefast ... in maydens shamefastnesse' (*The Physician's Tale* 55) was simultaneously more likely to try to avoid shame and also more predisposed to feel it.

Like Latin and various European vernaculars, Middle English had a term for this complex of ideas connected to averseness to shame: *shamefastness*. Although the word itself might describe the fear of any kind of general disgrace, when applied to women it referred more specifically to aversion to sexual shame – that is, shame that might attach to a woman deemed to be unchaste of body, mind, or habit. A woman's ability to secure her chastity (and therefore her honour) corresponded directly to her ability to practise shamefastness. Medieval English texts point to the various ways that women might seek to hone or mobilize their inward sense of shame by reflecting on what they would lose if disgraced (as the *Book of the Knight of La Tour Landry* proposes) and by inhibiting their motor impulses. They also highlight how a woman's honour depended on her ability to perform her virtue before others. The

Afterword

practice of shamefastness thus comprises a mix of interiorizing and exteriorizing habits that seem to pull against one another: on the one hand, women must be engaged in a constant kind of covering or withdrawal prompted by the fear of shame; on the other hand, these gestures are framed as a kind of exhibition of shamefastness, conspicuous evidence of inner virtue. After all, how else could one be sure of a woman's honour? Even physical examinations of a woman's body could not be expected to yield unquestionable proof of an unmarried woman's virtue (and, as the prologues to the *Sickness of Women* and *The Knowing of Woman's Kind in Childing* warn, such examinations might themselves pose risks to a woman's reputation or feelings). Yet the very persistence with which medieval conduct literature exhorts women to practise shamefastness is driven by the sense that female honour is a slippery thing, impossible to be certain of, and therefore impossible to prove.

As anti-feminist portrayals of female shamefastness make clear, the slipperiness of female honour was frequently linked to the perceived slipperiness and cunning of women themselves. In these contexts, the very nature of shamefastness as something to be practised is cause for suspicion: if recognizably shamefast conduct was something that could be learned and (in theory) perfected, it could also be counterfeited. Thus, in texts like the *Roman de la rose* female shamefastness is both an obstacle and a red herring, vilified as a performance meant simply to keep up appearances rather than to genuinely discourage male lovers. Indeed, as Lydgate's depiction of Medea suggests, women might even deliberately adopt the guise of shamefastness in order to conceal the lust in their hearts. In the *Roman de la rose*, this kind of logic leads *Ami* to suggest that male lovers should count women's protests, bashfulness, and standoffishness as 'not worth a husk' (*ne prisiez tretout une escorce*); they should recognize such behaviour as mere feigning, take what they desire 'by force' (*tout a force*), and thereby prove their manhood.[2] This is not to say that medieval literature presents this idea as unproblematic; Chaucer, for example, points towards its troubling implications in *Troilus and Criseyde* and most particularly in his narratives concerning Virginia and Lucrece, which seem to define female honour in relation to what Rachel Warburton has termed 'rapability', a woman's potential for violation by men.[3] Those texts that do meditate on the disturbing way in which female shamefastness and masculine aggression seem to be mutually constitutive and antithetical raise the issue without engaging with the question of what solutions might exist to the problem, although the problem itself is suggestive of certain solutions.

One solution would be the regulation of male behaviour. The narratives of Virginia and Lucrece are particularly stark examples of misdirected masculine aggression, but Christine de Pizan's discussion of how men slander women in the *Epistre au dieu d'Amours* suggests that even in contexts where women are not threatened by actual violence, men would do well to direct their energies towards a worthier goal:

> Dieux, quieulx parleurs! Dieux, quelles assemblees,
> Ou les honneurs des dames sont emblees!
> Et quel prouffit vient d'ainsi diffamer
> A ceulx mesmes qui se deussent armer
> Pour les garder et leur honneur deffendre?
>
> (Good God, what gossips! God, what gatherings,
> At which a lady's honor's stripped away!
> And where, in slander, is the profit for
> The very men who ought to arm themselves
> To guard the ladies and defend their name?)
> (Christine de Pizan, *Epistre au dieu d'Amours*, lines 163–7)

Rather than wasting time sullying the good name of innocent women, Christine argues, men should be prepared to take up arms to keep women safe from threats to their persons and to their reputations. This is the courtly ideal to which Troilus adheres in *Troilus and Criseyde*, and is held out as a more honourable path for men to choose. As the prologues of *Knowing* and *Sickness* likewise contend, it is only 'vncurteys men' who pose a threat to women's honour.

As Hoccleve's *La Male Regle* makes clear, the relationship of medieval men to female shamefastness was not restricted to the binary of aggressor or defender in the literature of later medieval England. A quasi-feminine shamefastness was also something that some categories of men (in Hoccleve's case, clerks) might be expected to exhibit; but Hoccleve demonstrates that, taken more literally, the femininity of clerkly shamefastness could also function as a kind of masquerade, a persona to be inhabited when adopting a pose of comical subjection before one's social and economic superiors. *La Male Regle* effectively lifts the gestures and conventions associated with female shamefastness from the social and cultural contexts in which that shamefastness normally operates, redeploying them in order to amuse Hoccleve's reader and ensure the success of his

Afterword

petition for payment. Only a male author could get away with treating female shamefastness so lightly, and the manoeuvre stands as a reminder of the extent to which both the fetishization of female chastity and shamefastness and so many of the medieval texts that reinforce it are male-authored. But it is also a reminder of the varied ways in which texts can be connected to emotional practice. Certain genres like affective meditation can function as 'intimate scripts', as McNamer has shown, whereas other literary and non-literary texts can be used in emotional practices, functioning (in Scheer's phrase) as 'templates of language and gesture', 'mediators of social norms', and as sources 'not only for discourses and implicit orders of knowledge, but also for emotives and other emotional practices'.[4] But literary texts also provide opportunities for experimentation and play with emotional practices, and for imagining how the interior processes associated with emotions might work (for instance, by giving them 'a body, a face, and a personality' in a personified figure within an allegorical narrative).[5] At the same time, reading across literary and non-literary texts can help us better understand the ways in which texts of all kinds contribute to the construction of emotional practices and the social and cultural values to which they are attached.

***

Shamefastness faded out of the English language sometime after the sixteenth century, when through an apparent etymological misinterpretation it was transformed into *shamefacedness*.[6] And yet I doubt that anyone could deny that traces of the link between shamefastness and female honour are with us still. When I began researching this link nearly a decade ago, the subject of 'honour killings' was making headlines in the United Kingdom, a painful reminder that violence is still viewed by some as the surest way to safeguard female chastity and familial honour. When I finished conducting the research for this book, the retrial of Bill Cosby for sexual assault was concluding in the United States, having gained new momentum in the wake of the #MeToo movement and the revelations concerning Harvey Weinstein's abuse and assault of women throughout his career. But the fetishization of female shamefastness may also be legible in what some might characterize as less sensational traumas – perhaps most obviously, in the questions inevitably asked of so many female victims of harassment or assault (what were you wearing? how much did you drink? did you lead him on? why didn't you leave?). Such questions hinge on the expectation that it is almost entirely women's responsibility to keep themselves from being harassed and assaulted: they must avoid the wrong sorts of places, the wrong sort of sex, the wrong amount of alcohol, the wrong sort of clothes, lest they be blamed for their own violation. Most insidiously of all, this logic can convince women that, if they experience unwanted sexual advances or intercourse, they have no one but themselves to blame. Indeed, if this book offers one potential refinement to Warburton's disturbing idea of 'rapability', it is that the shamefast practices that make women 'rapable' in fact make them 'rape-*worthy*'. It is not simply that these practices make women so attractive that men must have sex with them by any means necessary (the crude sense in which the term is sometimes used today), but that they make women establish their worth in terms that in turn establish them as violable subjects.[7] Shamefast women are thus women who are not only deserving of honour, but who are also deserving of recognition as victims when they are assaulted. The link between this idea of women's worth and the idea of what women deserve filters into a statement made by Stephanie Clifford, the adult film star professionally known as Stormy Daniels, who claimed to have had an affair with Donald Trump; when describing her alleged sexual encounter with Trump, Clifford declared, 'I was not a victim … I had it coming for making a bad decision for going to someone's room alone and I just heard the voice in my head, "Well, you put yourself in a bad situation and bad things happen, so you deserve this."'[8]

Just as I would not claim that female shamefastness is an emotional practice exclusive to medieval England or the Middle Ages, I would not claim that Clifford's statement is evidence that she or we are somehow 'stuck' in a medieval mindset concerning women's honour. But there are resonances here that should not be overlooked. A more wide-ranging study of the links between gender and shame would make the history of these resonances much clearer, and would also, I would venture, reveal the connections between the fetishization of female shamefastness I have sketched out here and contemporary expectations of female behaviour (many of which are shaped by a sense that women are somehow better suited to what has been termed 'emotional labour').[9] By attending to the practice of shamefastness in medieval texts, we can better understand the role played by emotional practices in constructing gendered identities in both the past and the present day, as well as how those emotional practices help to shape our sense of what honour entails.

Notes

1 Stearns, *Shame*, p. 8 (original emphasis).
2 Guillaume de Lorris and Jean de Meun, *Roman de la rose*, lines 7648–64; *Romance of the Rose*, pp. 144–5.
3 Warburton, 'Reading Rape in Chaucer'.
4 Scheer, 'Are Emotions a Kind of Practice', p. 218.
5 Flannery, 'Personification and Embodied Emotional Practice', p. 352.
6 *OED*, s. v. *shamefast, shamefaced*.
7 See, for example, the first two entries for *rapeworthy* listed on UrbanDictionary.com. Perhaps even more revoltingly, the third proposed definition is as an adjective describing a woman who is 'both sexually attractive and evil. Men know she doesn't deserve sexual pleasure, so they want to punish and degrade her by fucking her against her will.'
8 'Stormy Daniels Describes Her Alleged Affair With Donald Trump' (correspondent Anderson Cooper), www.cbsnews.com/news/stormy-daniels-describes-her-alleged-affair-with-donald-trump-60-minutes-interview/ [accessed 17 April 2018].
9 Arlie Hochschild is largely responsible for coining the term 'emotional labour', which describes the ability not only 'to display emotion at work, but to "really" feel it' (Jan Plamper, *The History of Emotions: An Introduction*, trans. by Keith Tribe (Oxford: Oxford University Press, 2015), p. 119); see Arlie Russell Hochschild, *The Managed Heart: Commercialization of Human Feeling* (Berkeley, CA: University of California Press, 1983); and Arlie Russell Hochschild, 'Emotion Work, Feelings Rules, and Social Structure', *American Journal of Sociology* 85 (1979), 551–75.

Bibliography

Primary sources

The Anglo-Norman Dictionary, www.anglo-norman.net/gate/ [accessed 22 April 2014].

Anglo-Saxon and Old English Vocabularies, Vol. 1: Vocabularies, ed. Thomas Wright and Richard Paul Wülcker (London: Trübner & Co., 1884).

Apollodorus' Library and Hyginus' Fabulae: Two Handbooks of Greek Mythology, trans. R. Scott Smith and Stephen M. Trzaskoma (Indianapolis, IN: Hackett Publishing Company, 2007).

Aquinas, Thomas, *Summa Theologiae: Volume 19, The Emotions: 1a2ae. 22–30*, ed. Eric D'Arcy (Cambridge: Cambridge University Press, 2006).

_____, *Summa Theologiae: Volume 20, Pleasure: 1a2ae. 31–39*, ed. Eric D'Arcy (Cambridge: Cambridge University Press, 2006).

_____, *Summa Theologiae: Volume 21, Fear and Anger: 1a2ae. 40–48*, ed. J. P. Reid (Cambridge: Cambridge University Press, 2006).

_____, *Summa Theologiae: Volume 43, Temperance: 2a2ae. 141–154*, ed. Thomas Gilby (Cambridge: Cambridge University Press, 2006).

Aristotle, *The Nicomachean Ethics*, trans. H. Rackham, The Loeb Classical Library (Cambridge, MA: Harvard University Press, 1926).

Augustine, *The City of God Against the Pagans, Vol. I: Books I–III*, trans. George E. McCracken, The Loeb Classical Library (Cambridge, MA: Harvard University Press, 1957).

_____, *The City of God Against the Pagans, Vol. IV: Books XII–XV*, trans. Philip Levine, The Loeb Classical Library (Cambridge, MA: Harvard University Press, 1966).

Certaine Worthye Manuscript Poems of Great Antiquitie, ed. J. S[tow?] (London: R. Robinson f. R. D[exter], 1597), STC 21499.

Chaucer, Geoffrey, *The Riverside Chaucer*, ed. Larry D. Benson et al., 3rd edn (Oxford: Oxford University Press, 2008).

_____, *The workes of Geffray Chaucer newly printed, with dyuers workes whiche were neuer in print before*, ed. William Thynne (London: Thomas Godfray, 1532), STC 5068.

Christine de Pizan, Jean Gerson, Jean de Montreuil, Gontier and Pierre Col, *Le Débat sur le Roman de la Rose*, ed. Eric Hicks (Paris: Editions Honoré Champion, 1977).

_____, *'La Querelle de la Rose': Letters and Documents*, ed. Joseph L. Baird and John R. Kane (Chapel Hill, NC: North Carolina Studies in the Romance Languages and Literatures, 1978).

Dante Alighieri, *Dante Alighieri Convivio*, ed. F. B. Ageno, 3 vols (Florence: Le Lettere, 1995).

_____, *Il Convivio (The Banquet)*, trans. R. H. Lansing (New York, NY: Garland, 1990).

Dictionnaire du Moyen Français, www.atilf.fr/dmf/ [accessed 22 April 2014].

Geoffrey de La Tour Landry, *The Book of the Knight of La Tour Landry*, ed. Thomas Wright, EETS OS 33 (London: N. Trübner & Co., 1868).

_____, *Le livre du Chevalier de la Tour Landry pour l'enseignement de ses filles*, ed. Anatole de Montaiglon (Paris: P. Jannet, 1854).

The Good Wife Taught Her Daughter, The Good Wyfe Wold a Pylgremage, The Thewis of Gud Women, ed. Tauno E. Mustanoja (Helsinki: Suomaleisen Kirjallisuuden Seuran, 1948).

Gower, John, *The Complete Works of John Gower: The French Works*, ed. G. C. Macaulay, EETS ES 81 (Oxford: Clarendon Press, 1899).

_____, *The English Works of John Gower*, ed. G. C. Macaulay, EETS ES 81, 82 (Oxford: Oxford University Press, 1900; repr. 1969).

_____, *John Gower: Confessio Amantis, Book 7*, ed. Russell Peck, TEAMS (Kalamazoo, MI: Medieval Institute Publications, 2004), available online, http://d.lib.rochester.edu/teams/text/peck-gower-confessio-amantis-book-7 [accessed 10 April 2018].

Guido delle Colonne, *Historia destructionis Troiae*, ed. Nathaniel Edward Griffin (Cambridge, MA: The Mediaeval Academy of America, 1936).

_____, *Historia destructionis Troiae*, trans. Mary Elizabeth Meek (Bloomington, IN: Indiana University Press, 1974).

Guillaume de Lorris and Jean de Meun, *Le Roman de la Rose*, ed. Felix Lecoy, Les Classiques Français du Moyen Âge 92, 95, and 98, 3 vols (Paris: Librairie Honoré Champion, 1965, 1966, 1970).

_____, *The Romance of the Rose*, trans. Charles Dahlberg, 3rd edn (Princeton, NJ: Princeton University Press, 1995).

_____, *The Romaunt of the Rose and Le Roman de la Rose: A Parallel-Text Edition*, ed. Ronald Sutherland (Berkeley, CA: University of California Press, 1967).

Guy de Chauliac, *The Middle English Translation of Guy de Chauliac's Treatise on Ulcers, Part I, Text: Book IV of the Great Surgery*, ed. Björn Wallner (Stockholm: Almqvist & Wiksell International, 1982).

Hilton, Walter, *The Scale of Perfection*, ed. Thomas H. Bestul, TEAMS (Kalamazoo, MI: Medieval Institute Publications, 2000).

Hoccleve, Thomas, *'My Compleinte' and Other Poems*, ed. Roger Ellis (Exeter: University of Exeter Press, 2001).

_____, *The Regiment of Princes*, ed. Charles R. Blyth, TEAMS (Kalamazoo, MI: The Medieval Institute, 1999), available online, http://d.lib.rochester.edu/teams/text/blyth-hoccleve-regiment-of-princes [accessed 13 April 2018].

The Holy Bible, Containing the Old and New Testaments with the Apocryphal Books, in the Earlist English Versions made from the Latin Vulgate by John Wycliffe and his Followers, ed. Josiah Forshall and Frederic Madden (Oxford: Oxford University Press, 1850).

How the Good Wife Taught Her Daughter, in *Codex Ashmole 61: A Compilation of Popular Middle English Verse*, ed. George Shuffelton, TEAMS (Kalamazoo, MI: The Medieval Institute, 2008), available online, http://d.lib.rochester.edu/teams/text/shuffelton-codex-ashmole-61-how-the-good-wife-taught-her-daughter [accessed 26 March 2018].

How the Wise Man Taught His Son, in *Codex Ashmole 61: A Compilation of Popular Middle English Verse*, ed. George Shuffelton, TEAMS (Kalamazoo, MI: The Medieval Institute, 2008), available online, http://d.lib.rochester.edu/teams/text/shuffelton-codex-ashmole-61-how-the-wise-man-taught-his-son [accessed 27 March 2018].

Hyginus, *Fabulae*, ed. Peter K. Marshall (Stuttgart: Teubner, 1993).

Idley, Peter, *Peter Idley's Instructions to His Son*, ed. Charlotte d'Evelyn (Boston, MA: D. C. Heath and Co., 1935; repr. 1975).

St Jerome, *Adversus Jovinianum*, in *Patrologiae cursus completus, series latina, vol. 23*, ed. J.-P. Migne (Paris, 1844–64), columns 211–338.

The Knowing of Woman's Kind in Childing: A Middle English Version of Material Derived from the Trotula and Other Sources, ed. Alexandra Barratt (Turnhout: Brepols, 2001).

Latin Vulgate and Douay-Rheims Bible, available online, www.latinvulgate.com/lv/verse.aspx?t=1&b=15&c=2 [accessed 21 March 2017].

Livy, *History of Rome, Vol. 1, Books 1–2*, trans. B. O. Foster, The Loeb Classical Library (Cambridge, MA: William Heinemann, Ltd, 1967).

———, *History of Rome, Vol. 2, Books 3–4*, trans. B. O. Foster, The Loeb Classical Library (Cambridge, MA: William Heinemann, Ltd, 1967).

Lydgate, John, *A Critical Edition of John Lydgate's Life of Our Lady*, ed. Joseph A. Lauritis (Pittsburgh, PA: Duquesne University, 1961).

———, *Lydgate's Fall of Princes*, ed. Henry Bergen, EETS ES, 121, 122, 123, 124, 4 vols (London: Oxford University Press, 1924–27).

———, *Lydgate's Troy Book*, ed. Henry Bergen, EETS ES, 97, 103, 106, and 126 (London: Kegan Paul, Trench, Trübner & Co., 1906; repr. 1996 of EETS ES, 97, 103, and 106 as one volume).

Mannyng, Robert, *Robert of Brunne's 'Handlyng Synne'*, ed. Frederick J. Furnivall, EETS OS 119 (London: Kegan Paul, Trench, Trübner & Co., Ltd., 1901).

Marie de France, *The Fables of Marie de France: An English Translation*, ed. and trans. Mary Lou Martin (Birmingham, AL: Summa Publications, Inc., 1984).

Medieval Conduct Literature: An Anthology of Vernacular Guides to Behaviour for Youths, with English Translations, ed. Mark D. Johnston and Kathleen M. Ashley (Toronto: University of Toronto Press, 2009).

The Medieval Craft of Memory: An Anthology of Texts and Pictures, ed. Mary Carruthers and Jan M. Ziolkowski (Philadelphia, PA: The University of Pennsylvania Press, 2002).

Medieval English Prose for Women: Selections from the Katherine Group and Ancrene Wisse, ed. Bella Millett and Jocelyn Wogan-Browne (Oxford: Clarendon Press, 1990).

Monica H. Green and Linne R. Mooney, *The Sickness of Women*, in M. Teresa Tavormina (ed.), *Sex, Aging, and Death in a Medieval Medical Compendium: Trinity College Cambridge MS R.14.52, Its Texts, Language, and Scribe*, 2 vols (Tempe, AZ: Arizona Center for Medical and Renaissance Studies, 2006), pp. 485–568.

The N-Town Plays, ed. Douglas Sugano, TEAMS (Kalamazoo, MI: The Medieval Institute, 2007), available online, http://d.lib.rochester.edu/teams/text/sugano-n-town-plays-play-15-nativity [accessed 17 November 2016].

Ovid, *Fasti*, trans. J. G. Frazer, rev. G. P. Goold, The Loeb Classical Library, 6 vols (Cambridge, MA: Harvard University Press, 1989).

Pecock, Reginald, *The Folewer to the Donet*, ed. E. V. Hitchcock, EETS OS 164 (London: Oxford University Press, 1924).

Poems of Cupid, God of Love: Christine de Pizan's Epistre au dieu d'Amours and Dit de la Rose, Thomas Hoccleve's The Letter of Cupid, ed. Thelma S. Fenster and Mary Carpenter Erler (Leiden: Brill, 1990).

Promptorium Parvulorum sive Clericorum, Dictionarius Anglo-Latinus Princeps, ed. A. Way, Camden Society 25, 54, 89, 3 vols (London: Camden Society, 1843–65).

Proverbs of Hendyng, ed. Susanna Greer Fein, in *The Complete Harley 2253 Manuscript*, Volume 3, ed. and trans. Susanna Greer Fein, trans. David Raybin and Jan Ziolkowski, TEAMS (Kalamazoo, MI: The Medieval Institute, 2015), available online, http://d.lib.rochester.edu/teams/text/fein-harley2253-volume-3-article-89 [accessed 27 March 2018].

Prudentius, *Prudentius I*, trans. H. J. Thomson, The Loeb Classical Library (Cambridge, MA: Harvard University Press, 1949).

Salutati, Coluccio, *Declamatio Lucretiae*, ed. Stephanie H. Jed, in Stephanie H. Jed, in *Chaste Thinking: The Rape of Lucretia and the Birth of Humanism* (Bloomington, IN: Indiana University Press, 1989), pp. 133–52.

Selections from English Wycliffite Writings, ed. Anne Hudson (Cambridge: Cambridge University Press, 1978).

Smith, William, and John Lockwood, *Chambers Murray Latin-English Dictionary* (Edinburgh: Chambers, 1933; repr. 2001).

Trevisa, John, *On the Properties of Things: John Trevisa's Translation of Bartholomaeus Anglicus De proprietatibus rerum. A Critical Text*, ed. M. C. Seymour et al., 3 vols (Oxford: Oxford University Press, 1975).

The Trotula: A Medieval Compendium of Women's Medicine, ed. and trans. Monica H. Green (Philadelphia, PA: The University of Pennsylvania Press, 2001).

Whiting, Bartlett Jere, *Proverbs, Sentences, and Proverbial Phrases from English Writings Mainly Before 1500* (Cambridge, MA: The Belknap Press, 1968).
Woman Defamed and Woman Defended: An Anthology of Medieval Texts, ed. Alcuin Blamires, with Karen Pratt and C. W. Marx (Oxford: Clarendon Press, 1992).
Women's Writing in Middle English: An Annotated Anthology, ed. Alexandra Barratt, 2nd edn (London: Routledge, 2006).
Wyclif, John, *Select English Works of John Wyclif*, ed. Thomas Arnold (Oxford: Clarendon Press, 1871).
Yonge, James, *The Gouernaunce of Prynces*, in *Three Prose Versions of the Secreta Secretorum*, ed. Robert Steele, EETS ES, 74 (London: Kegan Paul, Trench, Trübner & Co., 1898; repr. 1996), 121–248.

Secondary sources

Ahmed, Sara, *The Cultural Politics of Emotion* (Edinburgh: Edinburgh University Press, 2004; repr. 2010).
Allen, Mark, 'Mirth and Bourgeois Masculinity in Chaucer's Host', in Peter G. Beidler (ed.), *Masculinities in Chaucer: Approaches to Maleness in the Canterbury Tales and Troilus and Criseyde* (Cambridge: D. S. Brewer, 1998), pp. 9–19.
Allen, Valerie, 'Waxing Red: Shame and the Body, Shame and the Soul', in Lisa Perfetti (ed.), *The Representation of Women's Emotions in Medieval and Early Modern Culture* (Gainesville, FL: University Press of Florida, 2005), pp. 191–210.
Arnold, John H., 'The Labour of Continence: Masculinity and Clerical Virginity', in Anke Bernau, Ruth Evans, and Sarah Salih (eds), *Medieval Virginities* (Toronto: University of Toronto Press, 2003), pp. 102–18.
Ashley, Kathleen, 'The *Miroir des Bonnes Femmes*: Not for Women Only?', in Kathleen Ashley and Robert L. A. Clark (eds), *Medieval Conduct* (Minneapolis, MN: University of Minnesota Press, 2001), pp. 86–105.
Ashley, Kathleen, and Robert L. A. Clark, 'Introduction: Medieval Conduct: Texts, Theories, Practices', in Kathleen Ashley and Robert L. A. Clark (eds), *Medieval Conduct* (Minneapolis, MN: University of Minnesota Press, 2001), pp. ix–xx.
Ashley, Kathleen, and Robert L. A. Clark (eds), *Medieval Conduct* (Minneapolis, MI: University of Minnesota Press, 2001).
Axton, Richard, 'Gower – Chaucer's Heir?', in Ruth Morse and Barry Windeatt (eds), *Chaucer Traditions: Studies in Honour of Derek Brewer* (Cambridge: Cambridge University Press, 2009), pp. 21–38.
Baker, Denise, 'Chaucer and Moral Philosophy: The Virtuous Women of *The Canterbury Tales*', *Medium Aevum* 60 (1991), 241–56.

Barratt, Alexandra, 'Introduction to the First Edition (1992)', in *Women's Writing in Middle English: An Annotated Anthology*, ed. Alexandra Barratt, 2nd edn (London: Routledge, 2006), pp. 1–19.

Bates, Laura, *Everyday Sexism* (London: Simon & Schuster, 2014).

Beidler, Peter G. (ed.), *Masculinities in Chaucer: Approaches to Maleness in the Canterbury Tales and Troilus and Criseyde* (Cambridge: D. S. Brewer, 1998).

Benson, C. David, *The History of Troy in Middle English Literature: Guido delle Colonne's "Historia destructionis Troiae" in Medieval England* (Cambridge: D. S. Brewer, 1980).

_____, 'Prudence, Othea, and Lydgate's Death of Hector', *American Benedictine Review* 26 (1975), 115–23.

Bernau, Anke, *Virgins: A Cultural History* (London: Granta, 2007).

Bernau, Anke, Ruth Evans, and Sarah Salih (eds), *Medieval Virginities* (Toronto: University of Toronto Press, 2003).

Blamires, Alcuin, *The Case for Women in Medieval Culture* (Oxford: Clarendon Press, 1997).

_____, *Chaucer, Ethics, and Gender* (Oxford: Oxford University Press, 2006).

_____, 'Chaucer's Revaluation of Chivalric Honor', *Mediaevalia* 5 (1979), 245–69.

Bloch, R. Howard, 'Chaucer's Maiden's Head: "The Physician's Tale" and the Poetics of Virginity', *Representations* 28 (1989), 113–34.

Bolens, Guillemette, *Le style des gestes: Corporéité et kinésie dans le récit littéraire* (Lausanne: Bibliothèque d'histoire de la médecine et de la santé, 2008).

_____, *The Style of Gestures: Embodiment and Cognition in Literary Narrative* (Baltimore, MA: The Johns Hopkins University Press, 2012).

Bonavia, T., and J. Brox-Ponce 'Shame in Decision Making Under Risk Conditions: Understanding the Effect of Transparency', *PLoS ONE* 13 (2018), e0191990, https://doi.org/10.1371/journal.pone.0191990 [accessed 19 April 2018].

Boquet, Damien, 'Introduction: La vergogne historique: éthique d'une émotion sociale', *Rives Méditerranéennes* 31, special issue on *Histoire de la vergogne* (2008), http://rives.revues.org/2763 [accessed 22 April 2014].

Boquet, Damien (ed.), *Histoire de la vergogne*, special issue of *Rives Méditerranéennes* (31 (2008)).

Boquet, Damien, and Piroska Nagy, *Sensible Moyen Âge: Une histoire des émotions dans l'Occident* (Paris: Seuil, 2015).

Bornstein, Diane, 'Anti-feminism in Thomas Hoccleve's Translation of Christine de Pizan's *Epistre au dieu d'amours*', *ELN* 19 (1981), 7–14.

Bott, Robin L., '"O, keep me from their worse than killing lust": Ideologies of Rape and Mutilation in Chaucer's *Physician's Tale* and Shakespeare's *Titus Andronicus*', in Elizabeth Robertson and Christine M. Rose (eds), *Representing Rape in Medieval and Early Modern Literature* (New York, NY: Palgrave Macmillan, 2001), pp. 189–211.

Bourdieu, Pierre, *Outline of a Theory of Practice*, trans. R. Nice (Cambridge: Cambridge University Press, 1977; repr. 1987).

Bowers, John M., 'Rival Poets: Gower's *Confessio* and Chaucer's *Legend of Good Women*', in Elisabeth Dutton with John Hines and R. F. Yeager (eds), *John Gower, Trilingual Poet: Language, Translation, and Tradition* (Cambridge: D. S. Brewer, 2010), pp. 276–87.

Breen, Katharine, *Imagining an English Reading Public, 1150–1400* (Cambridge: Cambridge University Press, 2010).

Brewer, Derek, 'Honour in Chaucer', in *Tradition and Innovation in Chaucer* (London: Macmillan Press, 1982; repr. 1983), pp. 89–109.

Brockes, Emma, 'Me Too founder Tarana Burke: "You have to use your privilege to serve other people"', *The Guardian* (15 January 2018), www.theguardian.com/world/2018/jan/15/me-too-founder-tarana-burke-women-sexual-assault [accessed online 24 February 2018].

Brown, Brené, *I Thought It Was Just Me (But It Isn't): Making the Journey from 'What Will People Think?' to 'I am Enough'* (New York, NY: Avery, 2008).

_____, 'The power of vulnerability', talk delivered at TEDxHouston (June 2010), www.ted.com/talks/brene_brown_on_vulnerability?referrer=playlist-the_most_popular_talks_of_all [accessed 18 April 2018].

Brown, Jr., Emerson, 'What is Chaucer Doing with the Physician and His Tale?', *Philological Quarterly* 60 (1981), 129–49.

Brusendorff, Aage, *The Chaucer Tradition*, 2nd edn (Oxford: Clarendon Press, 1967).

Burger, Glenn, *Conduct Becoming: Good Wives and Husbands in the Later Middle Ages* (Philadelphia, PA: University of Pennsylvania Press, 2018).

_____, '"Pite renneth soone in gentil herte": Ugly Feelings and Gendered Conduct in Chaucer's *Legend of Good Women*', *The Chaucer Review* 52 (2017), 66–84.

Burrow, J. A., 'Honour and Shame in *Sir Gawain and the Green Knight*', in *Essays on Medieval Literature* (Oxford: Clarendon Press, 1984), pp. 117–31.

_____, *Thomas Hoccleve*, Authors of the Middle Ages, 4 (Aldershot: Variorum, 1994).

_____, 'Versions of "Manliness" in the Poetry of Chaucer, Langland, and Hoccleve', *The Chaucer Review* 47 (2013), 337–42.

Burrus, Virginia, *Saving Shame: Martyrs, Saints, and Other Abject Subjects* (Philadelphia, PA: University of Pennsylvania Press, 2008).

Bynum, Caroline Walker, 'The Female Body and Medieval Religious Practice in the Later Middle Ages', in Michel Feher, with Ramona Naddaf and Nadia Tazi (eds), *Fragments for a History of the Human Body* (New York, NY: Zone Books, 1989), pp. 181–238.

Callan, Norman, '"Thyn Owne Book": A Note on Chaucer, Gower, and Ovid', *Review of English Studies* n. s. 22 (1946), 269–81.

Carruthers, Mary, *The Book of Memory: A Study of Memory in Medieval Culture*, 2nd edn (Cambridge: Cambridge University Press, 2008; repr. 2011).
_____, *The Craft of Thought: Meditation, Rhetoric, and the Making of Images, 400–1200* (Cambridge: Cambridge University Press, 1998; repr. 2008).
Christoph, Siegfried, 'Honor, Shame and Gender', in Friedrich Wolfzettel (ed.), *Arthurian Romance and Gender/Masculin/Féminin dans le roman arthurien medieval/Geschlechterrollen im mittelalterlichen Artusroman: Selected Proceedings of the XVIIth International Arthurian Congress*, Internationale Forschungen zur Allgemeinen und Vergleichenden Literaturwissenschaft 10 (Amsterdam: Rodopi, 1995), pp. 26–33.
Cohen, Jeffrey Jerome, and Bonnie Wheeler (eds), *Becoming Male in the Middle Ages* (New York, NY: Garland, 1997).
Cole, Andrew, 'John Gower Copies Geoffrey Chaucer', *The Chaucer Review* 52 (2017), 46–65.
Collette, Carolyn P., *Performing Polity: Women and Agency in the Anglo-French Tradition, 1385–1620* (Turnhout: Brepols, 2007).
Copeland, Rita, and Peter T. Struck, 'Introduction', in Rita Copeland and Peter T. Struck (eds), *The Cambridge Companion to Allegory* (Cambridge: Cambridge University Press, 2010), pp. 1–11.
Critten, Rory G., 'Imagining the Author in Late Medieval England and France: The Transmission and Reception of Christine de Pizan's *Epistre au dieu d'Amours* and Thomas Hoccleve's *Letter of Cupid*', *Studies in Philology* 112 (2015), 680–97.
Crocker, Holly A., *Chaucer's Visions of Manhood* (New York, NY: Palgrave Macmillan, 2007).
_____, 'Medieval Affects Now', *Exemplaria* 29 (2017), 82–98.
_____, 'Performative Passivity and Fantasies of Masculinity in the Merchant's Tale', *The Chaucer Review* 38 (2003), 178–98.
Cummings, Brian, 'Animal Passions and Human Sciences: Shame, Blushing and Nakedness in Early Modern Europe and the New World', in Erica Fudge, Ruth Gilbert, and Susan Wiseman (eds), *At the Borders of the Human: Beasts, Bodies and Natural Philosophy in the Early Modern Period* (London: Macmillan Press, 1999), pp. 26–50.
Davis, Isabel, *Writing Masculinity in the Later Middle Ages* (Cambridge: Cambridge University Press, 2007).
D'Avray, David, *Medieval Marriage: Symbolism and Society* (Oxford: Oxford University Press, 2005).
Dearnley, Elizabeth, *Translators and Their Prologues in Medieval England* (Cambridge: D. S. Brewer, 2016).
De Gendt, Anne Marie, *L'Art d'éduquer les nobles damoiselles: Le livre du Chevalier de la Tour Landry* (Paris: Champion, 2003).
Desmond, Marilynn, 'The *Querelle de la Rose* and the Ethics of Reading', in Barbara K. Altmann and Deborah L. McGrady (eds), *Christine de Pizan: A Casebook* (New York, NY: Routledge, 2003), pp. 167–80.

―――――, *Ovid's Art and the Wife of Bath: The Ethics of Erotic Violence* (Ithaca, NY: Cornell University Press, 2006).
Dixon, Thomas, '"Emotion": The History of a Keyword in Crisis', *Emotion Review*, 4 (2012), 338–44.
―――――, *From Passions to Emotions: The Creation of a Secular Psychological Category* (Cambridge: Cambridge University Press, 2003).
―――――, 'Revolting Passions', *Modern Theology*, 27 (2011), 298–312.
Dodds, E. R., *The Greeks and the Irrational* (Berkeley, CA: University of California Press, 1951).
Dronzek, Anna, 'Gendered Theories of Education in Fifteenth-Century Conduct Books', in Kathleen Ashley and Robert L. A. Clark, *Medieval Conduct* (Minneapolis, MN: University of Minnesota Press, 2001), pp. 135–59.
Ebin, Lois A., *John Lydgate* (Boston, MA: Twayne Publishers, 1985).
Edwards, Robert R., 'Lydgate's *Troy Book* and the Confusion of Prudence', in Thomas R. Liszka and Lorna E. M. Walker (eds), *The North Sea World in the Middle Ages: Studies in the Cultural History of North-Western Europe* (Dublin: Four Courts, 2001), pp. 52–69.
Edwards, Suzanne M., *The Afterlives of Rape in Medieval English Literature* (New York, NY: Palgrave Macmillan, 2016).
Elsakkers, Marianne, 'In Pain You Shall Bear Children (Gen 3:16): Medieval Prayers for a Safe Delivery', in Anne-Marie Korte (ed.), *Women and Miracle Stories: A Multidisciplinary Exploration* (Leiden: Brill, 2001), pp. 179–209.
Evans, Ruth, 'Virginities', in Carolyn Dinshaw and David Wallace (eds), *The Cambridge Companion to Medieval Women's Writing* (Cambridge: Cambridge University Press, 2003), pp. 21–39.
Fernie, Ewan, *Shame in Shakespeare* (London: Routledge, 2002).
Ferster, Judith, *Fictions of Advice: The Literature and Politics of Counsel in Late Medieval England* (Philadelphia, PA: University of Pennsylvania Press, 1996).
Fewer, Colin, 'John Lydgate's *Troy Book* and the Ideology of Prudence', *The Chaucer Review* 38 (2004), 229–45.
Finlayson, John, 'Guido de Columpnis' *Historia destructionis Troiae*, The *"Gest Hystorial"* of the Destruction of Troy, and Lydgate's *Troy Book*: Translation and the Design of History', *Anglia* 113 (1995), 141–62.
Flannery, Mary C., 'A Bloody Shame: Chaucer's Honourable Women', *The Review of English Studies* 62 (2011), 337–57.
―――――, 'The Concept of Shame in Late-Medieval English Literature', *Literature Compass* 9 (2012), 166–82.
―――――, 'Emotion and the Ideal Reader in Middle English Gynecological Texts', in Rachel Falconer and Denis Renevey (eds), *Literature, Science and Medicine in the Medieval and Early Modern Periods* (Turnhout: Swiss Papers in English Language and Literature (SPELL), 2013), pp. 103–15.
―――――, 'Personification and Embodied Emotional Practice in Middle English Literature', *Literature Compass* 13 (2016), 351–61.

―――, 'The Shame of the *Rose*: A Paradox', in Jennifer Chamarette and Jennifer Higgins (eds), *Guilt and Shame: Essays in French Literature and Culture* (Oxford: Peter Lang, 2010), pp. 51–69.
Flannery, Mary C. (ed.), *Emotion & Medieval Textual Media* (Turnhout: Brepols, 2019).
Frevert, Ute, *Emotions in History – Lost and Found* (Budapest: Central European University Press, 2011).
Giaccherini, Enrico, 'Tradition as Collaboration: The Public and the Private in *The Physician's Tale*', in Silvia Bigliazzi and Sharon Wood (eds), *Collaboration in the Arts from the Middle Ages to the Present*, Studies in European Cultural Transition, 35 (Aldershot: Ashgate, 2006), pp. 7–15.
Gilbert, Sophie, 'The Movement of #MeToo: How a hashtag got its power', *Atlantic* (16 October 2017), www.theatlantic.com/entertainment/archive/2017/10/the-movement-of-metoo/542979/ [accessed 24 February 2018].
Graham, David A., 'What If Voters Don't Care About Infidelity At All?', *Atlantic* (17 February 2018), www.theatlantic.com/politics/archive/2018/02/presidential-infidelity-shame/553559/ [accessed online 18 April 2018].
Gravdal, Kathryn, *Ravishing Maidens: Writing Rape in Medieval French Literature and Law* (Philadelphia, PA: University of Pennsylvania Press, 1991).
Green, Monica H., 'The Development of the *Trotula*', *Revue d'histoire des textes* 26 (1996), 119–203.
―――, 'From "Diseases of Women" to "Secrets of Women": The Transformation of Gynecological Literature in the Later Middle Ages', *Journal of Medieval and Early Modern Studies* 30 (2000), 5–39.
―――, 'A Handlist of Latin and Vernacular Manuscripts of the So-Called *Trotula* Texts', *Revue Internationale des Études Relatives aux Manuscrits* 51 (1997), 80–103.
―――, *Making Women's Medicine Masculine: The Rise of Male Authority in Pre-Modern Gynaecology* (Oxford: Oxford University Press, 2008).
―――, 'Obstetrical and Gynecological Texts in Middle English', *Studies in the Age of Chaucer* 14 (1992), 53–88.
Green, Monica H., and Linne R. Mooney, 'The Sickness of Women', in M. Teresa Tavormina (ed.), *Sex, Aging, and Death in a Medieval Medical Compendium: Trinity College Cambridge MS R.14.52, Its Texts, Language, and Scribe*, 2 vols (Tempe, AZ: Arizona Center for Medical and Renaissance Studies, 2006), pp. 455–83.
Greetham, D. C., 'Self-Referential Artifacts: Hoccleve's Persona as a Literary Device', *Modern Philology* 86 (1989), 242–51.
Grigsby, John, 'A New Source for the *Livre du Chevalier de la Tour Landry*', *Romania* 84 (1963), 171–208.
Gundersheimer, Werner L., 'Renaissance Concepts of Shame and Pocaterra's *Dialoghi Della Vergogna*', *Renaissance Quarterly* 47 (1994), 34–56.

Guynn, Noah, *Allegory and Sexual Ethics in the High Middle Ages* (New York, NY: Palgrave Macmillan, 2007).

Hammond, E. P., 'Lydgate and Coluccio Salutati', *Modern Philology* 25 (1927), 49–57.

Hanawalt, Barbara, *Crime and Conflict in English Communities 1300–1348* (Cambridge, MA: Harvard University Press, 1979).

Hanson, Ann Ellis, 'Hippocrates: *Diseases of Women* 1', *Signs: Journal of Women in Culture and Society* 1 (1975), 567–84.

Harley, Marta Powell, 'Last Things First in Chaucer's Physician's Tale: Final Judgment and the Worm of Conscience', *Journal of English and Germanic Philology* 91 (1992), 1–16.

Hirsch, John, 'Modern Times: The Discourse of the *Physician's Tale*', *The Chaucer Review* 27 (1993), 387–95.

Hochschild, Arlie Russell, 'Emotion Work, Feelings Rules, and Social Structure', *American Journal of Sociology*, 85 (1979), 551–75.

_____, *The Managed Heart: Commercialization of Human Feeling* (Berkeley, CA: University of California Press, 1983).

Hoffman, Richard L., 'Jephthah's Daughter and Chaucer's Virginia', *The Chaucer Review* 2 (1967), 20–31.

Hogan, Patrick Colm, 'Fictions and Feelings: On the Place of Literature in the Study of Emotion', *Emotion Review* 2 (2010), 184–95.

Horobin, Simon, 'A New Fragment of the *Romaunt of the Rose*', *Studies in the Age of Chaucer* 28 (2006), 205–15.

Jed, Stephanie H., *Chaste Thinking: The Rape of Lucretia and the Birth of Humanism* (Indianapolis, IN: Indiana University Press, 1989).

Johnson, Christen A., and K. T. Hawbaker, '#MeToo: A timeline of events', *Chicago Tribune* (22 February 2018), www.chicagotribune.com/lifestyles/ct-me-too-timeline-20171208-htmlstory.html [accessed 24 February 2018].

Kao, Wan-Chuan, 'Conduct Shameful and Unshameful in *The Franklin's Tale*', *Studies in the Age of Chaucer* 34 (2012), 99–139.

Karras, Ruth Mazo, *From Boys to Men: Formations of Masculinity in Late Medieval Europe* (Philadelphia, PA: University of Pennsylvania Press, 2003).

Kaster, Robert A., *Emotion, Restraint, and Community in Ancient Rome* (Oxford: Oxford University Press, 2005).

_____, 'The Shame of the Romans', *Transactions of the American Philological Association* 127 (1997), 1–19.

Kelly, Kathleen C., 'Menaced Masculinity and Imperiled Virginity in the *Morte Darthur*', in Kathleen C. Kelly and Marina Leslie (eds), *Menacing Virgins: Representing Virginity in the Middle Ages and Renaissance* (London: Associated University Presses, 1999), pp. 97–114.

_____, *Performing Virginity and Testing Chastity in the Middle Ages* (London: Routledge, 2000).

Kelly, Kathleen C., and Marina Leslie (eds), *Menacing Virgins: Representing Virginity in the Middle Ages and Renaissance* (London: Associated University Presses, 1999).

Kempshall, M. S., *The Common Good in Late Medieval Political Thought: Moral Goodness and Political Benefit* (Oxford: Clarendon Press, 1999).

Kindrick, Robert L., 'Gawain's Ethics: Shame and Guilt in *Sir Gawain and the Green Knight*', Annuale mediavale 20 (1981), 5–32.

King, Peter, 'Emotions', in Brian Davies and Eleonore Stump (eds), *The Oxford Handbook of Aquinas* (Oxford: Oxford University Press, 2011), pp. 209–26.

———, 'Emotions in Medieval Thought', in Peter Goldie (ed.), *The Oxford Handbook of Philosophy of Emotion* (Oxford: Oxford University Press, 2010), pp. 167–88.

Knapp, Ethan, 'Bureaucratic Identity and the Construction of the Self in Hoccleve's *Formulary* and *La Male Regle*', Speculum 74 (1999), 357–76.

———, *The Bureaucratic Muse: Thomas Hoccleve and the Literature of Late Medieval England* (University Park, PA: The Pennsylvania State University Press, 2001).

———, 'Thomas Hoccleve', in Larry Scanlon (ed.), *The Cambridge Companion to Medieval English Literature 1100–1500* (Cambridge: Cambridge University Press, 2009), pp. 191–203.

Knuuttila, Simo, *Emotions in Ancient and Medieval Philosophy* (Oxford: Clarendon Press, 2004).

Krueger, Roberta L., 'Introduction: Teach Your Children Well: Medieval Conduct Guides for Youths', in *Medieval Conduct Literature: An Anthology of Vernacular Guides to Behaviour for Youths, with English Translations*, ed. Mark D. Johnston and Kathleen M. Ashley (Toronto: University of Toronto Press, 2009), pp. ix–xxxiii.

Kuskin, William, 'The Erasure of Labor: Hoccleve, Caxton, and the Information Age', in Kellie Robertson and Michael Uebel (eds), *The Middle Ages at Work* (New York, NY: Palgrave, 2004), pp. 229–60.

Langlands, Rebecca, *Sexual Morality in Ancient Rome* (Cambridge: Cambridge University Press, 2006).

Larrington, Carolyne, 'The Psychology of Emotion and Study of the Medieval Period', Early Medieval Europe 10 (2001), 251–56.

Lastique, Esther, and Helen Rodnite Lemay, 'A Medieval Physician's Guide to Virginity', in Joyce E. Salisbury (ed.), *Sex in the Middle Ages: A Book of Essays* (New York, NY: Garland, 1991), pp. 56–82.

Lawes, R., 'Psychological Disorder and the Autobiographical Impulse in Julian of Norwich, Margery Kempe, and Thomas Hoccleve', in Denis Renevey and Christiania Whitehead (eds), *Writing Religious Women: Female Spiritual and Textual Practices in Late Medieval England* (Cardiff: University of Wales Press, 2000), pp. 217–43.

Lawton, David, 'Dullness and the Fifteenth Century', English Literary History 54 (1987), 761–99.

Lee, Brian S., 'The Position and Purpose of the *Physician's Tale*', *The Chaucer Review* 22 (1987), 141–60.

Lees, Clare, *Medieval Masculinities: Regarding Men in the Middle Ages* (Minneapolis, MN: University of Minnesota Press, 2004).

Leys, Ruth, 'The Turn to Affect: A Critique', *Critical Inquiry* 37 (2011), 434–72.

Lidaka, Juris, 'Glossing Conception, Infancy, Childhood, and Adolescence in Book VI of *De proprietatibus rerum*', in Baudouin Van den Apeele and Heinz Meyer (eds), *Bartholomaeus Anglicus, De Proprietatibus Rerum: Texte latin et réception vernaculaire* (Turnhout: Brepols, 2005), pp. 117–36.

Lochrie, Karma, *Covert Operations: The Medieval Uses of Secrecy* (Philadelphia, PA: University of Pennsylvania Press, 1999).

Lombardo, Nicholas E., *The Logic of Desire: Aquinas on Emotion* (Washington, DC: Catholic University of America, 2011).

Lynch, Andrew, '"Manly Cowardyse": Thomas Hoccleve's Peace Strategy', *Medium Ævum* 73 (2004), 306–23.

———, '"What cheer?" Emotion and Action in the Arthurian World', in Frank Brandsma, Carolyne Larrington, and Corinne Saunders (eds), *Emotions in Medieval Arthurian Literature: Body, Mind, Voice* (Woodbridge: D. S. Brewer, 2015), pp. 47–63.

Lynd, Helen, *On Shame and the Search for Identity* (London: Routledge, 1958), 49–56.

Mann, Jill, *Chaucer and Medieval Estates Satire* (Cambridge: Cambridge University Press, 1973).

———, 'Parents and Children in the "Canterbury Tales"', in Piero Boitani and Anna Torti (eds), *Literature in Fourteenth-Century England: The J. A. W. Bennett Memorial Lectures, Perugia, 1981–1982* (Cambridge: D. S. Brewer, 1983), pp. 165–83.

McDonald, Nicola F., 'Chaucer's *Legend of Good Women*, Ladies at Court, and the Female Reader', *The Chaucer Review* 35 (2000), 22–42.

———, 'Games Medieval Women Play', in Carolyn Collette (ed.), *The Legend of Good Women: Context and Reception* (Cambridge: D. S. Brewer, 2006), pp. 176–97.

McGavin, John J., *Chaucer and Dissimilarity: Literary Comparisons in Chaucer and Other Late-Medieval Writing* (Madison, WI: Fairleigh Dickinson University Presses, 2000).

McNamer, Sarah, *Affective Meditation and the Invention of Medieval Compassion* (Philadelphia, PA: University of Pennsylvania Press, 2010).

———, 'Feeling', in Paul Strohm (ed.), *Oxford Twenty-First-Century Approaches to Literature: Middle English* (Oxford: Oxford University Press, 2007), pp. 241–57.

———, 'The Literariness of Literature and the History of Emotion', *PMLA* 130 (2015), 1433–42.

McTaggart, Anne, *Shame and Guilt in Chaucer* (New York, NY: Palgrave Macmillan, 2012).

Medcalf, Stephen, *The Later Middle Ages* (London: Holmes & Meier, 1981).
Meyer-Lee, Robert J., 'Laureates and Beggars in Fifteenth-Century English Poetry: The Case of George Ashby', *Speculum* 79 (2004), 688–726.
_____, *Poets and Power from Chaucer to Wyatt* (Cambridge: Cambridge University Press, 2007; repr. 2009).
Middleton, Anne, 'The *Physician's Tale* and Love's Martyrs: "Ensaumples mo than ten" as a Method in the *Canterbury Tales*', *The Chaucer Review* 8 (1973), 9–32.
Miller, William Ian, *Humiliation and Other Essays on Honor, Social Discomfort, and Violence* (Ithaca, NY: Cornell University Press, 1993).
Millett, Bella, and Jocelyn Wogan-Browne, 'Introduction', in *Medieval English Prose for Women: Selections from the Katherine Group and Ancrene Wisse*, ed. Bella Millett and Jocelyn Wogan-Browne (Oxford: Clarendon Press, 1990), pp. xi–xxxviii.
Mitchell, Jerome, *Thomas Hoccleve: A Study in Early Fifteenth-Century English Poetic* (Urbana, IL: University of Illinois Press, 1968).
Morse, Ruth, *The Medieval Medea* (Cambridge: D. S. Brewer, 1996).
Nagy, Piroska, and Damien Boquet (eds), *Le Sujet des emotions au Moyen Âge* (Paris: Beauchesne, 2009).
Neal, Derek G., *The Masculine Self in Late Medieval England* (Chicago, IL: The University of Chicago Press, 2008).
Nederman, Cary J., 'Nature, Ethics, and the Doctrine of "Habitus": Aristototelian Moral Psychology in the Twelfth Century', *Traditio* 45 (1989–90), 87–110.
Ngai, Sianne, *Ugly Feelings* (Cambridge, MA: Harvard University Press, 2005).
Nissé, Ruth, '"Oure Fadres Olde and Modres": Gender, Heresy, and Hoccleve's Literary Politics', *Studies in the Age of Chaucer* 21 (1999), 275–99.
Olsson, Kurt, 'Grammar, Manhood, and Tears: The Curiosity of Chaucer's Monk', *Modern Philology* 76 (1978), 1–17.
Orme, Nicholas, *From Childhood to Chivalry: The Education of the English Kings and Aristocracy, 1066–1530* (London: Methuen, 1984).
Paster, Gail Kern, *The Body Embarrassed: Drama and the Disciplines of Shame in Early Modern England* (New York, NY: Cornell University Press, 1993).
Patrick, Vanessa M., HaeEun Helen Chun, and Deborah J. Macinnis, 'Affective Forecasting and Social Control: Why Anticipating Pride Wins Over Anticipating Shame in a Self-regulation Context', *Journal of Consumer Psychology* 19 (2009), 537–45.
Patterson, Lee, *Chaucer and the Subject of History* (Madison, WI: University of Wisconsin Press, 1991).
Paxson, James J., *The Poetics of Personification* (Cambridge: Cambridge University Press, 1994).
Peck, Russell A., *Kingship and Common Profit in Gower's Confession Amantis* (Carbondale, IL: Southern Illinois University Press, 1978).

Peristiany, J. G. (ed.), *Honour and Shame: The Values of Mediterranean Society* (Chicago, IL: The University of Chicago Press, 1966).

Perkins, Nicholas, *Hoccleve's Regiment of Princes: Counsel and Constraint* (Cambridge: D. S. Brewer, 2001).

_____, 'Thomas Hoccleve, *La Male Regle*', in Peter Brown (ed.), *A Companion to Medieval English Literature and Culture, c. 1350–1500* (Chichester: John Wiley & Sons Ltd, 2009), pp. 585–603.

Phillips, Kim M., *Medieval Maidens: Young Women and Gender in England, 1270 – 1540* (Manchester: Manchester University Press, 2003).

Pitcher, John A., 'Chaucer's Wolf: Exemplary Violence in *The Physician's Tale*', *Genre* 36 (2003), 1–27.

Plamper, Jan, *The History of Emotions: An Introduction*, trans. by Keith Tribe (Oxford: Oxford University Press, 2015).

Porter, Elizabeth, 'Gower's Ethical Microcosm and Political Macrocosm', in A. J. Minnis (ed.), *Gower's 'Confessio Amantis': Responses and Reassessments* (Cambridge: D. S. Brewer, 1983), pp. 135–62.

Pouchelle, Marie-Christine, *The Body and Surgery in the Middle Ages*, trans. Rosemary Morris (Cambridge: Polity Press, 1990).

Probyn, Elspeth, *Blush: Faces of Shame* (Minneapolis, MN: University of Minnesota Press, 2005).

Pugh, Tison, and Marcia Smith Marzec (eds), *Men and Masculinities in Chaucer's Troilus and Criseyde* (Cambridge: D. S. Brewer, 2008).

Reddy, William M., 'Against Constructionism: The Historical Ethnography of Emotions', *Current Anthropology* 38 (1997), 327–51 (p. 331).

_____, *The Making of Romantic Love: Longing and Sexuality in Europe, South Asia, and Japan, 900 – 1200 CE* (Oxford: Oxford University Press, 2012).

_____, *The Navigation of Feeling: A Framework for the History of Emotions* (Cambridge: Cambridge University Press, 2001).

Reese, Neal J., and Mike Morrison, 'The Psychology of Counterfactual Thinking', *Historical Social Research* 34 (2009), 16–26.

Reeves, A. Compton, 'Thomas Hoccleve, Bureaucrat', *Medievalia et Humanistica* n. s. 5 (1974), 201–14.

Riddy, Felicity, 'Mother Knows Best: Reading Social Change in a Courtesy Text', *Speculum* 71 (1996), 66–86.

Robbins, Rossell Hope, 'Medical Manuscripts in Middle English', *Speculum* 45 (1970), 393–415.

Rosenwein, Barbara, *Emotional Communities in the Early Middle Ages* (Ithaca, NY: Cornell University Press, 2006).

Rowland, Beryl, 'The Physician's "Historial Thyng Notable" and the Man of Law', *ELH* 40 (1973), 165–78.

Salih, Sarah, *Versions of Virginity in Late Medieval England* (Cambridge: D. S. Brewer, 2001).

Saunders, Corinne, *Rape and Ravishment in the Literature of Medieval England* (Cambridge: D. S. Brewer, 2001).

Scanlon, Larry, *Narrative, Authority, and Power: The Medieval Exemplum and the Chaucerian Tradition* (Cambridge: Cambridge University Press, 1994).

Scheer, Monique, 'Are Emotions a Kind of Practice (And Is That What Makes Them Have a History)? A Bourdieuian Approach to Understanding Emotion', *History and Theory* 51 (2012), 192–220.

Scheff, Thomas J., 'Shame and the Social Bond: A Sociological Theory', *Sociological Theory* 18 (2000), 84–99.

Sedgwick, Eve Kosofsky, *Touching Feeling: Affect, Pedagogy, Performativity* (Durham, NC: Duke University Press, 2003).

Sharp, Michael D., 'Reading Chaucer's "Manly man": The Trouble with Masculinity in the *Monk's Prologue* and *Tale*', in Peter G. Beidler (ed.), *Masculinities in Chaucer: Approaches to Maleness in the Canterbury Tales and Troilus and Criseyde* (Cambridge: D. S. Brewer, 1998), pp. 173–85.

Shepherd, Lee, Russell Spears, and Antony S. R. Manstead, '"This Will Bring Shame on our Nation": The Role of Anticipated Group-based Emotions on Collective Action', *Journal of Experimental Psychology* 49 (2013), 42–57.

_____, 'When Does Anticipating Group-based Shame Lead to Lower Ingroup Favoritism? The Role of Status and Status Stability', *Journal of Experimental Psychology* 49 (2013), 334–43.

Sobecki, Sebastian, *Last Words: The Public Self and the Social Author in Late Medieval England* (Oxford: Oxford University Press, forthcoming).

Sponsler, Claire, *Drama and Resistance: Bodies, Goods, and Theatricality in Late Medieval England* (Minneapolis, MN: University of Minnesota Press, 1997).

Staley, Lynn, *Languages of Power in the Age of Richard II* (University Park, PA: The Pennsylvania State University Press, 2005).

Stanton, Robert, 'Lechery, Pride, and the Uses of Sin in *The Book of Margery Kempe*', *The Journal of Medieval Religious Cultures* 36 (2010), 169–204.

Stavsky, Jonathan, 'Hoccleve's Take on Chaucer and Christine de Pizan: Gender, Authorship, and Intertextuality in the *Epistre au dieu d'Amours*, the *Letter of Cupid*, and the *Series*', *Philological Quarterly* 93 (2014), 435–60.

Stearns, Peter N., *Shame: A Brief History* (Urbana, IL: University of Illinois Press, 2017).

'Stormy Daniels Describes Her Alleged Affair With Donald Trump' (correspondent Anderson Cooper), www.cbsnews.com/news/stormy-daniels-describes-her-alleged-affair-with-donald-trump-60-minutes-interview/ [accessed 17 April 2018].

Swann, Alaya, '"By Expresse Experiment": The Doubting Midwife Salome in Late Medieval England', *Bulletin of the History of Medicine* 89.1 (2015), 1–24.

Tavormina, M. Teresa (ed.), *Sex, Aging, and Death in a Medieval Medical Compendium: Trinity College Cambridge MS R.14.52, Its Texts, Language, and Scribe*, 2 vols (Tempe, AZ: Arizona Center for Medical and Renaissance Studies, 2006).

Taylor, Gabriele, *Pride, Shame, and Guilt: Emotions of Self-Assessment* (Oxford: University of Oxford Press, 1985).

Tentler, Thomas N., *Sin and Confession on the Eve of the Reformation* (Princeton, NJ: Princeton University Press, 1977).

Teskey, Gordon, *Allegory and Violence* (Ithaca, NY: Cornell University Press, 1996).

Tolmie, Sarah, 'The *priue scilence* of Thomas Hoccleve', *Studies in the Age of Chaucer* 22 (2000), 281–309.

─────, 'The Professional: Thomas Hoccleve', *Studies in the Age of Chaucer* 29 (2007), 341–73.

Torti, Anna, 'From "History" to "Tragedy": The Story of Troilus and Criseyde in Lydgate's *Troy Book* and Henryson's *Testament of Cresseid*', in *The European Tragedy of Troilus*, ed. by Piero Boitani (Oxford: Clarendon Press, 1989), pp. 171–98.

Trigg, Stephanie, 'Introduction: Emotional Histories – Beyond the Personalization of the Past and the Abstraction of Affect Theory', *Exemplaria* 26 (2014), 3–15.

─────, '"Shamed be...": Historicizing Shame in Medieval and Early Modern Courtly Ritual', *Exemplaria* 19 (2007), 67–89.

Tupper, Frederick, 'Chaucer and the Seven Deadly Sins', *PMLA* 29 (1914), 93–128.

Ussery, Huling E., 'How Old Is Chaucer's Clerk?', *TSE* 15 (1967), 1–15.

Vines, Amy N., 'The Rehabilitation of Patronage in Hoccleve's *Series*', *Digital Philology* 2 (2013), 201–21.

Warburton, Rachel, 'Reading Rape in Chaucer: or Are Cecily, Lucretia, and Philomela *Good Women?*', in Mihoko Suzuki and Roseanna Lewis Dufault (eds), *Diversifying the Discourse: The Florence Howe Award for Outstanding Feminist Scholarship, 1990–2004* (New York, NY: Modern Language Association of America, 2006), pp. 270–87.

Wasserman, Loretta, 'Honor and Shame in *Sir Gawain and the Green Knight*', in Larry D. Benson and John Leyerle (eds), *Chivalric Literature: Essays on Relations Between Literature and Life in the Later Middle Ages* (Kalamazoo, MI: Western Michigan University, 1980), 77–90.

Watson, Nicholas, 'Outdoing Chaucer: Lydgate's *Troy Book* and Henryson's *Testament of Cresseid* as Competitive Imitations of *Troilus and Criseyde*', in Karen Pratt (ed.), *Shifts and Transpositions in Medieval Narrative: A Festschrift for Elspeth Kennedy* (Cambridge: D. S. Brewer, 1994), pp. 89–108.

Watt, David, *The Making of Thomas Hoccleve's Series* (Liverpool: Liverpool University Press, 2013).

Watt, Diane, 'John Gower', in Larry Scanlon (ed.), *The Cambridge Companion to Medieval English Literature 1100–1500* (Cambridge: Cambridge University Press, 2009), pp. 153–64.

Weiher, Carol, 'Chaucer's and Gower's Stories of Virginia and Lucretia', *ELN* 14 (1976), 7–9.

White, Robert A., 'Shamefastness as *Verecundia* and as *Pudicitia* in *The Faerie Queene*', *Studies in Philology* 78 (1981), 391–408.

Williams, Tara, *Inventing Womanhood: Gender and Language in Later Middle English Writing* (Columbus, OH: The Ohio State University Press, 2011).

Index

affect 4, 7, 27n.27, 28n.33, 120n.42
Aquinas, Thomas 7, 17, 19, 27n.31, 21n.77–8, 120n.42
Augustine, St 7

Bailly, Harry 126, 129, 161, 163–5, 175, 182n.21
blushing 18, 31–2n.72, 175–6, 185n.51
  blenching and 109
  bride 164
Book of the Knight of La Tour Landry, The 21, 24n.8, 5n.21, 60–3, 76–83, 85n.11, 92, 169, 186
  see also Geoffrey de la Tour Landry
Bourdieu, Pierre
  theory of habitus 9, 28n.42

Caxton, William 76
chastity viii–ix, 1–3, 8, 10–23, 24n.8, 34–41, 51–2, 61–83, 90–114, 117n.20, 122–51, 161–2, 166, 186–90
  definition of 23n.4
  male chastity 54n.15
Chaucer, Geoffrey 11–14, 22, 65, 122–51, 155n.32, 163, 165, 186–7
  Boece 28n.38
  The Clerk's Prologue 126, 163–5

General Prologue, The 126, 163–5, 103
  Hoccleve and 161–73
  The Knight's Tale 125
  The Legend of Good Women 103, 140, 152n.5
  comparisons with Gower's *Confessio Amantis* 154n.30
  The Legend of Lucrece 22, 131, 144, 150
  The Man of Law's Tale 140, 158–9n.71
  The Merchant's Tale 65, 181n.18
  The Parson's Tale 29n.51, 38, 54n.12, 157n.51
  The Physician's Tale 22, 75, 85n.19, 122–51, 186
  Troilus and Criseyde 124–30, 187–8
  The Wife of Bath's Prologue 1, 10–13, 40, 125–6
  see also Romaunt of the Rose
Christine de Pizan 99, 118n.25, 161–75, 188
  Epistre au dieu d'Amours 161–72, 182–3n.27, 188
  see also Hoccleve, Thomas, *Letter of Cupid*
conduct literature 3–15, 20–1, 24n.8, 60–83, 85n.11, 85n.18, 91, 100, 106–9, 123, 141, 151, 187
Criseyde 127–30

Index

embarrassment 19, 23, 33n.88, 36, 45, 161–2, 173, 179–80n.5, 180n.7
emotion ix, xi, 2–7, 14–23, 26n.17, 26n.22, 27n.28, 28n.33, 33n.88, 35–52, 60–83, 90–114, 124–65, 179n.5, 186–90
  as performance 186
  as practice 165, 186, 189–90
emotives 4, 6, 189
exemplarity 15, 22, 122–51

Fourneval, Lord Thomas 160, 173–8

Geoffrey de la Tour Landry 24–5n.9, 60, 63, 79–83, 87n.37, 88n.48
gesture 3, 6, 20, 37, 44, 68, 71, 75, 110, 114, 150–1, 161, 187–9
  covering 13–14, 20, 35–7, 41, 45, 70–1, 149, 187
  sensorimotor inhibition 68, 75, 83, 109, 146–7, 164–5, 188
  uncovering 13–14, 36–7, 45
Good Wife Would a Pilgrimage, The 61–2, 69, 71, 75
Gower, John 14, 22, 37, 45, 52, 124, 130–50, 155n.32
  Confessio Amantis 22, 124, 130–50, 157n.55
    comparisons with Chaucer's *Legend of Good Women* 154n.30
  Mirour de l'Omme, Le 37, 45, 87n.32
Guido delle Colonne 106–14, 120n.42
  Historia destructionis Troiae 106–10
    relationship to Lydgate's *Troy Book* 119–20n.41, 121n.51–3

gynaecological practice 21, 45–9, 56–7n.35
gynaecological texts 20–1, 34–52, 52n.3, 53n.9, 59n.50

habit 1, 5, 6, 8–15, 23, 25n.13, 28n.38, 28n.45, 29n.48, 34–9, 51–2, 60–83, 90–1, 104–9, 123, 126, 129, 138, 149, 168–9, 187
  of shamefastness 10–15, 23, 61, 66, 73, 75, 107, 123, 129, 138, 149, 169
habitus 8–14, 25n.13, 28n.36, 109
Hali Meiðhad 2, 12, 24n.8, 29n.56, 42
Hoccleve, Thomas 14, 22–3, 160–79, 180n.8–9, 184n.46–7, 184–5n.48, 188–9
  'Address to Oldcastle' 165
  Chaucer and 161–73
  Dialogue with a Friend 168
  Letter of Cupid 23, 161–72
    see also Christine de Pizan, *Epistre au dieu d'Amours*
  Male Regle, La 23, 160–2, 173–9, 184–5n.48, 188–9
  Regiment of Princes 162, 165, 178, 185n.56
  Series 14, 168, 180n.8
honour viii–x, xiii, 1–23, 35–52, 60–83, 91–114, 164–79, 186–90
  definition of 30n.66
  dishonour 122–51
Honte see Shame (allegorical figure)
Host, The *see* Harry Bailly
How the Good Wife Taught Her Daughter 66–8, 70, 73–5, 109
How the Wise Man Taught His Son 74, 87n.40

kinesis *see* gesture
Knowing of Woman's Kind in Childing, The 20–1, 34–6, 41, 45–6, 49–52, 187

Livre du Chevalier de la Tour Landry, Le 21, 24n8, 60–1, 76
see also Geoffrey de la Tour Landry; *The Book of the Knight of La Tour Landry*
Livy 132–4, 137–8, 156n.42, 156n.46
History of Rome 132–4, 137–8
Lucrece 22, 140, 144–51, 159n.74, 187–8
Lucretia 22, 68, 122–4, 130–50
Lydgate, John 22, 38, 44, 90–2, 106–14, 122–3, 151, 187
Fall of Princes 38, 121n.51, 122, 151n.3
Life of Our Lady 44
Troy Book 22, 90–2, 106–14, 121n.51, 151
relationship to Guido delle Colonne's *Historia destructionis Troiae* 119–20n.41, 121n.51–3

maidenhead 122
see also chastity; virginity
maidenhood 39–40, 61–6
manuscripts
Aberystwyth, National Library of Wales, Brogyntyn MS II.1 (formerly Porkington MS 10) 84n.9
Cambridge, Cambridge University Library, MS Kk.1.5 (referred to as C) 23n.1
St John's College, G.23 (referred to as J) 23n.1
Trinity College, MS O.5.4 18
MS R.14.52 46, 58n.39

Edinburgh, 'Fragment B', Sutherland Estates Papers, Acc. 10225, Box I, File 4 119n.36
Glasgow, Glasgow University Library, MS Hunter 409 119n.36
London, British Library, MS Harley 221 17–18, 32n.80
MS Harley 1764 76
MS Sloane 249 46, 58n.39
MS Sloane 2463 46, 58n.39
Royal College of Surgeons, MS 129 46, 58n.39
Oxford, Bodleian Library, MS Ashmole 61 67, 74, 86n.24, 87n.40
San Marino, CA, Huntington Library, MS HM 111 184n.47
Worcester Cathedral Chapter Library, MS F. 174 17, 32n.80
masculinity 19–23, 51, 82, 97–102, 123–51, 161–79
clerkly 126, 161–79
force and 97–102, 111, 124–31, 139, 141
rape and 97–102, 122–51, 151n.2, 154n.26, 157n.55, 158–9n.71, 190
Medea 22, 91, 106–14, 120n.49, 121n.51–2, 151, 187
midwifery 42–50

Ovid 91, 98–9, 113, 123–33, 144–9
Ars Amatoria 91, 98–9, 115n.3, 154n28
Fasti 133, 144–9
Metamorphoses 121n.52

Pandarus 127–30, 147
Paul, St 11–13, 126
proverbs 10, 29n.48, 40, 90, 134, 153n.18, 178, 185n.56

Index

Prudentius
  Psychomachia 7, 22, 91–5, 111
pudicitia 17–18, 65, 91–105,
  116n.11, 117n.17, 132
  see also verecundia
Pudicitia (personification) 91–7,
  105, 116n.10, 116–17n.16
pudor 17–18, 41, 53n.9, 93,
  116n.11, 117n.21,
  121n.52–3
Pudor (personification) 93,
  116n.10, 121n.52

Querelle de la Rose 99–100, 166,
  182–3n.27

rape ix, 2, 87n.32, 99–101,
  118n.31, 123–4, 127–51,
  151n.2, 154n.26,
  158–9n.71
  rapability 127–8, 135, 187–90
  rapeworthiness 190, 191n.7
romance 62, 81–2, 118n.31, 125,
  128
Roman de la rose, Le 21–2, 91,
  95–106, 109–14, 118n.25,
  119n.35, 123, 138, 142,
  146, 166, 182–3n.27,
  187
Romaunt of the Rose 10, 29n.48,
  102–5, 115n.1, 119n.35–7

Salome 44, 56n.32, 56n.34
Secretum secretorum 132, 155n.34,
  155–6n.36
shame viii-x, xi, xiii, 1–23, 25n.11,
  34–52, 55–6n.30,
  56–7n.35, 60–83, 89n.60,
  90–114, 116n.11, 117n.21,
  122–51, 153n.13, 162–79,
  187–90
  -avoidance viii, 46, 48, 51,
    60–1, 66–7, 79, 126–7,
    147, 186
  definitions of 24–5n.9, 53n.9
Shame (allegorical figure) 95–105,
  128
shamefastness 2–23, 35–8, 45–52,
  61–83, 90–114, 116n.11,
  122–51, 159n.74, 160–79,
  187–90
  definitions of 24–5n.9, 25n.10,
    153n.18
shamefuls 20, 36–49, 71
Sickness of Women, The 20–1, 36,
  45–52, 57n.36, 57–8n.38,
  58n.44, 187–8

Thewis of Good Women, The 1–2,
  61–4, 70–6, 84n.10
Thynne, William 103
touching 5, 17, 43–4, 56n.34,
  64–5
Troilus 126–47, 188
Trotula 44
Trotula, The 49, 55–6n.30

verecundia 17–19, 32n.76, 32n.78,
  67–8
Virginia 22, 75, 122–51, 154n.30,
  157n.52, 157n.55, 186–8
virginity 2–3, 12, 18, 29n.55,
  38–45, 54n.15, 55n.22–4,
  61–3, 77, 87n.32, 128–41,
  164
Virginius 123, 136–43, 157n.54–5

EU authorised representative for GPSR:
Easy Access System Europe, Mustamäe tee 50,
10621 Tallinn, Estonia
gpsr.requests@easproject.com

www.ingramcontent.com/pod-product-compliance
Lightning Source LLC
Chambersburg PA
CBHW070238240426
43673CB00044B/1839